The Journal of Stained Glass

Volume XXVI

2002

The Journal of the British Society of Master Glass Painters

Published at the Offices of the Society
6 Queen Square, London WC1N 3AR
www.bsmgp.org.uk

Front cover illustration:
Detail of Edward V in East window (c. 1511)
of chantry chapel, St Matthew's Church, Coldridge, Devon.
Photograph by Peter Williams, © English Heritage.

Back cover illustration:
Caroline Benyon FMGP, *Three Kings,* details of three lancet
lights (2002), Lady Chapel, St Simon Zelotes, Chelsea, London.
Photograph © Peter Cormack

Publication of this volume has been assisted by
a generous grant from the Worshipful Company
of Glaziers and Painters of Glass.

© British Society of Master Glass Painters 2003
on behalf of the contributors.

Designed and typeset in Sabon 9/11 by Jude Keen 020 8355 4541

Printed in Great Britain by Henry Ling Limited,
The Dorset Press, Dorchester DT1 1HD

ISBN 0 9540457 2 6

British Library Cataloguing in Publication Data.
A catalogue record for this book is available from the British Library.

The Journal of Stained Glass, Vol. XXVI
Edited by Sandra Coley

Contents

Peter Cormack

Guest editorial

In this brief essay, I want to examine a number of issues affecting contemporary and historic stained glass in church buildings.

Some years ago, the few remaining art schools in the UK which still taught people to design and make stained glass decided to re-designate their courses 'Architectural Glass'. It was perhaps a sincere attempt to suggest the wider applications of the craft in the modern world, but it was also another hefty nail in the coffin to which the education system has been consigning all traditional art/craft teaching. With reference to ecclesiastical work, which still constitutes the largest quantity of commissions, it was a hopelessly inaccurate description of what was actually taught, for the one thing characteristic of almost all contemporary stained glass in churches has been its flagrant disregard for architectural context. The relatively few exceptions one sees are usually the work of experienced and senior practitioners whose training long preceded these innovations. Their methods and approach are, in effect, probably as remote to younger designer-makers as those of Thomas Glazier or John Thornton. In another couple of decades, this country's long tradition of ecclesiastical stained glass as a matter of disciplined design and craftsmanship will be virtually moribund, replaced all too often by the anarchy of novelty-seeking and 'self-expression'.

This gloomy prediction does not, I believe, *have* to transpire if those who care about this marvellous 'artistic craft' (to use a term from the early 1900s) truly take stock of the current realities and re-energise training and practice towards more positive and coherent goals. Some of the most egregious inadequacies stem from the educational system, where art/craft tutors have been demoralised by drastic economic constraints while increasingly being saddled with a poorly-defined academicising agenda. Institutions founded as art schools or technical colleges – and which for many years functioned very effectively in those guises – have now been lured into the deceptive world of modern academia which forces every subject, however inappropriately, into a degree format. In the process, the essentially visual and manual components in artistic training have been downgraded, with disastrous results.

In obvious defiance of all historical precedent, the teaching of Drawing seems to have been relegated to an optional status. I do not think you can successfully design stained glass if you cannot draw. There is a popular fallacy that the medium is 'all about colour'. It is not. It is about the *organised* and *controlled* use of colour, and that is impossible without Design, which can only be learned through the instinctual and intellectual faculties developed by Drawing. This involves looking at – and visually absorbing – things in an analytical way. Rigorously disciplined but hugely rewarding, it is the only way to achieve the skills essential not only for meaningful, expressive figure-drawing and composition, but also for lettering, heraldry and all kinds of decoration/ornamentation. In stained glass, the drawing and design processes additionally involve the skilful interplay of linear and tonal elements in glass painting, as well as organising rhythmic dynamics of colour, paint, leadlines and saddle-bars within the architectural framework – not just of a particular window but of an entire building. All these aspects are given especial prominence in the rich context of our church buildings, where for all sorts of reasons we might properly expect the highest standards of designing and technical skill – and of inspiration also – to be applied.

In my own experience of involvement with Church of England bodies responsible for scrutinising new stained glass projects, one is very rarely presented with drawings which suggest any real knowledge of (or indeed sympathy with) the cumulative artistic and historic character of our churches. All too often, it is almost as if the artist wished to express some antipathy not only towards the building which the new window is meant to adorn but, equally, towards all previous efforts in the craft (to say nothing of the piety of past worshippers/donors). This apparent arrogance is, however, invariably the product of ignorance rather than culpable intent. How can we address this failure to prepare those embarking on a career in stained glass for the actual world in which they will be working?

First, there needs to be a greater recognition within training institutions of the realities of today's stained glass profession. Like it or not – and I suspect many tutors do not like it – the churches do still provide the majority of work, whether through new window commissions or the bread-and-butter income from repair/restoration/conservation. Buildings in traditional styles, therefore, not the transient ephemera of modern architecture, continue predominantly to be the setting for today's craft. This should not be seen as an obstacle to creativity, but as an incomparable opportunity for nurturing in their highest form the skills I have outlined above.

But how can this possibly be achieved when courses now contain minimal teaching not just about architectural sensitivity but about the history of stained glass itself? It is as if the past had never existed, as if stained glass was some new 'orphan' medium. Yet anyone with common sense can see this couldn't be further from the truth, that for a thousand years the best efforts of stained glass workers have been stimulated by the achievements of their predecessors. So, *bring back History to stained glass courses*. Thereby students can learn the lessons of the past and have at their disposal as many formal and technical resources as possible to fire their own imagination and ingenuity. Acquiring the skills needed to design effective windows for historic church buildings, with all their layered complexity and subtlety, would – in my view – unquestionably equip them to work far more interestingly in modern secular architecture too.

The ideal course would foster an appreciation of architectural context. It would expound the notion of harmonising with existing schemes of glazing and with other elements of a building which give it its overall character. On this whole question, there is no wiser counsel than that written almost a century ago by Christopher Whall in the chapter 'On Architectural Fitness' in his classic *Stained Glass Work* (first published 1905; new edition by M. & J. Venables, 1999). It is a manifesto for modern art informed by knowledge of and respect for its antecedents.

Alongside a more historically- and architecturally-aware approach in the training of stained glass designers, there is equally a need for a greater understanding of symbolism and iconography, by which I mean the ways in which faith groups and others have sought to express in visual form their beliefs and historical narratives. In our society, with its crisis of cultural identity and plummeting educational standards, it would now be wrong to assume even quite elementary levels of knowledge among most trainee artists about, for example, the Old and New Testaments or the Saints. This is a massive and problematic deficiency and it is shared by just as many clergy (shockingly) as stained glass designers. There are no short cuts, but a good tutor should feel confident to recommend the right sort of reading – there is certainly no shortage of source material – and this could be supplemented effectively by slides and site-visits focussing on imagery as well as aesthetics and technical aspects. The aim should be to enrich the designer's expressive vocabulary, enabling him or her to articulate ideas clearly and, if possible, with some beauty and emotional force.

The dire situation in the educational field is matched by the polarising crisis in conservation. Here, a new methodology is required for the treatment of 19th- and 20th-century stained glass in churches. The dead hand of an inappropriate orthodoxy (derived from the quite different needs of medieval glass) has for too long stifled thinking in this field and it is time to explore and define different criteria for preserving what is, after all, the huge majority of our historic stained glass. These must include an informed and properly skilled approach not only to repair and conservation but also to *Restoration*. For whereas the generally accepted principles of minimum intervention and reversibility of treatment are wholly suited to the preservation of relatively rare medieval glass, however fragmentary and weathered, the same principles attract little support from clergy, church-folk and Diocesan Chancellors when applied to our much larger heritage of Victorian and later glass. In the latter case, to advocate such a deceptively high-minded approach is effectively to condemn windows to destruction or, at best, removal. Instead, the option of careful and properly-researched restoration should be given serious consideration as a means of preservation.

The reality is that there are thousands of windows dating from the last two centuries (well over 90% of all our ecclesiastical stained glass) about which we know – or can find out – far more than we will ever discover about medieval glass. In some cases we know the names not just of the studio and its designers and cartoonists but also of the glass painters and suppliers of most of the glass used. We can also often locate numerous examples of contemporary work by the same individual or firm, windows for which, on occasion, even the same cartoons were used. There exists therefore, at least potentially, a quantity of artistic and technical data available to the skilled restorer which can be utilised to ensure that a restored window will be as close as possible to its original state. Of course, restoration of 19th- and 20th-century stained glass does go on all the time, but in an *ad hoc* manner, not always with much skill applied and with no guarantee of preliminary research undertaken. So some basic ground-rules are sorely needed here, as well as a raising of skill-levels.

In one particularly contentious area, namely the treatment of windows whose glass-painting has deteriorated because of faulty pigments or under-firing, I would advocate that the old remedy of re-painting and re-firing should be systematically examined and its merits assessed. During the later nineteenth century, firms such as Morris & Company and John Hardman & Co regularly – and successfully – carried out 'repairs' (this was Morris & Co's usual term) to some of their earlier windows which had suffered from paint loss. The glass was first removed from the church and returned to the studio, where it was dismantled and cleaned; it was then painted and fired again, assembled and finally re-installed. I have seen several examples of such windows, 'repaired' more than a hundred years ago, and the remedial treatment seems to have worked very effectively. Even the unavoidable double-firing of silver-stain had in no way distorted the effects of the restoration process. I am not recommending a miraculous panacea, but it seems foolish and counter-productive consistently to reject this particular option when the alternative – as has happened as a result of some recent Consistory Court cases – is the loss of the historic window altogether.

Unfortunately, many of the critical issues affecting the preservation of 19th- and 20th-century stained glass remain undiscussed. It is surely time for a conference to be convened, involving the BSMGP, the Glaziers Company, the Council for the Care of Churches, SPAB and other interested parties, which should have two principal aims: to work towards a more informed consensus about permissible technical options for restorer-conservators in this field; and to promote greater understanding of and respect for our unique heritage of later post-medieval glazing.

Peter Cormack was Co-Editor of The Journal of Stained Glass *from 1985 to 1994.*

History

Tim Ayers

A West Country glazier in the fifteenth century: John Godwin of Wells, MP

PLATE 1 *(overleaf)*:
Gerdur Helgadóttir,
Ludovicus and
Fritz Oidtmann
working on
windows for
Skalholt, Iceland
in 1959.
(SEE p. 61)
© Kópavogur
Art Museum.

The exhibition *Gothic: Art for England 1400-1547* at the Victoria & Albert Museum in London has given due place to the richness and diversity of late medieval English glass painting. Although it is increasingly evident that this was a collaborative craft in many ways, the better survival of documentary evidence from the end of the middle ages allows glimpses into the careers of those who were responsible for glazing businesses, including John Thornton of Coventry, John Prudde, Richard Twygge, Thomas Wodeshawe and Bernard Flower.[1] They were supported by varied social and economic structures, and recent work for the Corpus Vitrearum project has been adding to this picture. David King's forthcoming study of the medieval glass in the parish church of St Peter Mancroft in Norwich will include much new material on Norwich glaziers in the fifteenth century.[2] The marriage of relatively plentiful documentary evidence with the monuments themselves allows rich insights into how glaziers worked together, and their place in local politics and the wider artistic life of a great city and trading port.

The present article draws attention to a documented glazier in a different urban context, John Godwin of Wells, although he also enjoyed considerable social and probably economic success. He has attracted brief notice,[3] but a study of the economy of medieval Wells and recent work by the present author on the fifteenth-century glass at the Cathedral justify a further look.[4] Godwin's career spans the first half of the fifteenth century and he probably belonged to the generation after Thomas of Oxford and John Thornton of Coventry, overlapping their later years. Unlike great commercial centres such as London or York, but in common with other smaller English towns, there were no craft guilds in Wells before 1500, determining a rather different social context for the trade.[5] This case study demonstrates the status that a glazing business and good contacts could generate in a small town.[6]

The first known reference to John Godwin, glazier, appears in the earliest act book of the Wells Corporation, in 1406, when he was made free of the city, by right of marriage to the daughter of a burgess.[7] Born in the mid-1380s (see below), he must have been in his early twenties. The act books then record that Godwin stood pledge for sixteen craftsmen receiving their freedom over forty years between 1416 and 1456.[8] A man called John Glasyer stood pledge in 1407, 1409, 1410 and 1424, and was appointed churchwarden of the city's only parish church, St Cuthbert's, by the Master on behalf of the corporation, six times between 1402 and 1409.[9] Godwin and Glasyer may well be one and the same, as the craft was often treated as an alternative surname; they never appear together and Glasyer first stands pledge in the year after Godwin became free. Godwin was elected Master (equivalent to mayor) of the city seven times over thirty years, between 1423 and 1455,[10] representing it also in Parliament in 1423 and 1427.[11] Other contemporary glaziers are known to have sat in Parliament, including Henry Smart of Winchester.[12] In 1446 Godwin was described as being aged sixty years and more,[13] but he was still alive in December 1458, when he and his wife Joan were granted leave to have masses said at an oratory in their town house in Wells.[14] This probably indicates that he was infirm and it is the last reference to him alive. No will survives and there is no evidence for a son and heir, but Godwins continued to be prominent in the town, as the act books reveal, especially in the sixteenth century, when one branch of the family were mercers.

Godwin had clearly established himself as a senior figure. He is described as a gentleman in the register of Bishop Beckington, in the documents just mentioned of 1446 and 1458. He was settled in a town house that was grand enough to have its own oratory and, as will be shown, had been called upon on the former occasion to vouch for the good name of a future Dean of Wells. There is some evidence for his ownership of property locally, but not enough to give a clear sense of the extent of his landed wealth.[15] An impression of Godwin's seal or signet on a deed of 14 August 1433 ('sigillum meum apposui', FIG. 1) includes a merchant's mark, comprising a shield bearing a saltire cross (particularly appropriate to Wells, where the Cathedral was dedicated to St Andrew), or possibly crossed grozing irons, with a moon, a sun (perhaps), a star and a lily between the arms (FIG. 2).[16] Above, there is a capital T (on the left) and a cross-shaft with pennons flying to sinister, forming either an interlaced W or nested Vs. Below, a small device is now unreadable. The elements are common in such marks, although the heavenly light sources are an interesting choice for a man whose business was illumination.[17] The initial T could suggest that the seal had been inherited, which would be consistent with the family nature of many glazing businesses. Shaw argues that Godwin belonged to an elite of urban gentlemen, mostly merchants, involved in trade but probably distinguished socially by rural landholding.[18] As Horrox pointed out, this group emerges in a new way in fifteenth-century England, confounding expectations that gentry should prefer to dissociate themselves from towns.[19]

Godwin's social status in the region is apparent from the fact that he is named as an executor of John Stourton of Preston Plucknett (d.1438), a leading member of the county gentry.[20] The Stourtons held land in both Wiltshire and Somerset, and Sir John Stourton 'junior' was elevated to the peerage as Baron Stourton in 1448.[21] John 'senior', of Preston Plucknett, was his uncle and involved with the county

FIG. 1:
A deed of John Godwin, burgess of Wells, releasing a messuage in St Cuthbert Street to John Palton, 14 August 1433 (Wells Cathedral, Dean and Chapter Archives, AH 171). Photograph by R. Neale. Reproduced by courtesy of the Dean and Chapter, Wells Cathedral.

FIG. 2:
Impression of
the seal of
John Godwin.
Photograph by
R. Neale.
Reproduced by
courtesy of the
Dean and
Chapter, Wells
Cathedral.

both through his landholdings (many acquired through marriage) and public activities, serving as JP, Sheriff and Member of Parliament.[22] He and Godwin both served as MPs in 1423. Stourton took an interest in many aspects of the ecclesiastical affairs of the region and was closely associated with the bishopric, acting as guardian of the temporalities after Bishop Bubwith's death in 1424 and as steward of the estates of the bishopric under Bishop Stafford. Godwin's co-executor was William Carent, MP (d.1476), husband of Stourton's niece and representative of another leading county family, whose brother Nicholas was Dean of Wells between 1446 and 1467.[23] John Godwin, 'gentleman', himself testifies at the confirmation of the Dean's election.[24] Such connections help to account for the glazier's success.

Shaw's account of the economy of Wells shows that many trades had grown up in the service of the rich cathedral community that dominated the town, and glazing may have been one of them.[25] We have no contracts to associate Godwin with any particular kind of work, but this was no jobbing glazier and the refenestration of the nave and transepts took place when Godwin was beginning to make his way in the town.[26] The three western lancets of the nave had been reglazed by Bishop Harewell (1366-1386), but on the limited surviving evidence there may then have been an interval before the other windows were remade. In the nave north clerestory were recorded the arms of Stanley, which imply a date after 1402, when Dean Thomas Stanley took office. Heraldry that was once on the east side of the south transept post-dated the change in the English royal arms that probably took place in late 1406. Fund-raising is recorded to have been underway in August 1415 and one of the windows in the south transept included an inscription for Alice, Countess of Kent (d.1416), in terms that suggest she is dead. The limited surviving glass, almost entirely in tracery lights, is in a variety of styles (not surprisingly given the vast area involved), all revealing awareness of International Gothic. It seems a plausible hypothesis that John Godwin played some part in this project and, conceivably, it had even brought him to the city.

In the 1420s and 1430s, there were fewer opportunities for glazing at the Cathedral once the nave and transepts had been refenestrated, but work was to be had in the town. The parish church of St Cuthbert is one of the largest in Somerset and Godwin's possible close association with it as churchwarden has already been mentioned. Although the rectorship was held by the Dean and Chapter, which appointed a perpetual vicar, the corporation controlled the appointment of two churchwardens and was responsible for most fabric funds, co-operating with the Cathedral authorities in maintaining and beautifying the building.[27] The date of the architecture remains to be resolved in detail and little glass survives beyond fragments in the east window of the south transept.

On the north side of the church stands the medieval hospital of St Saviour, the Blessed Virgin Mary and All Saints, commonly known as the almshouse in the middle ages (FIG. 3). John Leland recorded that Bishop Nicholas Bubwith (1407-1424) began the building, but that it was completed by his executors.[28] A deed of agreement to commence building was agreed in late September 1435, in fact, according to the terms of the bishop's will; arrangements for the maintenance of a chaplain were finalized in September 1445 and statutes followed shortly after.[29]

Such foundations were very popular in the later middle ages.[30] At the east end stands a small chapel, beyond the original hall of the twenty-four inmates, with a five-light East window. From the tracery there survive four coloured shields, with an inscription naming Nicholas Bubwith, architecture and part of a delicately painted angel in white glass with silver stain (now in nII; FIG. 4), all of which were described and drawn there in the early nineteenth century.[31] The glass is technically accomplished, with drilled inserts, stipple shading, stickwork and back-painting. The little that survives does not relate obviously to any glass at the Cathedral.

Bubwith's shield was in the first of the four tracery lights. As an executor of Bubwith's will,[32] John Stourton had been a party to the foundation of the hospital, but his arms are not present, perhaps suggesting that the glass post-dated his death. However, the arms of Sydenham impaling Stourton (Stourton's daughter married John Sydenham) appeared in the third light within a Garter, supported by an angel under a canopy. John Sydenham is named in association with other parties involved in securing the endowment of the almshouse in January 1446.[33] The other two shields are of the English royal arms, again within a Garter (the pair to the preceding), in the second light, and for Bishop John Stafford (1425-1443) in the fourth (the pair to Bubwith's shield). Henry VI and Bishop Stafford were specifically to be remembered in the terms of grants towards the almshouse in October 1441 and August 1442.[34]

Although the initiative had come from Bishop Bubwith, the hospital was administered jointly by the town and the Cathedral.[35] Demonstrating the close relationship between corporation and almshouse architecturally, a new guildhall was built at the west end of the same block.[36] The provision of this meeting place, presumably planned from around the time of the foundation, was almost exactly contemporary with the establishment of new statutes for the corporation. This close association of guildhall and hospital was a forcible reminder of the gap between the rich and the poor or unfortunate, and the responsibility of one for the other before God – but also a way of binding the town to the fulfilment of that responsibility. At the other end of the complex, it seems plausible that the glazing in the chapel went to Godwin's business, the dominant glazier in the city and a prominent officer in its government at this time. He is among the burgesses witnessing an indenture establishing endowment for the chaplain in September 1445, as well as other documents relating to the almshouse foundation.[37]

Godwin must have worked widely, taking advantage of his connections with county gentry like the Stourtons and the Carents to provide glass for the many windows in the new building work underway in the region. A boom had been going on since the later fourteenth century and Godwin was surely a direct beneficiary. He must be the John Glazier of Wells recorded in the churchwardens' accounts of St Mary's parish church in Bridgwater, for 1414-15, for example.[38] He was paid the substantial sum of £3 4s 2d for glazing the new chapel of Holy Trinity with his team ('servientibus suis'). He may have benefited from

FIG. 3:
The Hospital of St Saviour or Bishop Bubwith's Almshouse, Wells, a view from the north-east showing the East window of the Chapel. Photograph by the author.

a longer family association with this major port. In 1378, before the MP was born, a John Godwin was paid £4 6s 8d for repairing ('emendando') windows in the same church, perhaps his father or uncle.[39] Both may have been related to the armigerous Godwin family, which held the local manor of Godwinsbower, helping to explain the glazier's later social standing.[40] Within three years of the foundation of the almshouse, Godwin would be an executor of John Stourton's will, as mentioned above. This sets out that Stourton wished to be buried at Stavordale Priory, which he had rebuilt and where glazing is explicitly stated as remaining to be done, another plausible project for Godwin to have undertaken.[41]

In looking at the wider context in the south-west of England, it is impossible to avoid what Woodforde called the 'Somerset School of Glass Painting', which dominated the region in the second half of the fifteenth century, in fact far beyond the county boundary, into Wiltshire, Dorset, Devon and Cornwall.[42] Marks has argued plausibly that this was not so much a school, as a single workshop operating over a long period.[43] The Corpus Vitrearum surveys have not yet been carried out for the south-western counties, but the style is probably found before mid-century in glass removed from the choir of Sherborne Abbey, just over the county boundary in Dorset.[44] A study of the glass at Exeter Cathedral has suggested that the workshop was based in that city, a hypothesis which remains to be proven.[45]

In Wells itself, these or related glaziers were probably employed by Bishop Beckington (1443-1466) to fill a window in the south aisle of the choir (sX) opposite his monument, which was established over a decade before his death; and to fill the windows on the Chain Gate, the bridge that he had built between the Cathedral and the hall of the Vicars Choral (constructed 1459-60).[46] In the windows of the Cathedral library, probably made in the 1450s, are found the distinctive quarry types of the same workshop. John Godwin had presumably ceased working, so perhaps a new workshop had moved into the region, but it is also worth considering whether this was a successor to his enterprise.

FIG. 4:
Heraldic glass and other fragments, c.1440, from the East window of the Chapel of the Hospital of St Saviour, Wells (now in nII, a low window on the north side). Photograph by the author.

NOTES

[1] R. Marks and P. Williamson (eds.), *Gothic: Art for England, 1400-1547*, exhib. cat. (London: Victoria & Albert Museum, 2003), 96-97, cat. nos. 22, 89, 292, 317.

[2] D. King, *The Medieval Stained Glass of St Peter Mancroft, Norwich*, Corpus Vitrearum Medii Aevi Great Britain, 5 (London, forthcoming). See also D. King, 'A Glazier from the Bishopric of Utrecht in Fifteenth-Century Norwich' in *Utrecht: Britain and the Continent, Archaeology, Art and Architecture*, ed. E. de Bièvre, British Archaeological Association Conference Transactions XVIII (1996), 216-25.

[3] L. S. Colchester, *Stained Glass in Wells Cathedral*, 2nd edn. (Wells: The Friends of Wells Cathedral, 1956), 38; R. Marks, *Stained Glass in England during the Middle Ages* (London: Routledge, 1993), 42.

[4] D. G. Shaw, *The Creation of a Community, The City of Wells in the Middle Ages* (Oxford: Clarendon Press, 1993); T. Ayers, *The Medieval Stained Glass of Wells Cathedral*, Corpus Vitrearum Medii Aevi Great Britain, 4 (London: forthcoming 2004).

[5] Shaw 1993, chapter 3, section 5; chapter 5, section 4.

[6] On the smaller English town, see *ibid.*, chapter 2. See also D. Keene, 'National and Regional Identities' and 'Civic Institutions', and J. Grenville, 'The Urban Landscape', in *Gothic: Art for England* (2003), 46-55, 262-64, 254-56.

[7] Wells, City Archives, 'Wells, Acts of the Corporation, A.D. 1378-1450', 166; D. O. Shilton and R. Holworthy (eds.) *Wells City Charters*, Somerset Record Society, vol. xlvi (1932), 134. I am grateful to the archivist William Smith for his help.

[8] *Ibid.*, 137, 140-43, 146-49.

[9] 'Acts of the Corporation, 1378-1450', 169, 178, 182, 205 (standing pledge; in the last case for another glazier, John Hampton); 148, 164, 167, 170, 174, 177 (churchwarden).

[10] 'Acts of the Corporation, 1378-1450', 240, 256, 281, 303, 322, 324; '1450-1553', 16.

[11] 'Acts of the Corporation, 1378-1450', 240, 255 (the elections); J. C. Wedgwood, in collaboration with A. D. Holt, *History of Parliament, Biographies of the Members of the Commons House, 1439-1509* (London: HMSO, 1936), 383.

[12] J. D. Le Couteur, *Ancient Glass in Winchester* (Winchester: Warren & Son, 1920), 136.

[13] *The Register of Thomas Bekynton, Bishop of Bath and Wells, 1443-1465*, ed. H. C. Maxwell-Lyte and M. C. B. Dawes, vol. II, Somerset Record Society, l (1935), 433, no. 1637.

[14] *Ibid.*, vol. I, xlix (1934), 311, no. 1175.

[15] Shilton and Holworthy 1932, 105, charter no. 200 (1413), acquiring land.

[16] Wells Cathedral, Dean and Chapter Archives, AH 171 (oval impression in red wax, surrounded by an impressed rush). I am indebted to Frances Neale for observations on the impression and to Richard Neale for photographs.

[17] E. M. Elmhirst, *Merchants' Marks* (London: Harleian Society, 1959), nos. 484, 630, 974; F. A. Girling, *English Merchants' Marks* (London/New York/Toronto: Oxford University Press, 1964), 11, 13, 17.

[18] Shaw 1993, 155-56, 173.

[19] R. Horrox, 'The Urban Gentry in the Fifteenth Century', in *Towns and Townspeople in the Fifteenth Century*, ed. J. A. F. Thomson (Gloucester: Sutton, 1988), 22-44.

[20] F. W. Weaver (ed.), *Somerset Medieval Wills (1383-1500)*, Somerset Record Society, xvi (1901), 145-46; J. S. Roskell, L. Clark and C. Rawcliffe, *The History of Parliament, The House of Commons, 1386-1421*, vol. IV (Stroud: Alan Sutton, 1992), 490-92. He was to receive £10 for his work and to act also for Stourton's recently deceased brother, Master Richard Stourton (d.1437), a canon of Wells: J. Le Neve, *Fasti Ecclesiae Anglicanae 1300-1541*, vol. VIII, *Bath and Wells Diocese*, comp. B. Jones (London: Institute of Historical Research, 1964), 24.

[21] G. E. C[okayne], *The Complete Peerage of England, Scotland, Ireland, Great Britain and the United Kingdom, Extant, Extinct and Dormant*, revised edn., vol. XII (London: St Catherine Press, 1910-59 edn), 301-302.

[22] Roskell, Clark and Rawcliffe 1992, vol. IV, 490-92.

[23] *Ibid.*, vol. II, 480-82.

[24] Maxwell-Lyte and Dawes 1935, 433, no. 1637.

[25] Shaw 1993, 66-69; chapter 8, section 1.

[26] For details of what follows, see Ayers, forthcoming.

[27] T. Serel, *Historical Notes on the Church of Saint Cuthbert, in Wells; the Priory of St. John, College of La Mountery, and Chapels formerly at Southover, Southway, Polsham, and Chilcote* (Wells: J. M. Atkins, 1875), 35-55; Shaw 1993, 258-61.

[28] L. Toulmin Smith (ed.), *The Itinerary of John Leland, in or about the Years 1535-1543*, vol. 1 (London: George Bell & Sons, 1907; reprinted Southern Illinois University Press, 1964), 145, 292.

[29] Wells Cathedral, Dean and Chapter Archives, AH 178 (deed of agreement), AH 193 (endowment of chaplain); J. H. Parker, *The Architectural Antiquities of the City of Wells* (Oxford and London: J. Parker & Co., 1866), 43-68 (by T. Serel), esp. 60-64 (statutes); W. Paley Baildon ed., *Calendar of the Manuscripts of the Dean and Chapter of Wells*, vol. 2 (London: Historical Manuscripts Commission, 1914), 73, charters 611-13, 621.

[30] There is a substantial literature, but see recently N. Orme and M. Webster, *The English Hospital, 1070-1570* (New Haven and London: Yale University Press, 1995).

[31] British Library, Add. MS 17463, ff.210v-211r. A watercolour of the window, showing the glass and dated 1847, is in the collection of the Somerset Archaeological and Natural History Society, Taunton (Braikenridge Collection, Wells, no. 31). I am indebted to Dr Matthew Reeve for a xerox and librarian David Bromwich for the reference. Serel reports, however, that the glass was moved to its present position from the 'common kitchen' in 1850, as part of the general restoration of the chapel: Parker 1866, 68. At this time, 'the eastern window was opened, repaired, and filled with stained glass (by Bell)', which remains in the tracery lights, deriving in design from the medieval remains, with shields of Bishops Bubwith, Still (1593-1608), Willes (1743-1773) and Bagot (1845-1854).

[32] *The Register of Henry Chichele, Archbishop of Canterbury, 1414-1443*, ed. E. F. Jacob with the assistance of H. C. Johnson, vol. II (Oxford: Canterbury and York Society, 1937), 300.

[33] Wells Cathedral, Dean and Chapter Archives, AH 197.

[34] Pailey Baildon 1914, charter 611; Wells, Dean and Chapter Archives, AH 185.

[35] Parker 1866, 50; Shaw 1993, 241-42.

[36] Parker 1866, 68-72.

[37] Wells Cathedral, Dean and Chapter Archives, AH 193.

[38] T. B. Dilks ed., *Bridgwater Borough Archives*, III, *1400-1445*, Somerset Record Society, lviii, 1945, 49, no. 576.

[39] T. B. Dilks ed., *Bridgwater Borough Archives*, II, *1377-1399*, Somerset Record Society, liii, 1938, 189, no. 426.

[40] R. W. Dunning (ed.), *A History of the County of Somerset, Andersfield, Cannington, and North Petherton Hundreds (Bridgwater and Neighbouring Parishes)*, VI (London: Oxford University Press, 1992), 210.

[41] Weaver 1901, 143, 145.

[42] C. Woodforde, *Stained Glass in Somerset, 1250-1830* (Oxford: Oxford University Press, 1946), chapter II; C. Woodforde, *English Stained and Painted Glass* (Oxford: Clarendon Press, 1954), 23-24. For medieval glass in Devon and Cornwall, photographed by the late Professor Christopher Brooks, see the CVMA website (www.cvma.ac.uk).

[43] Marks 1993, 193-94.

[44] Marks 1993, 193.

[45] C. Brooks and D. Evans, *The Great East Window of Exeter Cathedral* (Exeter: University of Exeter, 1988), 107.

[46] For a discussion of these, see Ayers, forthcoming.

Chris Brooks and Martin Cherry

The Prince and the Parker:
a speculative essay on the Evans chantry glass
at Coldridge, Devon, and Tudor propaganda

Contemporary representations of Edward V in any medium are so rare that the survival of one in glass in deepest rural Devon raises intriguing questions as to patronage and purpose. Set high in the East window of a chantry chapel and looking down upon an ensemble of coeval fittings and fixtures, the figure of the boy king, one of the Princes in the Tower, challenges the onlooker to understand the message he was designed to convey. The patron of the chantry remains elusive, being almost wholly absent from the documentary record, but a mixture of firm evidence and inference provides a plausible story that sheds light on the propaganda functions of royal representations in the early Tudor period.[1]

FIG. 1:
Exterior view of Coldridge Church showing chantry chapel to fore. Photograph by Chris Brooks.

John Evans and the Coldridge chantry

Coldridge is a parish in mid-Devon, north of the granite mass of Dartmoor and still quite remote. The village stands on high ground, one of a line of such hill-top settlements in this part of the county. The nearest large town is Crediton, ten miles to the south east, with Exeter some six or seven miles beyond.

Coldridge parish church, standing in the centre of the village and dedicated to St Matthew, is principally Devon Perpendicular of the fifteenth century. In the early sixteenth century the north chancel aisle was built – or possibly remodelled – as a chantry chapel (FIG. 1). Architecturally it is unpretentious enough, and its endowment was modest, providing for an anniversary and five candles, its value recorded at four shillings by the commissioners who dissolved it in 1548.[2] The chantry has its own small door on the north side, three-light straight-headed windows in the north and east walls, and a two-bay granite arcade giving into the chancel, its western arch crudely adjusted to the north aisle arcade – a clumsiness that would originally have been hidden by the roodloft to the screen. Modest as it is though, this little chantry links Coldridge, far down in the south west, with the turbulent reign of Richard III and the demise of the House of York, and with the dynastic history of the Tudors.[3]

The chantry was built by John Evans for the use of himself and his family. Both chancel aisles have, or had, inscriptions in plenty. Carved on the granite imposts above the capitals of the chantry arcade, and still coloured with its original red paint, is the legend ORATE PRO IHOHANNES EVANS. Although the original furniture of the chantry has largely gone, some benches and a prie-dieu survive in the south chancel aisle. Here, on the desk of the prie-dieu, Evans spelt things out at greater length: ORATE P[RO] JOH[ANNES] EVANS PARCARIUS DE COLRUG FACTOR ILLIUS OPUS ANNO REGNI REGIS REGIS HENRICO OCTAVIO TERCIS. That is, 'Pray for John Evans, Parker of Coldridge, maker of this work in the third year of the reign of King Henry the Eighth'. Other seating provided by Evans survived in the family aisle until the 1880s, only to disappear in a subsequent restoration of the church. Among this was another prayer desk with a further inscription, recorded by the Exeter architect Edward Ashworth in 1882: ORATE P[RO] BONA STATU JOH[ANN]IS EVANS QUI FIERI FECIT EX P[RO]P[ER]IS EXPENSIS A[NNO] D[OMI]NI MCCCCXI S[E]C[UN]DA DIE AUGUSTA: 'Pray for the good estate of John Evans, who caused this to be made at his own expense, the second day of August in the year of the Lord 1511'.[4]

Evans's freestone effigy survives in the north wall of the chantry chapel, reclining below a shallow ogival arch that is far cruder than the effigy itself. Though battered, it is evident that it must originally have been of some quality and is reminiscent in terms of its pose and modelling to the effigy in Exeter Cathedral of Sir John Speke,[5] who owned land in Brushford, close to Coldridge, and died in 1518. Wearing full plate armour over chain mail, Evans lies in a relaxed pose, the hands originally clasped in prayer at the waist, the head, turned slightly to one side, resting on a tasselled pillow supported by a podgy-limbed cherub. Against the

pillow is propped a small shield carrying, yet again, Evans's name: JOH[ANN]IS EVA[N]S – the surname oddly contracted. In the very small body of secondary material about Coldridge, Evans is referred to as Sir John, but there is no contemporary evidence to suggest that he was so termed in his lifetime. The fact that the shield carries only his name could imply that Evans was not even armigerous, and the full armour does not prove beyond doubt the profession of arms. Probably a soldier, John Evans – as the inscription on the surviving prie-dieu reveals – was certainly a parker, responsible for the upkeep of a hunting chase and its stock and taking a share of its emoluments and pleasures. The long, loose surcoat that the effigy shows over his armour probably represents his robe of office (FIG. 2).

In the fifteenth century the deer park at Coldridge that was Evans's responsibility had been part of the estates of the Bonville family, for more than half a century the most potent rivals in the south west to the Courtenay Earls of Devon. With the failure of the male line, the great bulk of these lands passed to Cecily Bonville – one of the great heiresses of late medieval England. In 1474 she married Thomas Grey, Earl of Huntingdon, son of Elizabeth Woodville and thus stepson of Edward IV. In April 1475, Grey became Lord Harington and Bonville by right of his wife, and assumed the Bonville lands along with the title. Later in the same year he was created first Marquess of Dorset. Subsequently a Knight of the Garter and Privy Councillor, Dorset was a key figure in the Woodville faction and controlled the southwest of England in the interest of the King, his stepfather Edward IV. In the power struggle that followed the King's death in 1483, the Woodville faction was decisively worsted by Richard Duke of Gloucester, soon to be Richard III. Stripped of his offices and grants, and subsequently attainted, Dorset fled the country under circumstances that we will revert to later. The attainder was reversed by Henry VII who reconfirmed Grey in all his lands in November 1486.[6]

A 1525 survey of the Bonville lands makes it clear that it was during the reign of Henry VII that John Evans – still alive with his wife Margaret when the survey was made – came to Coldridge.[7] The parkership was a valuable post: the 1525 survey says that the park was 3000 yards in circumference, with 140 beasts of the chase and good timber. The deer park formed a rough oval and lay immediately north of the village and traces of it still survive. As well as the parkership, the 1525 survey also records that John Evans held a sixty-year lease on the manor of Coldridge, and a life leasehold on the adjoining farm of Birches, along with other smaller properties. The house belonging to the manor was Coldridge Barton, still surviving as a farm but with little if anything from Evans's time. The manor lands totalled 152 acres, plus two gardens and four closes, while Birches, which remained in the Evans family until the eighteenth century, ran to 240 acres.

Evans would have been a figure of considerable standing in the local community. But he was not a local man, and there is no record of a family called Evans in mid-Devon before John Evans's time at Coldridge. The surname suggests a Welsh origin, especially since it is quite unusual in public records outside Wales at this date. In addition, a later entry in the Coldridge burial registers records the name of one of the family as John ApEvans, a specifically Welsh form.[8] How then did the first John Evans get to Coldridge? The grant of the manor and parkership must have been made on the authority either of Thomas Grey or of his wife Cecily, presumably as a token of good service. There is, however, no firm evidence as to the precise nature of that service, or of Evans's connection to the Grey/Bonville affinity. But, remembering the Welsh connection, there is a well-established link between Wales and the Woodville faction, of which Grey was such a key member. For Wales was one of the Woodvilles' principal power bases, held during the reign

FIG. 3:
View of the
parclose screen
between the
chancel and the
Evans chantry
chapel, Coldridge
Church.
Photograph by
Peter Williams.
Copyright
English Heritage.

of Edward IV by Anthony Woodville, second Earl Rivers, the brother of the Queen and the uncle of Thomas Grey, Marquess of Dorset. Evans could well have come to Grey from the affinity of his uncle, for that affinity was thrown into disarray by the arrest and summary execution of Rivers in 1483, after Richard III's seizure of power.

Evans's likely Welsh origin is suggestive in another way as well. He was established at Coldridge, it will be remembered, during the reign of Henry VII, who was born and brought up in Wales and who was, of course, the first monarch of the Welsh House of Tudor. Grey's successful establishment at Henry's court would not only have put him in a good position to reward his servants – hence, on this argument, the grant of Coldridge to Evans – it would also have meant access to royal patronage. And here, despite Evans's general elusiveness, there is suggestive documentary evidence that may tie Evans both to the Tudor court and to the patronage of the crown. In 1516, the published *Letters and Papers* of Henry VIII record a John Evan in the capacity of yeoman of the crown, receiving six pence a day for life, the grant specifically noted as having been made by Henry VII.[9] As was remarked earlier, Evans is an uncommon name in English public records at this date; nor need the spelling without a terminal 's' worry us, for Evans's name is spelt indiscriminately with and without it in the 1525 survey of the Bonville lands.

If this John Evan is the Coldridge John Evans, then very likely it was the same man, again described as a yeoman (presumably in this context a king's yeoman), who was present at the funeral in 1511 of the infant son of Henry VIII and Catherine of Aragon, Henry Prince of Wales – an occasion on which the chief mourner was none other than Thomas Grey, second Marquess of Dorset, the son and heir of Evans's original patron. We also know that Dorset occasionally travelled to Devon to visit his aunt, Katherine Courtenay, Countess of Devon and, significantly, one of the sisters of the Princes in the Tower. Out of favour and imprisoned during the later years of Henry VII's reign, Katherine was rehabilitated by Henry VIII in 1511 and restored to her estates. From this time on she began to style herself 'the excellent Princess Katherine, Countess of Devon, daughter, sister and aunt of kings'. This, the date also when Evans adorned his chantry, suggests that the Coldridge glass might be the sole vestige of a local cult of the Princes centred around the person of their sister.[10]

The furnishing of the chantry chapel

With this nexus of relationship, patronage, and possible affinity in mind, we can return to the chantry chapel at Coldridge, and to the most remarkable of its fittings – its parclose screen and the remains of its stained glass. Firstly the parclose. The fine rood screen of Coldridge church, the north section of which divides the Evans chantry from the north aisle, is characteristic West Country work of the late fifteenth century. The parclose is quite different: rectangular openings are divided by spiral-shafted columns, the heads filled with Flamboyant forms containing a restless filigree of tiny tracery motifs, and wainscot panels decorated with linenfold (FIG. 3). Two other Devon churches have screenwork like this. The chancel screen of the little church of Brushford – literally on the next hill west of Coldridge under a mile away – has all the same elements, though the openings are only divided into two. In Colebrooke parish church – four miles south-west of Coldridge – are two further such screens, somewhat more complex, but of similar character and composition. They separated off the east end of the north aisle for the Coplestone family, considerable magnates in the later medieval period, Lords of the Manor of Colebrooke and also related to the Bonville family. The screens in these three churches form a group unique in Devon and perhaps in England. But they are not English at all. Stylistically, they are akin to the late fifteenth-century screenwork of southern Brittany, and are particularly close in detail and design to the screen below the loft of the great jubé of St Fiacre le Faouet, which is dated to 1480.[11]

The existence of the screens all within a small area of mid-Devon, without parallel elsewhere in the county, cannot be coincidental. It strongly suggests that they came from the same source at the same time – that they were all in the same batch, as it were, when they arrived in Devon. They did not come in the normal way of trade, for although there was regular trade between Brittany and the south Devon coast, it did not include church fittings. Moreover, these screens were not designed for the positions they now occupy. The Brushford screen fits best, but its reverse side has vertical mouldings chopped short, and only half its wainscot has linenfold decoration. The screen on the chancel side at Colebrooke has its muntins fairly roughly cut to fit the arcade, and both the screens are incomplete in a way that cannot be simply the result of loss and damage over time. At Coldridge, the adjustment to position is roughest of all, with wainscot and tracery crudely chopped through to make the fit and, interestingly, re-assembled so that the fairer side faced into the chantry rather than the chancel.[12]

These screens, then, were obtained from Brittany as a single lot, presumably soon after their manufacture in the 1480s, and were later reassembled in Devon. In one case several components are missing, in another, a whole bay of the screen is clumsily cut through. All this is decidedly odd, but suggestively so, for Brittany in the 1480s was where Henry Tudor, Earl of Richmond, assembled his forces for his attempt on the throne of England. And among the people who joined him there were Thomas Grey, Marquess of Dorset, and his supporters. Although some thought that Dorset was present in June 1483 at the coronation of Richard III – not the last time there was to be a certain ambiguity in his relationship to Richard – it is unlikely and, by October he was a leading figure in Buckingham's rebellion, the stated object of which was to place Richmond on the throne.[13] On 18 October Dorset proclaimed Henry in Exeter, with a large number of local gentry assembled in support. The rebellion was a fiasco, and the rebels fled before Richard and his army reached the city in early November. They escaped through the ports of south Devon to Brittany, whither Henry himself had already returned, having been unable to effect a landing on the English coast. Within a few days he learnt that Dorset and other supporters had arrived at Vannes. They were to remain in Brittany and France until 1485. It

seems very probable that the screens that finished up in Coldridge, Brushford, and Colebrooke, had their origin in this sojourn, either obtained at the time or through contacts made then. Grey could have obtained them himself, but their highly localised distribution in Devon suggests a local resident, and that points to the Coplestones of Colebrooke. While it has not been possible to confirm that members of the family were in Brittany between 1483 and 1485, Philip Coplestone, the former head of the family, was related by marriage to Grey having married during the reign of Edward IV, Anne Bonville, heiress of the Bonville family seat of Shute in east Devon. The other, and greater, Bonville heiress, it will be recalled, was Anne's cousin Cecily, whose inheritance included the manor of Coldridge and its deer park.

The glass, its meaning and context

The circumstantial evidence surrounding the person of John Evans – the Welsh connection, the likely nature of his relation-ship to Grey and the Woodville faction, the pension from Henry VII, the Breton screens – is all brought sharply into focus by the glass that remains in the East window of the chantry. It is very incomplete. There are two principal elements. In the centre light survives the figure of a boy

FIG. 4:
Evans chantry chapel. Detail of the stained glass figure depicting Prince Edward, son of Edward IV. Photograph by Peter Williams. Copyright English Heritage.

prince (FIG. 4, SEE ALSO FRONT COVER) and, set lower down on the right, the head and torso of another figure to whom we will return. The significance and purpose of the glass is discussed below. It is not certain which *atelier* (or *ateliers*) produced this glass. Evans probably shopped locally, most likely from the Exeter workshop that produced so much glass for West Country clients in the late fifteenth century (although its output was on the wane by the early sixteenth century). The contrasting styles in evidence here – the refined, sensitive, 'soft' representation of the Prince and the harder, more realistic and expressive head and torso – could have been produced by the same workshop where a variety of techniques and vocabulary would have been available. At the same time, of course, Evans's likely court connections may have tempted him to commission work from another source, although neither figure closely resembles metropolitan work of the period.

The Prince carries a book and sceptre and wears a coronet, though above his head hangs another and far larger royal crown. He wears an ermine tippet and an ermine-lined robe over a short gold tunic, and has on the hose and round-toed shoes of the early sixteenth century. The polygonal base on which he stands bears the legend *prenys edward the feyte*. Pieced in above the crown is a fragment that looks like a falcon within a fetterlock, the badge used by Edward V, as depicted at Bishop King's chantry in St George's Chapel, Windsor, and by his brother, Richard, Duke of York, as in the 'Royal' window at Canterbury Cathedral – both representations to which we shall return. Prince Edward the Fifth was the elder of the two Princes in the Tower. Their disappearance in the summer of 1483, and their supposed killing on the orders of Richard III came to be the central dramatic component in Tudor propaganda. The murdered innocent, whose death lingeringly retold by Tudor historians gave a moral justification to Henry VII that far outweighed his less than convincing claim to the throne, thus provided moral legitimacy for the whole Tudor dynasty.

In his book, *Richard III and the Princes in the Tower*, A. J. Pollard states that there are four contemporary or near contemporary representations of Prince Edward.[14] This Coldridge example, which Dr Pollard did not know, brings the total to five. That of itself would make the figure sufficiently remarkable, but there are aspects of the representation that make it more unusual still. Two of the other representations are also in stained glass – but wholly unlike the Coldridge figure. The best known is from the so-called Royal Window at Canterbury Cathedral, completed before 1482, in which Edward Prince of Wales is shown with the rest of the royal family, including his sister Princess Cecily (illustrated elsewhere in this issue, FIG 1, p. 159.) These figures were originally kneeling along the foot of the window in the conventional pose of donors.[15] Very similar in conception is the representation in the East window of Little Malvern Priory, a window commissioned by Bishop Alcock of Worcester, a member of Edward IV's Council, and dating from 1481, in which the Prince was also shown with the rest of the royal family (although only he now survives intact), and appears again in the attitude of a donor.[16] Made during the Prince's lifetime, the Canterbury and Little Malvern figures image Edward as pious benefactor, in which role he can of course be paralleled by hundreds of other donor figures in medieval glass. But they do not help us understand the meaning of the representation of Edward at Coldridge, where he is not shown as a donor.

One other representation dates from Edward's lifetime: it illustrates the Lambeth Palace manuscript *Sayings of the Philosophers* and shows the Prince with his father Edward IV and mother Elizabeth Woodville receiving the work from the Queen's brother Anthony Woodville, second Earl Rivers – uncle to the Prince as he was also uncle to Evans's patron, Thomas Grey.[17] That connection is tantalising, but perhaps coincidental – one would expect the Woodvilles to figure in material closely related to the royal family in the 1470s and early 1480s. Certainly this representation of the Prince does not seem to relate in any significant way to the Coldridge figure.

That is not the case with the fourth representation that, as in the Coldridge window, but unlike the others, is posthumous. It is a painting from the back of the stalls opposite the entrance to the chantry of Bishop Oliver King in the south choir aisle of the royal chapel of St George at Windsor and dates from around 1495 (FIG. 5).[18] The figure of Edward V stands alongside three other royal figures who were patrons of Bishop King – Edward Prince of Wales who died at Tewkesbury in 1471, Edward IV, and Henry VII. Although painted on wood, the Windsor artist modelled his composition on glazing designs, the figures being set against quarry grounds.[19] Despite the obvious differences of costume detail between the Windsor and Coldridge figures of Edward V, there are clear parallels in the way they are posed. Both stand on polygonal, sculptural bases that carry their name. The figures are also conceived in the same way, presented to the onlooker not as donors – as at Canterbury and Little Malvern – and not as participants in court ceremony – as in the Lambeth Library manuscript – but as iconic statements, independent images for the viewer's contemplation and interpretation.

But there is a further, and crucial, similarity: although the Coldridge Edward wears a coronet and the Windsor Edward does not, both are shown with the crown of England suspended above them – in the case of Coldridge a crown almost as large as the figure itself. The iconographical point, of course, is that Edward, although the legitimate heir to the throne, was never crowned: and that is a point made expressly against Richard III, who justified his assumption of the throne by claiming that both the Princes were bastards. In other words, the depictions of Edward at both Windsor and Coldridge are politically charged, the representations consciously determined ideologically. At Windsor, the composition is particularly telling. The four figures are not arranged chronologically but in such a way that Edward V (second panel from left), a child, who stands shorter than the others but with his crown hovering above him at the same level as the other kings, looks upward towards his father, Edward IV, in the third panel. As well as reinforcing Bishop King's own anti-Ricardian credentials – he was deprived of his offices and imprisoned by Richard in June 1483 – the group also implicitly presents Henry VII, the concluding figure in the series, as, co-extensively, the remedy for both personal and dynastic wrongs. So what should we make of the Coldridge representation? What reasons, personal and political, may have underlain John Evans's choice of a figure of Edward V for the East window of his chantry chapel?

The answers one can provide are necessarily tentative, and it seems likely that the motives involved were complex. Central to them could well have been concern over the role of the Woodville faction and, in particular, of Evans's patron, Thomas Grey, Marquess of Dorset, in the murky events that took place in the late spring of 1483. Anthony Woodville, second Lord Rivers, was the governor of Edward, Prince of Wales and head of his household. He was with him at Ludlow when the news of the death of Edward IV arrived. Rivers, accompanied by Richard Grey – Dorset's brother – then set out with the Prince for London, where a swift coronation was being planned by the Queen and by Dorset. At Northampton on 29 April, the Dukes of Gloucester and Buckingham effectively intercepted the royal party on its way to London and, having arrested Rivers and Richard Grey, took control of the person of Edward V. When the news of the coup reached London, Dorset, the Queen, and her children, fled to sanctuary in Westminster. Within a few weeks there followed Richard's usurpation of the throne and the disappearance of the Princes. What we need to recognise here is the potentially – and perhaps actually – compromised position of the Marquess of Dorset. His uncle and his brother had had charge of the person of the young King, and he was thought by some to have still been Constable of the Tower (although this is unlikely). In fact, Richard's coup, masked as an assertion of his rights as protector, secured control of the King, while the Woodvilles were stripped of office. But contemporary chroniclers were wholly uncertain about the sequence of events, or of who was responsible for them – and Richard did nothing to relieve that uncertainty. Although the Tudor version of events, promoted after 1485, made the monstrous Richard responsible for everything, ambiguity still surrounded Dorset's role. Nor was this helped by the compromised nature of some of Dorset's own actions. As was remarked earlier, some thought he had attended Richard's coronation. Certainly, he had rebelled and joined Henry Tudor in Brittany, but Dorset's loyalty to the Tudor cause became questionable when his mother apparently secured a reconciliation between him and Richard's court, and Henry had to prevent his returning to England. In consequence, Dorset did not take part in the expedition that finished with the victory at Bosworth, but was left in Paris as a surety for a loan of money. So, even after his establishment at the Tudor court, Thomas Grey had, as we would put it today, a problem of credibility; and it was a problem that related back very directly to the key issue of responsibility for the person of the young Edward V in those fateful late spring months of 1483. As a client of Dorset, presumably well disposed towards him, John Evans would have been concerned for the reputation of his patron – such concern being a proper part of the response to good lordship. In such a context we can read the commemorative icon of the dead Prince at Coldridge as explicitly endorsing the Tudor version of his deposition and death at

FIG. 5:
The Windsor
Edward V,
Chantry Chapel
of Bishop King,
St. George's
Chapel. (c. 1495).
Copy photograph
by Chris Brooks.

the hands of Richard, and thus implicitly recruiting Grey, his lord and patron, into that endorsement, simultaneously exculpating him and aligning him unambiguously to the Tudor cause.

There may have been something more personal as well. If, as was suggested earlier, Evans came into Grey's service from that of Rivers, following the latter's dramatic demise at the hands of Gloucester and Buckingham, was Evans in the party accompanying Edward V to London? Indeed, as Rivers was Edward's governor, did Evans, through Rivers' household, have experience of service to the young Prince? Without documentary support such questions are merely speculative, yet they are given point by some aspects of the Coldridge representation. The fact that the figure is crowned and yet not crowned, and that the name around the base, Prince Edward the Fifth, conflates his title as heir apparent with his title as monarch, seems to emphasise the poignancy of his situation – and poignancy was certainly available to an early sixteenth-century sensibility, as Tudor versions of the murder of the Princes amply demonstrate. More telling perhaps, indicative of a subtly different status to the Coldridge image of the boy king, is that he is holding a book in his left hand, whereas in the Windsor representation he is holding an orb. Iconographically, a book means holy writ, which means piety: in later Tudor propaganda, launched in the religious troubles of the 1530s, representations of Henry VIII holding a book prepare for his assumption of the role of Defender of the Faith. Here at Coldridge, the book functions to elevate Edward's spiritual standing: not only a murdered innocent but

a pious murdered innocent, poignantly robbed of his rightful throne. That is a potent combination, and one that suggests that Edward may have been – for Evans and in Coldridge at least – a figure of veneration. Indeed, is that not actually invited by his iconic representation in the East window of the chantry chapel towards which from his tomb recess, Evans gazes in perpetuity?

And there is a further element in this representation. The prayer desk inscriptions from the south chancel aisle date the completion of Evans's work to 1511 – one of them indeed to 2 August 1511. Although one cannot unreservedly give this as the date for the completion of the chantry chapel, it is at least highly plausible – and it would be right for the costume detail of the East window figure. We think it possible (inferring from documentary evidence already cited) that John Evans was present in February of that year at the funeral of Henry Prince of Wales – a funeral that followed ironically hard on the heels of the great tournament that the King had summoned to celebrate the birth. How far might Evans's experience of the obsequies of one Prince of Wales influence his commemoration of an earlier prince, one who had been on the very point of coronation? Indeed, how far is the Coldridge Edward V invocatory of other royal heirs who died young? For the icon that dominates the image of the Prince is the great crown, inviting contemplation of the relationship between the individual royal personage and the divine validation of regal authority, coronation itself. And Evans's lifetime had seen the deaths of uncrowned princes enough. Before the Henry whose funeral he had attended – the son of Henry VIII and Catherine of Aragon – there had been Catherine's first husband, the eldest son of Henry VII, Prince Arthur, who had died a youth in 1502 at Ludlow, from whence, nineteen years before, Edward V had set out for the coronation that never happened. And before that Edward was the other Edward, who features in the screen paintings at Windsor, Henry VI's eldest son, killed after the battle of Tewkesbury in 1471 – a killing, contemporary chroniclers said, in which a principal hand was taken by the then recently created Earl of Huntingdon, none other than Evans's patron-to-be, Thomas Grey. That rather sinister connection somehow epitomises the semantic density of the Coldridge image of Edward V: for it is an image in the very marrow of the dynastic anxiety of the Tudors, and of the guilt that insistently fed that anxiety.

There is little other painted glass remaining in the East window of Evans's chantry, and what there is is highly fragmentary – the beginning of the *Orate pro...* legend at the bottom left, a few more or less uninformative scraps of background. But one piece survives that is every bit as unusual as, and in some ways more puzzling, than the figure of Edward V. Low down in the right-hand light is a single head (FIG. 6). It is vigorously conceived, strongly shaped and moulded with a bold use of stipple shading and much expressive stick-work detail. Above all, it is not a conventionalised face, and its marked individuation suggests a measure of deliberate portraiture. It seems not to be by the same hand that produced the Edward V and may thus have been in a different window originally – perhaps that in the north wall of the chapel – although it is certainly contemporaneous. The care taken in the depiction shows that this was not a subsidiary figure. Indeed, given that the ratio of head to body would have been the same as that of the Edward V, then the whole figure would have stood some 19.5 inches high – three inches taller than the Prince. He is depicted bare-headed with shoulder-length straight hair; he wears a heavy garment – it is difficult to decide quite what – on top of what appears to be an undershirt with a v-opening at the neck. Fixed to the shoulder is some kind of heraldic badge, a seven-petalled flower perhaps, the significance of which is as yet unknown. At the bottom of the fragment, below the badge, is the top of a crown, its alternation of cross and fleur-de-lis the same as that which appears on the royal crown that hangs above the head of Edward V.

It is the crown that gives one clue to the possible identity of this figure. John Evans, it will be remembered, was a yeoman of the crown under both Henry VII and Henry VIII. The relatively few depictions of men of this status which survive, largely on memorial brasses, show them wearing a representation of the crown in the form of a large shoulder badge.[20] If it is such a badge that is shown in the Coldridge glass, in association with another as yet unrecognised flower badge, then this head must be what remains of the figure of John Evans himself. If this were so, however, it is odd that he was not so emblazoned on his own stone effigy.

So, such an identification is not wholly satisfactory. The crown does not look like a badge, it looks as if it is meant to represent the thing itself; and its position is odd – it is not set on the shoulder but appears far more centrally, as if held in front of the chest. There is another possible identity. The strongly-individuated features – in particular, the long rather bony face, set lips, and pronounced chin and jaw – all appear in the earliest known portrait of Richard III, that held by the Society of Antiquaries of London. And these features remain constant in the sixteenth-century series derived from the somewhat later portrait in the royal collection. Both types are believed to be based on a lost original. And there is a further suggestive feature to the Coldridge representation. The line of the figure's shoulder, as the hair falls upon it, is unnaturally high – precisely the deformity that Tudor propaganda so successfully assigned to Richard, and that, as we now know, was added to the portrait in the royal collection. Careful analysis of the figure by David Evans shows that the lead line dividing the head is a break and not an original constructional lead. By digitally stitching the two pieces together we get a perfect fit (FIG. 7). The countenance appears to have been given a deliberate twist with the mouth displaced and the upper lip omitted in the interests of deformity.[21]

If this is a representation of Richard III then it is a wholly politicised one, the earliest propaganda image of him, and one that depicts him uniquely and directly as usurper, holding before him the crown that he stole. Attributing heads in medieval glass to specific likenesses is fraught with danger and in many cases – perhaps this – involves the use of the eye of faith. Would local people have been familiar with royal portraits? Would not a propaganda point be better made with the use of an heraldic device such as Richard's boar? But, as we have seen, John Evans's neighbours were not all rustic boors. Some were sophisticated men of affairs with a keen and direct interest in recent events. We cannot know how this

FIG. 7:
Possible representation of Richard III. Digitally manipulated image by David Evans to remove repair leading. Copyright David Evans.

image related to that of Edward V. Yet, so singular is it, and so unusual – in some particulars unprecedented – is the representation of the Prince, and so odd the historical circumstances of the chantry, that we could well have here the fragmentary remains of a unique political and religious iconography. It seems quite conceivable that at Coldridge John Evans, approaching the end of his life, conscious of grave dynastic uncertainty, and mindful of his own experiences and of the tainted ambiguities of his patron's career, sought to resolve doubts, quiet guilts, and seek repose for his soul, perhaps with that of others, by bringing into confrontation the demonised king of Tudor mythology and the sanctified image of his most pathetic victim.

March 1992, revised 2003

NOTES

[1] The late Chris Brooks and I worked intermittently together for many years on this and other Devon church matters and he read a version of this paper to the Royal Archaeological Institute in 1992. Comments received then from Dr P. W. Hammond and Dr Charles Tracy are gratefully acknowledged. The paper also benefited from discussions with various friends, notably Jo Cox, David Evans, Sarah Brown, David Stocker and Anna Eavis. New photography was taken by Peter Williams.

[2] N. Orme, 'The Dissolution of the Chantries in Devon, 1546-8', *Transactions of the Devonshire Association* CXI (1979): 104.

[3] There are no other royal representations in glass of this period surviving in Devon and, of the many painted panels on screens of the late-fifteenth and early-sixteenth centuries, there is only one of a roughly contemporary king, that of the Henry VI (who had acquired semi-saintly status by the end of the fifteenth century) at Whimple. A full list of painted panels (some now gone) is given in C. E. Keyser, 'On the Panel Paintings of Saints on the Devonshire Screens', *Archaeologia* LVI (2nd series, VI), part 1, (1898): 183-222.

[4] Edward Ashworth, 'Notes on Some North Devon Churches', *Transactions of the Exeter Diocesan Architectural Society* V, new series (1892): 7. High quality Barnstaple-style tiles, now re-arranged around the altar, may have formed part of the original ensemble. The detailing looks early sixteenth century. If so, this would push back the accepted dating of the earliest Barnstaple tiling by more than a generation. See Elizabeth Eames, *English Tilers* (London: British Museum Publications, 2000).

[5] Observation by Peter Cormack FSA.

[6] There is a substantial secondary literature on the last years of Edward IV and Richard III's usurpation and short rule. The most accessible authorities that are relevant to this paper are: Charles Ross, *Edward IV* (London: Eyre Methuen, 1974) and his *Richard III* (London: Eyre Methuen, 1981); Rosemary Horrox, *Richard III: a Study in Service* (Cambridge: Cambridge University Press, 1989); Ralph A. Griffiths and Roger S. Thomas, *The Making of the Tudor Dynasty* (Gloucester: Alan Sutton, 1985); Louise Gill, *Richard III and Buckingham's Rebellion* (Stroud: Sutton Publishing, 1999); and, of particular value A. J. Pollard, *Richard III and the Princes in the Tower* (Gloucester: Alan Sutton, 1991).

[7] T. L. Stoate (ed.), *A Survey of West-Country Manors 1525. The Lands of Cecily Marchioness of Dorset, Lady Harington & Bonville in Cornwall, Devon, Dorset, Somerset, Wiltshire* (Bristol: privately published, 1979).

[8] The Evans family retained its status throughout the greater part of the sixteenth century, marrying into neighbouring gentry families. They were still local farmers in the eighteenth century.

[9] *Letters and Papers, Foreign and Domestic, of the Reign of Henry VIII*, vol. II, part 1(London: Longman, 1864), no. 2736 (p. 876).

[10] *Letters and Papers, Foreign and Domestic, of the Reign of Henry VIII*, vol. I, (London: HMSO, 1920), no. 707 (p. 382). Margaret Westcott, 'Katherine Courtenay, Countess of Devon, 1479-1527' in Todd Gray, Margery Rowe and Audrey Erskine (eds.), *Tudor and Stuart Devon. The Common Estate and Government* (Exeter: Exeter University Press, 1992), 13-38, especially pp. 23, 29.

[11] F. Bligh Bond and Dom Bede Camm, *Roodscreens and Roodlofts*, 2 vols (London: Pitman & Sons, 1909). Brief descriptions of the three screens are given in vol. II, pp. 300, 306-7 and photographs, all in vol. II, at plates LXXXV, XCIX (Brushford); LXXXV, XCVIII, XCIX, CI (Colebrooke); and LXXVI and C (Coldridge); and in Aymer Vallance, *English Church Screens: Being Great Roods, Screenwork & Rood-lofts of Parish Churches in England & Wales* (London: Batsford, 1936), 54, pl. 153 (detail of Colebrooke). More recent analysis of the screens may be found in Charles Tracy, *Continental Church Furniture in England. A Traffic in Piety* (Woodbridge: Antique Collectors' Club, 2001), 12, 207-11 (Brushford); 214-16 (Coldridge); 216-18 (Colebrooke).

[12] Dr Tracy (*op. cit.*) considers it unlikely that the screens were imported and discerns some stylistic evidence of local work. He believes that the Brushford screen was made for its present position by English workmen under Breton supervision. Perhaps, but it does not fit entirely comfortably and the others have clearly been introduced from elsewhere. It seems implausible that all three screens were assembled in England at some point after c.1480 and then moved to three adjacent Devon parishes within fifteen years or so.

[13] Anne Sutton and P. W. Hammond, *The Coronation of Richard III: The Extant Documents*, (Gloucester: Sutton Publishing, 1983), 350-51.

[14] Pollard, *op. cit.* 16-17 where all the images are illustrated. Michael Hicks's *Edward V* (Stroud, Tempus, 2003) came out as this article went to press. Professor Hicks illustrates the Coldridge Edward but its significance is not discussed in the text. This book, especially chapter 5 ('The Politics of the Family, 1475-83') adds useful material for better understanding the motives of the Grey family.

[15] M. H. Caviness, *The Windows of Christ Church Canterbury Cathedral*, CVMA Great Britain II (London: Published for the British Academy by Oxford University Press, 1981), 256-62.

[16] Discussed in Richard Marks, *Stained Glass in England during the Middle Ages* (London: Routledge, 1993), 203-04 where its quality is compared unfavourably with the work of the Canterbury 'Royal' window. Both the Canterbury and Little Malvern glass are discussed and illustrated in Richard Marks and Paul Williamson (eds.), *Gothic: Art for England* 1400-1547 (London: V&A Publications, 2003), 40 (Little Malvern); 177-78 (Canterbury with a full-page detail of Princess Cecily).

[17] Discussed in Pamela Tudor-Craig, *Richard III* (London: National Portrait Gallery, 1973), 31, 89.

[18] W. H. St John Hope, *Windsor Castle: An Architectural History* (London: Country Life, 1913) vol. II, p. 414 places the construction and decoration of the chapel as between 1492 and 1496. It is illustrated and discussed in E. Croft-Murray, *Decorative Painting in England, 1537-1837*, vol. I (London: Country Life, 1962), 14, 174 (no. 55); Pl. 7.

[19] As noted by Marks, *Stained Glass in England*, pp. 55-56.

[20] One example is the 1471 brass to Roger Kyngdon and his wife at Quethiock in Cornwall. The second of their sons, Edward Kyngdon, was a yeoman of the crown (mentioned as such in 1461 and again in 1484), and appears on the brass among the Kyngdon children with a crown badge on his left shoulder. Professor Marks points out another, in glass, at Stanford-upon-Avon, Northants., see yeoman of the crown donor in *The Medieval Stained Glass of Northamptonshire*, CVMA Great Britain IV (London: Published for the British Academy by Oxford University Press, 1998), 267.

[21] Personal communication. Dr Evans considers the head to be the work of the 'Doddiscombsleigh' school (in fact based in Exeter) and closely reminiscent of the technique of the Cadbury Master. For a discussion of this workshop, the variety of styles executed within it, and an illustration of a head of Christ by the Cadbury Master, see Chris Brooks and David Evans, *The Great East Window of Exeter Cathedral: a Glazing History* (Exeter: Exeter University Press, 1988), 107-12.

Joseph McBrinn

Frank Brangwyn and stained glass: The Earl of Iveagh memorial windows at Dublin and Elveden

Although today little associated with the history of stained glass, Frank Brangwyn (1867-1956) produced several noteworthy windows throughout his long and varied career. In July 1937 his largest window and greatest statement in stained glass, the memorial to his friend and champion Edward Cecil Guinness, the 1st Earl of Iveagh, was installed in St Patrick's Cathedral, Dublin. Only minor attention was paid in the press, although his murals had, to date, brought him international acclaim. The same year, William Gaunt identified Brangwyn in 'English Painting of Today' as a 'Kipling chastened by the Socialism of Morris, and dipping a brush in Jordaens's paint-box', and as the greatest modern decorative painter, producing 'vast canvases riotous with tropical fruits and ablaze with blast furnaces'.[1] Indeed by this time Brangwyn's versatility as a designer, encompassing everything from mural and mosaic decoration, furniture, carpets and ceramics to book illustration, etching, lithography and stained glass, had been widely acknowledged, prompting *Studio* Editor Geoffrey Holme to declare in 1941 (the year Brangwyn received a knighthood), that 'every new medium tackled was engaged with a dash and determination that could only mean success in the finish.'[2]

It may be surprising to some, but Brangwyn's *début* as a decorative artist at the 1895 remodelling and decoration of the Paris gallery of Siegfried Bing, the Svengali of Art Nouveau, did in fact include several stained glass panels – visual 'equivalents' of music, they anticipated Christopher Whall's rather Whistlerian call for the sensory harmony between 'colour, light and shade, and design' in glass as in music.[3] Several stained glass commissions in England after 1900 and before the First World War established Brangwyn as one of the few painters willing to submit to the disciplines of working in 'coloured light', although he clearly diverged from Whall's 'Neo-Pre-Raphaelite'[4] style so suited to ecclesiastical art. Although Walter Shaw-Sparrow made a perfunctory mention of Brangwyn's 'modern' stained glass designs in his 1910 book on the artist, by 1924 his glass merited an entire section in Herbert Furst's mammoth survey of Brangwyn's career as a decorative artist. By 1968, however, Brangwyn was to receive only a cursory mention in John Piper's survey of stained glass: 'Brangwyn did a window or two, reflecting his own painterly mannerisms too strongly for the glass to be finally agreeable, or influential.'[5]

In 1937 Brangwyn completed a pair of monumental stained glass windows for two venerable medieval buildings, St Patrick's Cathedral in Dublin and the Church of St Andrew and St Patrick at Elveden, Suffolk. Both were memorials to the 1st Earl of Iveagh, and surely rate amongst his greatest achievements.[6] Although the Dublin window attracted little press attention at the time, Dublin's eminent stained glass studios, most notably Harry Clarke's studio and Sarah Purser's An Túr Gloine, quickly made tenders for the commission.[7] And given the remarkable achievements of early twentieth-century Irish stained glass artists, why did such a prestigious commission instead go to Brangwyn, who by the mid-1930s had not designed a window in over ten years, and whose career as a painter, after the rejection of his mural decorations for the House of Lords in 1931, was in eclipse?

Essentially, Brangwyn's windows commemorate his friendship with Iveagh, which had evolved after his appointment in 1924 to paint a series of murals, the 'Empire' panels, to form part of the Peers' First World War Memorial at the House of Lords, which had been proposed and entirely funded by Iveagh.[8] The commission had come about after discussions between Iveagh, his secretary C. H. Bland and the Marquess of Lincolnshire, concluding that Brangwyn was the only modern artist capable of such a monumental scheme, and who had not previously been employed on the successive mural projects at the Palace of Westminster between 1909 and 1924. The original idea of war scenes for the murals was replaced by more uplifting images 'celebrating the Empire', but after Iveagh's death in 1927 the project floundered and by 1931 the panels were rejected, only reaching a resolution in 1934 when they were purchased by the Guildhall in Swansea.

This article aims to identify the Earl of Iveagh memorial (1931-7) as a two-part commission encompassing the windows at Dublin and Elveden. These relate both iconographically and stylistically to Brangwyn's Empire panels, which have been

FIG. 1:
Lithograph poster for S. Bing's *L'Art Nouveau*, exhibition at the Grafton Galleries, London (1899).

recognised as the culmination of his career and the apotheosis of his philosophical and pictorial beliefs. It will also highlight the role of Arts and Crafts traditions in Brangwyn's work and emphasise a greater importance of stained glass in his *œuvre* than has previously been credited or investigated.

Arts and Crafts beginnings and Art Nouveau achievement

In 1882 Arthur Mackmurdo 'discovered' the fifteen year old Frank Brangwyn sketching in the South Kensington Museum, and soon introduced him to William Morris.[9] Perhaps aware of his father, W. Curtis Brangwyn, an ecclesiastical architect and decorator who worked for a long period in Bruges and had produced stained glass,[10] Morris employed him as a copyist of Flemish tapestries at the Queen Square workshop and made the (unrealised) suggestion that he be apprenticed to 'the glass-workers' job'.[11] Morris was the first to recognise Brangwyn's versatile abilities, and helped him to cultivate a love for medieval tapestry-like effects in large-scale work as well as an interest in colour and natural motifs. In 1885, at eighteen years of age, Brangwyn made his *début* as a painter at the Royal Academy and in 1891 his *Funeral at Sea* won a medal at the Paris Salon, bringing him to the attention of the European vanguard. He quickly affiliated himself with influential Continental groups such as the Secessionists in Munich and Vienna.

Almost certainly Brangwyn's success at the Paris Salon led to his introduction to Siegfried Bing, who was seeking a painter in sympathy with the Belgian and French designers creating external decorations for his rue de Provence Gallery in Paris's chic 9th *arrondissement*. As noted above, this was Brangwyn's first decorative commission, involving a series of murals and also several stained glass panels. The latter, like designs by Bonnard, Vuillard, Denis, Sérusier, de Feure, Grasset, Ranson, Besnard, Ibels, Vallatton and Toulouse-Lautrec, were made up by Louis Comfort Tiffany's workshops in New York. Brangwyn recalled that the panels were 'not stained or painted glass in the ordinary manner, but were moulded out of solid junks [*sic*] of glass modelled like a clay relief'.[12] Bing was not entirely satisfied with Brangwyn's preliminary designs for the exterior murals (courting Victor Horta, through Henri Van der Velde, to submit additional designs),[13] but he seems to have been pleased with the stained glass panels, and commissioned more for his 1899 *L'Art Nouveau* exhibition at London's Grafton Galleries, for which Brangwyn also designed the poster (FIG. 1). The exhibition included work by Colonna, Meunier, Lalique, Gallé and Tiffany, shown alongside Brangwyn's *Music* (FIG. 2) and *The Baptism of Christ* (FIG. 3).[14] As a consequence, the British, French and German art press devoted considerable coverage to Brangwyn not only as a mural painter but as a stained glass designer.[15] As a 'picture painter of real originality and exceptional strength, a colourist who delights in rich harmonies and daring combinations, and a manipulator who is absolutely free from any fear of his materials' his transition to stained glass from painting came as little surprise as he was a 'un artiste pur et un artisan pratique' whose designs on canvas, furniture, textiles and in glass provided an example to other 'ouvriers'.[16]

Although Brangwyn later claimed that he worked for several firms producing designs for stained glass, his next known commission was not until 1911: a three-light window for the Church of St Mary, Bucklebury in Berkshire (FIG. 4), where he subsequently completed another two windows after the war.[17] In 1920 he designed a four-light First World War memorial window at the Congregational Church, Northampton (FIG. 5).

During the 1920s Brangwyn began to turn increasingly to religious subject matter, completing paintings of the Stations of the Cross for Arras Cathedral and for a Leper Colony in Pretoria, South Africa, and returning to the same theme in 1931 in a series of lithographs. At this point, he was asked by a young admirer, William de Belleroche, on behalf of his friend Dom Gaspard Lefèbvre, if these could be reproduced in the Belgian ecclesiastical magazine *L'Artisan Liturgique*. De Belleroche also suggested an exhibition of Brangwyn's religious art at the Abbey of St André, Zevenkerken, in Bruges[18] along with an accompanying exhibition which ultimately led to the establishment of a permanent display of his art in the city.[19] Lefèbvre was so enraptured by Brangwyn's lithographs that de Belleroche reported, 'The Abbot told me your Stations of the Cross would hang all round their Chapter House and hoped that one day they might be able to commission you to design stained glass windows so that the whole room would be your work.'[20] Not long afterwards, Brangwyn began work on a series of windows for the Chapter House of the Abbey.[21]

When de Belleroche visited Brangwyn at Ditchling, he saw the series of 'ten large cartoons' destined for the Abbey,[22] and recorded their ensuing discussion. It is perhaps Brangwyn's only known exposition on his stained glass and gives some insight into his windows. In each cartoon Brangwyn put 'a certain incident' or emblems connected with the life of each saint, but he was primarily concerned with the 'play for colour and pattern', telling de Belleroche, 'I want these windows to be *rich* and *luminous*… and the sun to pour through the room throwing the many colours over the white robes of the Abbot and monks during one of their *big services*…'[23]

FIG. 2:
Music (1895), designed for S. Bing's Maison de L'Art Nouveau, Paris, and published in *The Studio* (1899).

The Iveagh memorial window in St Patrick's Cathedral, Dublin

Edward Cecil Guinness, the 1st Earl of Iveagh, heir of the famous Irish brewing dynasty, was a well-known benefactor, philanthropist and patron of the arts.[24] He had formed his philanthropic ideals during the 1880s-1890s, investigating with Lord Rowton the social conditions in the East End of London.[25] Iveagh's father, Benjamin Lee Guinness, had restored St Patrick's Cathedral in Dublin between 1858-65 and Iveagh dedicated himself between 1893-1915 not only to conserving and restoring the Cathedral but also to rejuvenating its medieval *quartier*. From 1901-5 the Iveagh Buildings were erected, consisting of a series of new artisans' dwellings, flats and recreational spaces, including baths and a hostel, all reported with much enthusiasm in the Irish press.[26] Iveagh was deeply impressed by Walter Besant's writings about the East End of London, committing himself to financial support of Besant's 'People's Palace'.[27] At the heart of the redeveloped St Patrick quarter was a similar 'Play Centre', a recreational building aimed at moral as much as educational improvement.[28] Iveagh's humanitarianism would clearly have won Brangwyn's admiration.

Following the death of the Earl of Iveagh in 1927, a paper was discovered in his desk stating that if any memorial should be erected to him he wished it to be in the National Cathedral of St Patrick in Dublin, the building on whose restoration he and his father had invested, with much contention, a great deal of time and money. When Brangwyn was approached by Iveagh's private secretary, C. H. Bland,[29] on behalf of the Iveagh Trust and family, to design the memorial in the form of a stained glass window, he confessed to de Belleroche that he had already thought of the idea himself.[30]

Ironically, with no available space in the Cathedral at the time of Iveagh's death, F. S. Barff's window *The Ascension of Our Lord*, which had been donated by Iveagh's father in 1862-63, was removed, although Barff's highly inventive clerestory windows of Celtic knotwork patterns in rich blues and reds have survived.[31] The proposal to fill a large and prominent space in such an eminent Dublin building aroused some interest. A surviving An Túr Gloine minute book indicates that they had begun a proposal as early as May 1928.[32] Healy's eventual design 'was unanimously rejected by both the Board and the Chapter and Miss Purser refused to make any alteration.'[33]

Several different designs for the Iveagh memorial window have survived and show that Brangwyn was deeply concerned with finding a subject which would reflect his admiration for Iveagh. In a letter to the Bishop of Dublin, he asked, 'Do you think it should represent our Lord? Or just a fine face suggestive of Love and Charity.'[34] Brangwyn later told de Belleroche that the window,

> was to represent charity – a quality which so fitted the character of the old Lord [Iveagh]. He was one of the kindest persons I've ever known – one of the best... one who went through life doing good and helping his fellow-men... I've often wondered whether my friend would not have preferred having the money for this window spent otherwise. Still, it was up to us to do something to foster his memory – and the suggestion of the family to have a design representing Charity – CHARITY – was excellent in my opinion.[35]

FIG. 3:
The Baptism of Christ (1895), designed for S. Bing's Maison de L'Art Nouveau, Paris, and published in *The Studio* (1899).

FIG. 4:
Cartoon for
The Crucifixion
(1911), Church
of St Mary,
Bucklebury,
Berkshire.
Published in
The Studio
(1923).

FIG. 5:
*The Descent from
the Cross* (1920),
Congregational
Church,
Northampton.
Published in
H. Furst, *The
Decorative Art of
Brangwyn* (1924).

The William Morris Gallery has three sketch designs in watercolour, black chalk, ink and pencil for the Dublin window, one of which corresponds closely to the glazing as finally executed.[36] One design depicts 'The Great Feast' (FIG. 6) in a style reminiscent of Renaissance traditions, following the example of Veronese and other Italian painters whom Brangwyn admired.[37] The other two designs depict a central figure of Charity surrounded by the poor and sick of all ages, with a broad scroll beneath inscribed 'But the greatest of these is Love'.[38] One of these shows a landscape background with a few ruined buildings against a dramatic dawn or sunset sky (FIG. 7), the other, which is closest to the window as executed, shows the Charity figure beneath a spreading fruit tree with the Pelican and its young in the upper branches (FIG. 8).[39] Brangwyn had been occupied for much of the late 1920s with his Empire panels and in the early 1930s by several mural commissions in Britain and America, and several images from his Iveagh window designs can clearly be traced from these murals.[40]

Iveagh's humanitarian interests evidently prompted Brangwyn to choose Charity as a theme but he had earlier employed the subject for an unrealised mural design, exhibited at the New Gallery in 1900. Shaw-Sparrow pointed to elements and qualities in this design that are apparent in the window:

quaint and graceful costumes, a felicitous grouping of figures under a low horizontal pole, contrasts between crippled age and youth, and a subtle blend of colour having a rare beauty – strange modulated blues, pale russets and pearly greys, faint carnations, and crimsons. A Lady Bountiful in a blue robe, with ailing children gathered around her, gives alms to a couple of old men, one halt, the other blind, while a mother awaits her turn, carrying tenderly in her arms a little nude baby. The draperies are all made in the factory of Brangwyn's mind and are all good. The old fellow with the crutch under his arm is naked nearly to the waist; there a heavy garment gathers itself into a girdle of folds and falls down about the legs in uncertain lines of light and shade very suggestive of physical weakness. The children are all charming: with bare necks, their light dresses of a rustling softness. The note of optimism is found in every part, for this charity is given and accepted in the same spirit – with joy and without parade.[41]

Brangwyn's imagery of abundant and resplendent flora, fauna and peoples of the 'Empire' does not immediately suggest a religious subject. A Romantic pantheism is evident in the beauty and bounty of nature, as well as in the monumental compositional structure, closely following the composition and theme of the 'Empire' panels. The central, and unifying, symbol of the tree was often used by Brangwyn, who exploited the decorative potential of verticals, reflecting his admiration of Japanese prints which often featured trees as vertical framing devices. This decorative symbolism also harked back to his study of Mantegna at South Kensington.[42] David Lawrence has

suggested that the images of suffering in the window reflect not only the Iveaghs' 're-imaging' of a medieval Dublin quarter but are also a comment on the First World War, in which one of Iveagh's sons had been in service. Clare Willsdon has further suggested that the portrayals of 'the old, infirm and young' are related to those in Brangwyn's mosaics in St Aidan's Church, Leeds.[43] Although the window bears some relation to its architectural setting, Brangwyn never visited the Cathedral and it seems possible that the Dublin window may have originated in his *juvenilia* design for a mural.

Brangwyn's window was executed in Edinburgh by the stained glass artist Alexander Strachan (brother of Douglas Strachan), whose Livingston window in Dunfermline, also of 1937, bears a striking affinity to it, particularly in the upper tracery with its flower and fruit symbolism and use of blue-greens and deep fiery oranges (FIG. 9).[44] Strachan's use of the allegorical 'Pelican in its Piety' as well as pomegranates is very close to the iconography of Brangwyn's Dublin design (which used pears rather than pomegranates). However, Brangwyn's use of the pelican iconography may equally have been inspired by Burne-Jones's well-known cartoon

FIG. 6:
Sketch for Earl of Iveagh memorial window, Dublin (1931-37). William Morris Gallery, London.

FIG. 7:
Sketch for Earl of Iveagh memorial window, Dublin (1931-37). William Morris Gallery, London.

(1880), for part of the East window of St Martin's, Brampton, which may well have been familiar to him from his early apprenticeship with Morris & Company. In fact, Burne-Jones's *Pelican* cartoon was purchased by Brangwyn in 1936 from the art dealer D. Croal Thomson's Barbizon House gallery.[45]

Brangwyn employed a succession of glaziers, including James Sylvester Sparrow and Paul Turpin as well as Alexander Strachan. He nevertheless felt that understanding the technical processes of stained glass was fundamental to design and always regretted not being able to execute his windows himself. He also wanted his collaborators to leave at least some imprint of their own (although if they went too far a quarrel would ensue, as happened with Sparrow). Faithful to his Arts and Crafts origins, Brangwyn believed that the 'designer should also be the technician... the job should be more or less done by one man as in the olden days'[46], that the 'worker and the designer should always be *one*'.[47] He explained his own situation, 'That's what I should have liked to have done... but it's a full-time job, and I had so many other jobs on the go that I couldn't do it.'[48] When de Belleroche claimed that designers wouldn't have the patience to carry out their designs in glass, Brangwyn retorted 'Why the devil not?' declaring that the stained glass designer/worker should be both patient and experimental:

> There are so many opportunities in this field... effect of light, effect of colour, effect of pattern, design—and... leadwork. Painters have explored the work of the Old Masters... but what about our great stained glass artists? Some of these fellows worked in obscurity, just for the love of the thing... . Every day one hears of wonderful old windows in churches, windows which are as fine as a painting by Greco or those tapestries which were executed after Lucas van Leyden's cartoons at the Prado for the Escurial... . And, besides, anyone who is a real artist shouldn't be afraid of craftsmanship.'[49]

FIG. 8:
Sketch for Earl of Iveagh memorial window, Dublin (1931-37). William Morris Gallery, London.

FIG. 9:
Alexander Strachan, Detail of Livingston window (1937), Dunfermline Cathedral. Photograph by Juliette MacDonald.

FIG. 10:
The Earl of Iveagh memorial window
(1937), National Cathedral and
Collegiate Church of St Patrick, Dublin.
Photograph by the author.

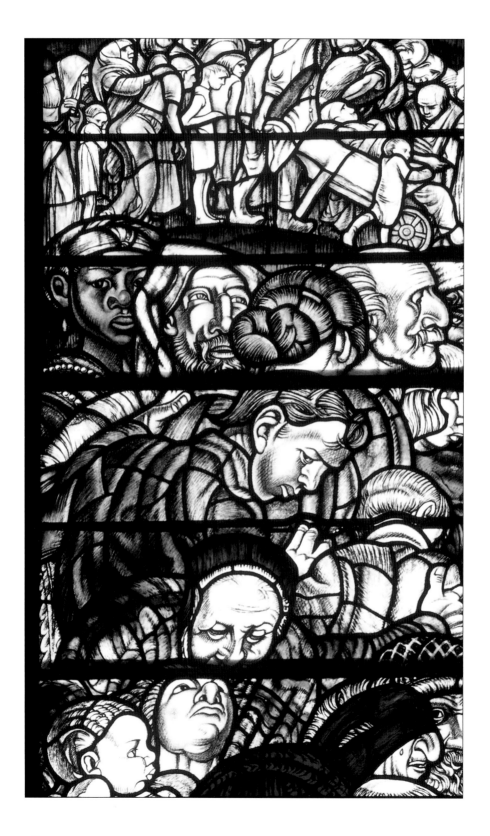

With three lights and over forty feet high, the Iveagh memorial window in St Patrick's was Brangwyn's largest window (FIGS. 10, 11). It bears the inscription: 'THE WINDOW HAS BEEN ERECTED BY HIS CHILDREN IN MEMORY OF EDWARD CECIL GUINNESS, FIRST EARL OF IVEAGH. BORN 1847 DIED 1927'. It was unveiled and dedicated at a ceremony on 25 July 1937 in which the Rev. Vivian W. Darling spoke of the window's 'message of love' and of Iveagh's commitment to the Church of Ireland, 'our ancient Irish church.'[50] The ceremony took place during a momentous month in Irish history as it saw the opening of the new Irish Free State Parliament, the Dáil Éireann – in fact the window's dedication was held amidst special services at St Patrick's to coincide with the Dáil's inauguration. It is intriguing that Lord Newton suggested Brangwyn's 'Empire Panels' could be installed in a public building 'such as Dáil Éireann' (after they had been rejected in 1931 and had languished at Elveden Hall).[51]

The Iveagh memorial window in the Church of St Andrew and St Patrick, Elveden
When Brangwyn was approached to prepare designs for the Iveagh memorial window in Dublin he was also asked to make a second window for the family's chapel in the parish church at Elveden (FIG. 12). Iveagh had purchased the Elveden estate in Suffolk in 1894 after the death of its owner, the Maharajah Duleep Singh, and had been deeply committed to its development.[52] As well as refurbishing Elveden Hall, he also initiated a brick works, laid roads and attempted to improve the farms, and between 1899-1904 he restored and altered the 13th-century Church of St Andrew.[53] Arts and Crafts architect W. D. Caröe was employed to add a new nave and chancel in harmony with the existing medieval structure,[54] dedicating the alterations to St Patrick.

The four-light memorial window at Elveden at twelve feet high was on a somewhat smaller scale than the Dublin commission. Executed once again by Alexander Strachan, it was completed in 1937, and dedicated and unveiled on 17 July 1938. It bears the identical inscription as the Dublin window, and like its counterpart, its imagery equally celebrates the 'beauty of nature' and the 'endless variety'[55] of plant life – but here also includes the two figures of SS Andrew and Patrick. Iveagh had been a member of the Order of St Patrick and Brangwyn had earlier completed a mural depicting St Patrick at Christ's Hospital Chapel in Horsham, Sussex (FIG. 13).[56] The theme of 'Charity' was again chosen and Brangwyn wrote to the Rector of Elveden to explain his symbolism:

> Charity and Education. Charity like Mercy, is twice blessed, enriching both the giver and the recipient. The tree both blesses, and is blessed by, man: it brings forth flowers and fruit; it yields shade, and birds shelter in its branches; it symbolises Charity. Education, as it increases knowledge, also increases understanding, and breeds compassion.
>
> On the right side of the window are a Schoolmaster and his pupils; on the left, a Mother and her children. In the centre, children whose lot is happy, and who have been trained to share their happiness, bring gifts for the less fortunate.

FIG. 11:
Detail of The Earl of Iveagh memorial window (1937), National Cathedral and Collegiate Church of St Patrick, Dublin. Photograph by David Lawrence.

Charity and Education are under the direct guidance of the Saints and Angels. St Andrew and St Patrick look down with approval on the happy scene, and help the good work, as it were, with their intercessions; and the Angels are glad… . The Window suggests the quality of completeness that belongs to the man who has a charitable heart and serves his fellow men.'[57]

Thus the imagery of the Elveden window follows that set out in Dublin but the introduction of St Andrew and St Patrick perhaps reflects an attempt at a more intimate symbolism reflecting the particular significance of the window itself, as adorning the Iveagh chapel.

Conclusion

Early on, Brangwyn clearly recognised the difference between 'stained cloth' and 'stained glass' and like many of his contemporaries was fascinated by the translation of his designs on canvas into actual light. However, he produced too few windows to resolve fully the complexities of working in such different mediums and was left with too little time between mural commissions to learn thoroughly the craft of stained glass. Brangwyn's rejection from the State-sponsored mural schemes at the Palace of Westminster in the early twentieth century was a result in some ways of his unique style which was much more in line with Continental painting, and in contrast to the promoters of a distinctly English Pre-Raphaelite style in mural decoration and stained glass. Brangwyn's 'modern' Continental style was, in essence, a form of realist expressionism.

His approach to stained glass design fundamentally demonstrates Piper's later formulation of a 'positive constructive relation' between stained glass and decorative painting. The connections between his Iveagh windows and his Empire panels are as much pictorial and ideological as compositional or technical, and are testament to Brangwyn's ability to translate his designs into mural painting as well as into glass work. As such, he can be linked to his European counterparts and schemes like Kolomon Moser's decorations at the Church of St Leopold 'am Steinhof' in Vienna or Alfons Mucha in his murals and windows at the Obecní dúm (Municipal House) in Prague.

When asked by de Belleroche why he became a decorative painter Brangwyn pointed to the two formative influences in his early life, his father and William Morris, who had both 'done glass'.[58] And as to the future of stained glass Brangwyn hinted at more diverse developments:

FIG. 12:
The Earl of Iveagh memorial window (1937), Church of St Andrew and St Patrick, Elveden, Suffolk. Photograph by Neville Turner.

A rich man came to see me one day and said he wanted a window with no design – only colour. I thought him a madman. But he kept on insisting. I told him it couldn't be done, and eventually sent him to a fellow who made a fine and costly window... . This, when completed was laid on the floor and broken all over into hundreds of little bits... then leaded together without any design – all haphazard... . I was told the result was fine and the client satisfied.'[59]

When de Belleroche suggested it may have looked like a 'Rouault', Brangwyn retorted, '*Better* – maybe? There's no telling what the result of this window may have been. Wish I'd seen it'.[60]

ACKNOWLEDGEMENTS
The author would like to gratefully acknowledge the help and encouragement of the following people in the preparation of this article: in particular Sandra Coley and Peter Cormack for invaluable information and suggestions; Nicola Gordon Bowe; Clare Willsdon; Juliette Macdonald; Gillian and Neville Turner; The Earl of Iveagh; David Caron; David Lawrence; and Laurence Van Kerkhoven.

FIG. 13:
Frank Brangwyn,
St. Patrick in the Forest A.D. 450
(1912-23), mural painting in the Chapel of Christ's Hospital, Horsham, Sussex. Photograph by the author.

NOTES

[1] W. Gaunt, 'English Painting of Today', *The Studio*, vol. CXII, no. 351 (June 1937): 297-98.

[2] G. Holme, 'Frank Brangwyn', *The Studio*, vol. 121 (Jan.-June 1941): 71.

[3] C. W. Whall, *Stained Glass Work* (London: J. Hogg, 1905), 222.

[4] The term 'Neuprärefaeliten' or 'Neo-Pre-Raphaelite' was coined by Herman Muthesius, in 'Kunst und Leben in England', *Zeitschrift für bildende Kunst* (1902), 66, to describe the most progressive styles in British decorative painting which, as evident in the work of the Birmingham group and the muralists of the East Corridor at the Palace of Westminster, betrayed a powerful and conscious debt to the Pre-Raphaelites. Muthesius also included the more 'Baroque and Continental influenced' work of Brangwyn, although Brangwyn quickly developed away from Pre-Raphaelitism, which had become by the early twentieth century a common style in both stained glass and mural painting. The connection between Brangwyn and the 'Neo-Pre-Raphaelites' was identified by Clare A. P. Willsdon and is discussed in detail in her *Mural Painting in Britain, 1840-1940: Image and Meaning* (London: Oxford University Press, 2000).

[5] John Piper, *Stained Glass: Art or Anti-Art* (London: Studio Vista, 1968), 38.

[6] Two recent publications have drawn attention to Brangwyn's Iveagh Memorial windows: Gillian Turner, *The Church of St Andrew & St Patrick: A History & Guide* (Elveden: Elveden Parochial Church Council, 2002) and Lesley Whiteside and David Lawrence, *The Stained Glass of St Patrick's Cathedral, Dublin* (Dublin: St Patrick's Cathedral, 2002). Whiteside attributes the Dublin window to Alexander Strachan, crediting only the cartoon to Brangwyn. However, Brangwyn's window is discussed in full in David Lawrence, *The National Cathedral and Collegiate Church of St Patrick, Dublin: Stained Glass Windows – Art Historical, Technical Report and Photographic Record* (Representative Church Library, Dublin: August 2001), 22, from which all Whiteside's information is drawn.

[7] Although Harry Clarke died in 1931, his studio did prepare a design for the Iveagh window. Information kindly supplied by Dr Nicola Gordon Bowe.

[8] Iveagh had also contributed a posthumously published introduction on Brangwyn's murals to Frank Rutter's *The British Empire Panels by Frank Brangwyn R.A.* (Leigh-on-Sea: F. Lewis, 1933).

[9] See Isabelle Anscombe and Charlotte Gere, *Arts & Crafts in Britain and America* (London: Academy Editions, 1978), 208-9, and Lionel Lambourne, *Utopian Craftsmen: The Arts & Crafts Movement from the Cotswolds to Chicago* (London: Astragal Books, 1980), 190-91.

[10] As Brangwyn later recalled, see William de Belleroche, *Brangwyn's Pilgrimage: The Life Story of An Artist* (London: Chapman & Hall, 1948), 45.

[11] William de Belleroche, *Brangwyn Talks* (London: Chapman & Hall, 1944), 35.

[12] de Belleroche (1948), 45.

[13] See Martin Eidelberg and Suzanne Henrion-Giele, 'Horta and Bing: An Unwritten Episode of L'Art Nouveau', *The Burlington Magazine*, no. 896, vol. CXIX (Nov. 1977): 747-52.

[14] These designs by Brangwyn have been discussed in Alastair Duncan, *Tiffany Windows* (New York: Simon and Schuster, 1980), 129; Gabriel P. Weisberg, 'Siegfried Bing and Frank Brangwyn: The Gallery L'Art Nouveau in Paris in 1895', *Jaarboek 1985-6, Stedelijke Musea Brugge* (1987): 277-86; and Gabriel P. Weisberg, *Art Nouveau Bing: Paris Style 1900* (New York and Washington: Harry Abrams and the Smithsonian Institution, 1986).

[15] See 'Stained Glass Designs by Frank Brangwyn', *The Studio*, XVI (1899): 252-59, H. Fiérens-Gevaert, 'Frank Brangwyn', *Art et Décoration*, vol. VI (July-Dec. 1899): 23-31, and *Dekorative Kunst* (1899): 122.

[16] See *The Studio* (1899): 252, and *Art et Décoration* (1899): 31.

[17] See Libby Horner, 'Pea Pods, Banana Skins and Brangwyn', *Ecclesiology Today: Journal of the Ecclesiological Society*, 25 (April 2001): 25-28.

[18] See Rodney Brangwyn, *Frank Brangwyn* (London: William Kimber, 1978) and de Belleroche, (1944).

[19] Brangwyn had recently given a large bequest of his work to the William Morris Gallery in London, and had also given generously to several public collections throughout Europe, in Italy, France, the Netherlands and to Ireland's Hugh Lane's Municipal Gallery of Modern Art in Dublin. See six letters written between 1904 and 1914 from Frank Brangwyn to Hugh Lane, concerning the bequest of a painting to the Dublin Municipal Gallery (National Library of Ireland, MS. 35, 823/1/12).

[20] de Belleroche (1944), 56.

[21] Brangwyn's father had designed the Church of St André (Sint-Andries/St Andrew) in Bruges, and around the time of his stained glass commission at the Abbey, Brangwyn designed a memorial tablet commemorating the work of his father. See de Belleroche (1944), 104-05.

[22] de Belleroche (1948), 44.

[23] *Ibid*.

[24] Edward Cecil Guinness had inherited the Guinness Brewery in 1876 and sold part of it in 1886, making him a millionaire. He was made Baronet in 1885, Baron 1891, Viscount in 1904 and the 1st Earl of Iveagh in 1919.

[25] For information concerning the excursions of Guinness and Rowton (Montague William Lowry-Corry, 1st Lord Rowton) see *The Times* (10 November 1903). Rowton's philanthropic building schemes in London also served as a conscious model for Iveagh's building schemes in Dublin and London. Rowton's 'hostel' was famously described by George Orwell in *Down and Out in Paris and London* (London, 1933), 170.

[26] For instance see, 'Lord Iveagh's Gift to Dublin', *The Irish Builder* (1 January 1899).

[27] See *The Echo* (20 November 1889).

[28] This was inspired by Besant's novel *All Sorts and Conditions of Men* (1882) in which the heroine (and heiress) Angela Messenger (her friend and helper is a brewery heir) sets up a 'Palace of Delight' to regenerate Stepney, an area of London's 'degenerate' East End.

[29] As Brangwyn developed a friendship with the Earl of Iveagh, he also developed a friendship with Bland, whose son Roger became an assistant to Brangwyn in the late 1920s.

[30] de Belleroche (1948), 214.

[31] See 'Stained Glass at St Patrick's Cathedral', *The Dublin Builder* (15 June 1862): 150, and 'Restoration of St Patrick's Cathedral', *The Dublin Builder* (15 November 1863): 184. Barff's 'Ascension' window was originally placed in the south transept in 1862 and moved to the north transept in 1863 'as the light in the south side was too strong for the picture'.

[32] See David Caron, 'An Túr Gloine and Michael Healy (1873-1941)', unpublished PhD thesis, (Trinity College, Dublin, 1991), 151-52, and also C. P. Curran, 'Michael Healy: Stained Glass Worker, 1873-1941', *Studies*, vol. XXV (March, 1942): 80.

[33] Quoted in David Lawrence (2001), 22.

[34] Undated letter from F. Brangwyn to the Bishop of Dublin, St Patrick's Cathedral Archives, Representative Church Body Library, Dublin.

[35] de Belleroche (1948), 214-15.

[36] Information supplied by Peter Cormack.

[37] This design is in the William Morris Gallery, London.

[38] These two designs are also in the William Morris Gallery.

[39] Information on the designs for the Iveagh window in the William Morris Gallery has been generously supplied by Peter Cormack.

[40] For instance his murals for the Rockefeller Center in New York (1930-34), and the mural for Odham's Press, London (1936).

[41] Shaw-Sparrow (1910), 116-17. However, as Peter Cormack has pointed out, the figure of Charity in the Dublin designs is not in fact female, but most probably intended to represent Christ, as in the 'anonymous' depiction of Christ in the last of the Rockefeller murals.

[42] It was Mackmurdo who suggested that Brangwyn copied Mantegna's 'sketch of the Roman Triumph, with elephants' an image which would reappear in his 'Empire' panels; see also Walter Shaw-Sparrow, *Frank Brangwyn and His Work* (London: Kegan Paul, Trench, Trübner & Co., 1910), 11. As well as receiving support and encouragement from Mackmurdo, the young Brangwyn had also met Harold Rathbone at South Kensington, who taught him the 'hard outlines' evident in much of his mural work, which were so suitable to the leading of stained glass.

[43] This comparison was first suggested by C. Willsdon in correspondence with the author, 8 April 2001. For the mosaics, see Arthur Finch, 'Recent Decorative Work by Frank Brangwyn A.R.A.: II. Mosaic Designs for St Aidan's Church, Leeds', *The Studio*, LXXII, no. 298 (January 1918): 142-47, and Willsdon (2000), *op. cit.*

[44] I am very grateful to Juliette MacDonald for information regarding Alexander Strachan and for photographs of the Livingston window at Dunfermline.

[45] The Burne-Jones cartoon was subsequently donated to Walthamstow Borough as part of the 'Brangwyn Gift'. See 'Reproductions of Some of the Principal Pictures Sold from Barbizon House, 1936' in Lockett Thomson, *Barbizon House 1936. An Illustrated Record* (London: Barbizon House, 9 Henrietta St, Cavendish Square, London W1, 1936): 27. I am greatly indebted to Peter Cormack for pointing out this reference.

[46] de Belleroche (1944), 35.

[47] de Belleroche (1948), 46.

[48] *Ibid.*

[49] *Ibid.*

[50] According to Darling, Brangwyn's window was commissioned 'at the request of' the 2nd Earl of Iveagh, Rupert Edward Cecil L. Guinness. See 'The Late Lord Iveagh: Memorial Window Unveiled: Ceremony at Saint Patrick's', *The Irish Times* (26 July 1937): 8-9.

[51] See Willsdon (2000), *op. cit.* 162.

[52] For a description of Iveagh's development of Elveden Hall and the Church of St Andrew and St Patrick see Nikolaus Pevsner, *The Buildings of England : Suffolk* (Penguin, 1974), 199-200; Birkin Haward, *Nineteenth Century Suffolk Stained Glass* (Woodbridge: The Boydell Press, 1989); and Turner, *op. cit.*

[53] *Ibid*, 1-4. I am greatly indebted to Gillian and Neville Turner at Elveden for their help in the preparation of this article.

[54] See Jennifer Freeman, *W. D. Caröe, RstO FSA: His Architectural Achievement* (Manchester: Manchester University Press, 1990), 33.

[55] De Belleroche (1944), 59.

[56] See Arthur Reddie, 'Mr. Frank Brangwyn's Mural Paintings in Christ's Hospital Chapel', *The Studio*, LXVI, no. 273 (December 1915): 151-52, W. R. Macklin and H. A. Rigby, *The Decorative Paintings in Christ's Hospital Chapel* (Ditchling: St Dominic's Press, 1925), and Willsdon (2000), *op. cit.* chapter 8.

[57] Letter from Frank Brangwyn to the Rector of the Church of St Andrew and St Patrick, quoted in the *Parish Magazine*, 1940. I am indebted to Gillian Turner for pointing this source out to me and providing me with a copy of it.

[58] de Belleroche (1948), 45.

[59] *Ibid.*, 46-47.

[60] *Ibid.*, 47. Brangwyn may have been referring to Alfred Wolmark's Ellerman memorial window (1915) at St Mary's, Slough, for which J. Sylvester Sparrow made sample panels. I am grateful to Peter Cormack for this reference.

Adam Goodyear

Hugh Ray Easton (1906-1965)

My first encounter with the work of Hugh Easton was as a student at Swansea College of Art, when we were shown a slide of his war memorial window in Durham Cathedral. Admiring the dramatic composition and draughtsmanship, the design appealed to me, although my fellow students were far from impressed. While I am not impervious to certain failings in some of Easton's work, their disapproval was in common with many comments and reactions I was to find in the ensuing twenty-two years of research: 'painfully obtrusive';[1] 'quite unbelievably behind the times and moreover terribly genteel and thin blooded';[2] 'naturalistic and very crude';[3] 'appalling'.[4] That a successful and prolific artist is often dismissed and at times reviled makes him a more fascinating subject for research. These few pages are an attempt to give a bare account of Easton's life and work; a book is intended for the future.

Hugh Ray Easton was born on 26 November 1906 to Dr Frank Easton and Alice Muriel Easton (née Howland). The family lived at 12 Devonport Street, Hyde Park West, London, where Dr Easton had a successful career as a general practitioner. Easton was the younger of two sons, his brother John Lawrence Howland Easton was born in 1903 and would follow in his father's and grandfather's footsteps to become a G.P.[5]

At the start of the summer term of 1920, aged thirteen, Easton began his studies at his father's old school, Wellington College, Berkshire (FIG. 1).[6] He did

FIG. 1:
Hugh Easton (top row, 4th from left), aged 16 at Wellington College, July 1923. Reproduced by permission of Wellington College.

not distinguish himself in any field and showed no talent for art. He left Wellington aged sixteen, considered a rather stupid boy, and with an uncertain future. He was sent to Tours University to study French. Aged nineteen and back in England, his future was no clearer. However it was at this time that an aptitude towards drawing and painting finally emerged, coinciding with bicycling tours to do brass rubbings at the instigation of a master at his brother's school who was interested in church architecture in general and stained glass in particular.

As a result of this new-found talent Easton was sent c.1925 to work under William Henry Randoll Blacking (1891-1958) who had an architectural and church furnishing practice in Guildford. Blacking had been articled to J. N. Comper and following service in the Great War established a practice c.1919, in which he collaborated with another Comper pupil, Christopher Rahere Webb (1886-1966).[7] Family history has it that Easton was encouraged in his early career by Webb and Comper, although quite when he was introduced to the latter is uncertain.[8]

Happy with Easton's vocation in ecclesiastical art, his family set him up in premises in 1930 at 2 Free School Lane in Cambridge, and in 1932 he moved to 13 Botolph Lane where he remained until the outbreak of war.[9] Both of these premises appear to be residential; a separate studio is thus far unknown. His early diaries make occasional references to visiting Christopher Webb, now established in St Albans, and allude to painting, but did he use Webb's studio for glass painting?

Possibly his earliest commission for stained glass was in 1930 for Romsey Abbey (FIG. 2). A single-light window depicting *The Annunciation*, it must have appeared quite striking at the time. The colours are rich and set against a white background and the matting is used in a bold, stylised manner. The design suffers (as do a number of his commissions) in the positioning of the saddle bars in relation to important elements of the design, namely the Virgin's hands. Canon Corban, possibly the anonymous donor wrote, 'the colouring is fine & clean, and it is an instance of how colour can be brought in without darkening the church'.[10]

During the early years of his career in Cambridge his personality and confidence developed and he found many friends amongst the undergraduates. Easton's tiny note books, with minuscule pencilled entries, give details of journeys to clients and friends, commissions for church furnishings as well as stained glass and lists whom he dined with, often indicated only by initials or a nickname, such as 'The White Devil'. At other times the names are given in full and frequently through 1930 Easton dined two or three times a day with Anthony Blunt and Guy Burgess.

Another friend acquired at this time was Uvedale Lambert Jnr., who in 1932 commissioned Easton to convert an existing Morning Chapel into a Lady Chapel at the wonderful barn church of

FIG. 3:
Bas-relief for
reredos at St
Philip and All
Saints, North
Sheen (1932).
V&A Picture
Library.

St Philip the Apostle and All Saints, North Sheen, Surrey, in memory of his parents. The design involved cedar panelling, an oak altar and four silvered wooden candlesticks, all executed by C. Hammond of Kew. The focal point, a *bas-relief* reredos depicting the Madonna and Child surrounded by playing children (FIG. 3), was carved by Easton.[11]

Other commissions were for an altar at Eltham (1931), a lectern for Warwick (date unknown), a bronze corpus figure (date unknown) made by W. Frank Knight,[12] altar furnishings and a three-light window at Pebmarsh in 1934.[13] Pevsner, discussing the Clayton & Bell East window at Pebmarsh says, 'So much is said (and done) nowadays against Victorian glass that one should consider seriously whether Clayton & Bell's is not more legitimately stained glass than Mr Easton's which is always reminiscent of line drawings daintily water coloured'.[14]

In October 1934 Easton prepared a design for a two-light window at Belford church, Northumberland, *Gideon Chooses Three Hundred Men*. Although happy with the sketch, the DAC were unsure of one element, 'the figure of Jehovah', as it was thought unacceptable to illustrate God as human. They sought the advice of the Bishop who felt, 'such a representation is most undesirable'. Easton replaced this area of the design with a hand in blessing and rays of radiating light.[15]

April 1936 saw the dedication of the first of Easton's eleven windows in Durham Cathedral. A three-light window in memory of Basil Philpott Blacket KCB, it depicted St Gregory Naziansen, 'an early Greek Saint whose writings were translated into English by Sir Basil. 'The upper part of the window and the tracery are filled with a representation of God the Father with outstretched arms ready to receive the saint...'.[16] It is interesting that Durham didn't share the qualms of neighbouring Newcastle diocese and more particularly that Easton wished to pursue this type of image. 1935 had brought an important commission at Exeter Cathedral, for his friend Denzil Fortescue in memory of his father Hugh 4th Earl Fortescue. The window depicted St George and the patron saint of huntsmen St Hubert, 'symbolising his love of the chase'.[17] It was soon vandalised by an elderly gentleman protesting against hunting,[18] and was then destroyed on 4 May 1942 when the Luftwaffe attacked Exeter.

In May 1936 an enthusiastic report of Easton's recent commission at Burwell appeared in *The Cambridge Review*, describing the four-light double-tiered window of the *Annunciation* above *The Adoration of the Magi* in detail:

FIG. 4:
I saw a New Heaven and a New Earth, St Paul's, King Cross, Halifax (1937). Photograph by Adam Goodyear.

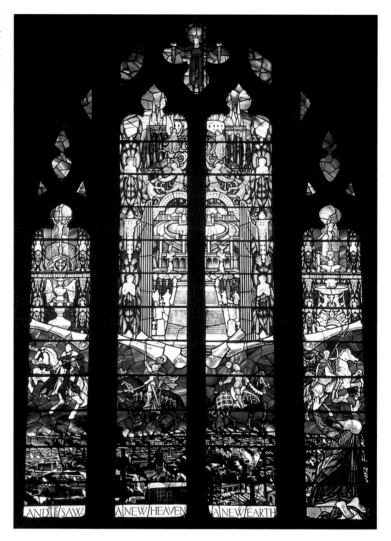

the immediate impression on entering the church is a blaze of blue... . It should be noted that all this blue is clear glass, an unusual treatment which risks over intensity in the deep shades, but which has the great advantage of the shimmering effect obtainable when there is, as here, a background of trees in the church yard... . The individual drawing is excellent, the character of the negro king being specially remarkable... Mr Easton may be congratulated on achieving a fine and original thing... Mr Easton might be said to belong to the romantic school but in the Burwell window his romanticism has the solid background of 16th Century handling.[19]

The reviewer was Theodore Fyfe,[20] architect, author and husband of Mary Nina Fyfe, at whose girls' school, Owlstone Croft, Cambridge, Easton was drawing master during the 1930s. One of his former pupils remembered that the girls regarded him as 'something of a heartthrob',[21] a fact not lost on Easton who related this to a friend.[22]

1936 was also the year of Easton's first window at Clare College, Cambridge,[23] following the removal of the Wailes windows. It depicts Bishop Latimer and Nicholas Ferrar kneeling before a green cross and the crucified Christ with Ferrar's 'Protestant Nunnery', Little Gidding, in the background. It was reviewed by Eric Milner-White, then the Dean of Cambridge:

> For nearly a hundred years the interior of Clare Chapel has been suffocated by an atrocious series of windows. Like the window at Burwell, so this by its brilliance will be found startling at first glance. Continue to look, and its lasting merits declare themselves. Its style may be said to carry over from the half-Gothic, half-Renaissance idiom of the King's Chapel glass to a full Renaissance manner which never arrived in England, or, to any appreciable extent, elsewhere. What with the Burne-Jones windows in Jesus, Humphry's in Pembroke, Strachan's in Westminster, and now this, the College Chapels of Cambridge are contributing a fine chapter to the revival of glass-painting.
>
> The design has the boldness and bigness appropriate to a large unmullioned window, and which few glass painters to-day dare to attempt… . Nor does the artist do more painting than is necessary; he leaves the glass (e.g., of the green Cross) to display its own quality and variety of tone, clear and naked. This is true "painting on light," and since the draughtsmanship is as bold as the design, it is a window of which the College is not likely to repent. To imagine a series of such, if only it might be, is to see a feast of colour which increases rather than diminishes the light of the Chapel, and relieves, without lessening, its dignity.[24]

Pevsner on the other hand, commenting on the departure of the Wailes windows and the arrival of Easton's says, 'time will show whether the change was wise'.[25]

In August 1936 a faculty was granted for the West window at St Paul's, King Cross, Halifax. A gift of the parish in memory of the vicar, the subject is St John's vision of the New Jerusalem (FIG. 4), one Easton depicted a number of times. St John looks up to the golden city surrounded by seraphim. Beneath the city ride the Four Horsemen of the Apocalypse set against an unpainted streaky blue sky, an idea previously used at Belford and Warwick in 1935 and praised by Fyfe in 1936. The lower register is taken up with a detailed panorama of Halifax in all its dark satanic splendour, the first use by Easton of a panoramic scene, but a theme often revisited: Durham in 1948, Derby in 1949, Stepney in 1950, and so on. The overall effect is very dramatic, a blaze of colour in a dark area of the church. It is one of the few occasions where Easton used gold-pink glass to any extent. The local press reported events in full, 'In workmanship and design the window is unique', and referred to Easton as 'one of the foremost modern artists in stained glass… . It is claimed to be the masterpiece of the artist, and has cost about £500'.[26]

1938 was an even busier year with windows for parish, college and cathedral. Easton was commissioned to provide three windows in the east apse of Ypres Cathedral, 'the gift of prominent personages in the Ypres district'.[27] The twenty-foot tall lights set high in the chancel wall depict St Martin, St Maurice and St Michael (FIG. 5). The figures are set against a rather medieval, red and blue chequered background, a device first used at Hockerill the previous year and again at Gloucester, also in 1938.[28] The Ypres windows were made in Coulpaert's studio in Brussels,[29] the reason as yet unknown. Two more windows were added to the Cathedral at a later date.

This was also the year of Easton's first commission for the Worshipful Company of Glaziers, whom he had joined in 1935 and in which he took an active role, acting as one of the judging panel in the annual competition. A two-light window in Tonbridge School Chapel (where the chaplain Rev. D. H. Booth was a close friend of Easton's until his death) was a gift to the Skinners Company, of which the school is a foundation. It is a striking image of St Martin seated on a rearing grey horse, dividing his cloak for the beggar. At the luncheon following the dedication Lord Carisbrooke, chairman of the Glaziers Company stained glass window committee said, 'the great aim of the Glaziers Company was to revive the art of glazing and to encourage those who practised it'.[30] A second commission for the Glaziers came in 1939 – the Coronation window at Winchester Cathedral.[31] In the nine years since Easton opened his studio his style had evolved greatly. Particularly apparent is the development of figures from the stylised treatment at Romsey, through the windows at Barnack and Baddingham where they are slender and flowing – perhaps showing some influence of Christopher Webb, to the latter commissions where his figures are more dramatic and at times very muscular.

Whilst Easton's work had gone from strength to strength and commissions had flowed in for prestigious locations from influential donors, receiving fine reviews, his work was not without criticism. Sir Eric Maclagan, chairman of the Victoria & Albert Museum and of the Winchester DAC, commented that Easton 'was a good artist but not a good designer of stained glass.'[32]

Family history maintains that Easton enlisted as soon as war was declared. Certainly in 1940 Easton was no longer teaching at Owlstone Croft,[33] and it is possible that he was living at the Strand Hotel, London. How he was filling his life is thus far unclear as his war record does not begin until April 1942,[34] in the RNVR based at the Admiralty in the press division, as 'naval advisor to the Censorship Division of the Ministry of Information…'.[35]

The Times of 11 May 1944 reported that, 'Commander Hugh Easton… well-known artist in stained glass, has been commissioned to design the window for the RAF Chapel in Westminster Abbey'. On 29 March 1946 Easton was released from service[36] and he moved to 14A Downshire Hill, a partially bomb-damaged property on the edge of Hampstead Heath. As numerous war memorial commissions rolled in for all services, British as well as American (e.g. USAF memorial at Elveden Church, Suffolk, 1947), work progressed on what was to become Easton's best-known commission. The Battle of Britain memorial window in Westminster Abbey commemorates the 1495 men who gave their lives in this momentous conflict. Easton's aim in the design was 'to create in glass a jewelled curtain of such brilliance as to be a translucent painting, a fresco shot through by flames, taking its place in the richness of the Henry VII's Chapel. Each light in its own way tells the story of the Battle of Britain, each light has its own meaning, but the whole is subservient to the architectural frame.'[37] The window was unveiled on 10 July 1947, the seventh anniversary of the first day of the battle.

The window and the whole memorial chapel was praised: 'It is a window that must give, so long as it endures, unfailing artistic delight to those who go to examine it…';[38] and 'The memorial, one of the most important in the eyes of the world at the present moment, is distinguished by reticence and simplicity'.[39]

However, it did not find favour in all quarters. John Betjeman was beginning to make his name as an architectural writer and critic. He had met Ninian Comper in 1937, and befriending the architect, who was at a low ebb in both his professional and private life, he proceeded to cultivate this friendship, introducing a number of people to the isolated Comper, including John Piper.[40] Comper writing to Betjeman of his reminiscences, says:

> I may add that I had another young friend, Hugh Easton, who I fear has really gone to the bad because you tell me that he announces that he only does glass for cathedrals! And Sebastian tells me that his glass is not good, and the glass merchants that he has a large establishment. But he used to stay with me sometimes and show me some 30 or more diaries full or the most exquisite outline drawings of side and back views of naked youths as on a Greek vase. It is therefore a worse fate which has befallen him: for sins of the spirit are far worse than sins of the flesh. He is much too grand to know me now! And he knows that I should convict him out of his own mouth and writing.[41]

A month after the dedication Betjeman replied, 'I am horrified by the Easton glass at Westminster. It is as coarse as the new coinage and utterly disregards that delicate tracery and subtle Prout-like light and shade of Henry VII Chapel. I went to see it yesterday. Oh goodness it must not occur in any other window.'[42]

Betjeman had introduced Sir Kenneth Clarke, Director of the National Gallery, to Comper in 1940. Following the RAF window Comper tried unsuccessfully to enlist the help of Clarke in the prevention of Easton securing any further commissions in the Abbey.[43] In his letters to Comper written at intervals through the following year, Betjeman, who was now championing John Piper, continued to rail:

'Easton! Do Mr Piper and I hold any brief for him? We LOATHE his windows... . A campaign of ridicule may do some good as I am told he is now "Only booking orders for Cathedrals"... . Your admirers increase daily – and they are the young. Easton is vieux jeu.'[44]

Another who disapproved of this and subsequent commissions at the Abbey was Stephen Dykes Bower, a friend and one-time champion of Easton's. The friendship cooled as Dykes Bower wrote against the windows to F. C. Eeles, then chairman for the Council for the Care of Churches, and to W. I. Croome, who sat on a number of DACs.[45] Croome had also supported Easton's early work but would come to disapprove of later commissions.

According to family history, at this point Easton felt that his popularity might be on the wane and advised his assistants Robert L. Hendra (1912-1968) and Geoffrey F. Harper (1913-1966), who had worked for Martin Travers and Hardman's respectively and had been with Easton since the mid 1930s, to leave his employ and establish their own studio. How accurate this is I am unsure, but certainly their partnership starts in 1947. As well as their own work, they and their apprentices continued to paint Easton's considerable output, seemingly unabated by the efforts of Betjeman, Comper and Dykes Bower. 'Once a week Easton would travel down from London to the studio at Harpenden to check on the work in progress... . Every 2 or 3 months he would read out a list of future windows which rarely represented less than 18 months work'.[46]

A month after the dedication of the Battle of Britain window, Rolls Royce proposed a commission for a large single-light window in the foyer at the Derby works (FIGS. 6-7). The window was to commemorate the pilots of the RAF and the work of the Derby factory in providing the engines for their planes. W. Lappin of Rolls Royce wrote to Lord Tedder Marshall of the RAF, asking him to unveil the window and telling him that the artist was Hugh Easton, saying: 'He claims that it will be his masterpiece'.[47] A commemorative booklet was produced in which Easton describes his design:

> In the centre of the window stands the figure of a typical Fighter Pilot of the Royal Air Force. Ready for the Battle, in flying-boots and 'Mae West,' his helmet in his hand, he stands on the spinner of an airscrew, its three blades dominating the lower part of the window. Behind it are stretched out in long lines the sheds and buildings of the Derby factory which produced these engines with which the pilots won the Battle of Britain. In the lower part, therefore, I have tried to symbolise the work of man's hands, the machine or, one might say, the structure, the bones and muscles. In the centre, I felt, the pilot should represent the brain. Above and behind him, with outstretched wings, ready to strike, is a golden eagle; here is the heart and spirit.

FIG. 7: Window commemorating pilots of the Battle of Britain and the workers of Rolls Royce who provided their engines, Rolls Royce, Derby (1949). Reproduced by permission of Rolls Royce.

FIG. 6: (opposite) Full size preparatory drawing in position at Rolls Royce, Derby (c.1948). V&A Picture Library.

Beyond, and framing the eagle and dominating all the top of the window, is the resplendent sun in all its glory, symbol of that for which the Battle was fought, and towards which Humanity lifts up her eyes.[48]

In the planning of the ceremony Easton, ever reserved, requested to remain in the background as one of the spectators.[49] Following the unveiling Lappin wrote to Easton, 'I hope that you feel we did credit to your magnificent window. I must congratulate you most sincerely and we feel proud that this window will be a permanent feature of the building...'.[50] Easton replied: 'Your letter pleased me so very much. You could not have written anything nicer. I do believe that we have achieved something quite exceptional in that window.'[51]

How frequently Easton took his cartoons to a location I don't know (SEE FIG. 6). Certainly he would produce numerous preliminary cartoons or full-size sketches of part, or all of a window, on very thin paper. Some were very sketchy whilst others were highly finished as he got nearer to the effect he desired. This is one of the few windows in which Easton uses Norman Slab glass.

In 1950 Easton moved to 6A Holbein Place off Sloane Square, Chelsea. The following years saw a vast amount of work with particularly large windows and series of windows: thirteen windows for St George's Church, Royal Naval Barracks, Chatham (1950); seven windows for Oundle School Chapel (1950, FIG. 8); eleven windows for Wellington College (1953); twelve windows for St George's Chapel, Biggin Hill (1955). That year also saw the completion of Easton's enormous seven-light two-tier West window at Holy Trinity Coventry, the *Te Deum*. Christ reigns in glory before a green cross, seated on a rainbow with his feet resting on the globe. In all, the window contains 113 figures. Unfortunately, saddle bars were once again allowed to cut through heads, and Christ's foot is cut off by a mullion. Conversely, the rainbow which forms a circle also cuts across a number of the faces, giving the striking and technically taxing effect of these faces being streaked with vivid bands of colour. The East window, blown out by the bomb which destroyed the Cathedral, was replaced in the same year by Comper. One can only muse at what the two men felt about their respective windows staring at each other.

The workload continued apace through 1956 although the following years were seemingly quieter – with no less prestigious commissions, however, such as a replacement for the 4th Earl Fortescue window destroyed at Exeter Cathedral and a window in Lloyds New Building in Lime Street, opened by The Queen Mother in November 1957. The following year was the last in which Easton included a list of his work in the *BSMGP Directory*. In common with his earlier entries, the listings are fairly comprehensive and as previously he does not include any commissions prior to 1936. Easton contributed greatly to the Society, serving on the Council between 1951 and 1955, and the *Journals* refer to his ability as an after-dinner speaker and his great sense of humour.

In 1959 E. Liddall Armitage published *Stained Glass: History, Technology and Practice*, the final section of which is given over to accounts by contemporary artists of their working methods. Easton's is interesting, not just for what it reveals about his own approach but for the percentage of the piece devoted to those whom he employed.

FIG. 8:
The Lover from *The Seven Ages of Man,* Oundle School Chapel (1950). Photograph by Tim Lewis.

FIG. 9:
The workforce
at Little Gables,
Leyton Road,
Harpenden
(c.1949).
Showing painting
in progress for
Nurses window,
Westminster
Abbey. From L/R:
1) Unidentified;
2) Edward Wigzell;
3) Either Hendra
or Harper;
4) Peter Ryall;
5) Unidentified.
V&A Picture
Library.

I like to develop the design as I go on and not tie myself down to a scale drawing... . I prefer to do the roughest of small drawings, sufficient to indicate to my client what can be done with the window. Then, I consider the design and its possibilities in my mind for as long as possible, turning over and working out different ways of treating the subject. Then I like to work out the whole window full-size in a drawing... and I am prepared to make several full-size drawings until I get what I want.

As for the work itself, I have been most fortunate in having Robert Hendra and Geoffery [*sic*] Harper who for many years have understood what I wanted in my work and have always been able to interpret my slightest drawing in paint (SEE FIG. 9). We have worked together for a long time and they came to me first when I was young and they were very young. Latterly, they have been doing their own work as well as mine and their technical knowledge and experience is, in my opinion unrivalled. Although I painted my earliest windows myself, I soon found that if one was fortunate enough to discover an artist who could paint and interpret one's drawings, a far greater technical mastery was achieved, when one had to spend so much time on the designing and drawing and carrying on the business of dealing with clients and committees. As far as the cutting and glazing of the windows is concerned, I have also been lucky in finding two perfect craftsmen, father and son: T. G. and Denis Harris,[52] and they have glazed practically all my windows... as the years go by I feel it is better to do fewer windows and take longer and longer over them.[53]

Most of Easton's post-war windows give credit to Hendra and Harper by the inclusion of their initials in Easton's distinctive weathervane rebus (FIG. 10). Occasionally quite pointed messages are hidden away in a discreet corner of the window, which one must assume Easton initiated: *Oundle 1950 – Hugh Easton gets all the credit for the windows but we – R. L. Hendra, G. F. Harper, A. E. Wigzell, A. J. Harper, S. H. Davy, P. Ryall and C. R. Watkiss did all the work*.

1959 was another quiet year in terms of the number of commissions although the East window of St Luke's, Chelsea, contains 450 square feet of glass, then 'the largest stained-glass window to be put into any London church since the war.'[54] The heraldic design 'incorporated not only the devices of the evangelists, apostles, and great doctors of the Church but also those of 105 of the saints'.[55]

In 1960 Easton was diagnosed with cancer of the hip. A friend of many years felt that his health had suffered as a result of concern for his aged parents.[56] In 1962 or early 1963, Easton was asked by his friend Denzil George Fortescue, Viscount Ebrington, to design an East window for the village church at Ebrington, Gloucestershire, on the *Parable of The Sower*. Surviving papers reveal the opposition the design met with and the feelings aroused in all concerned. The window in question was large and had long created a problem with its plain glazing allowing too much light into the chancel, making the altar all but invisible. The points of concern with the new design were the use of contemporary costume and that there would be insufficient stained glass in the lower part of the design to reduce the glare. The fact that the design crossed the mullions caused certain disquiet to Will Croome, chairman of the Gloucester DAC and an inveterate letter writer. He wrote:

> I got my reply from Hugh Easton; very cordial to me, thanking me for my efforts in the past; cursing Garth-Moore (Diocesan Chancellor) for having "gone to another committee over my head without telling me first"; but saying he would neither modify this design, nor attempt another, but washed his hands of the Commission altogether… . But with it came also another long letter from Denzil Fortescue; which said he and Easton had had a long talk after receiving the Chancellor's, and my, letters. That Easton was furious; that he was deeply interested in this window and wanted to execute it; that he had already made many experiments on it in glass … I replied… and pointed out that once Easton used to "respect" the form of a window; e.g. the Coronation "White Horse" at Winchester where all the tour-de-force of draughtsmanship had been directed to keeping the figure within the mullions; but that the present phase of ignoring the shape, and drawing a mere "picture" of furrows and Sower stretching over all lights and past heavy mullions was really against the best results from glass, and must create a continuing problem.[57]

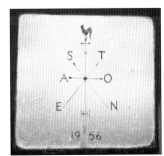

FIG. 10: Ninth and final version of Weathervane rebus, incorporating Hendra's and Harper's initials, St John's, Morecambe 1956. Photograph by Adam Goodyear.

From this difficult position Viscount Ebrington wished to re-submit the original design or for Easton to prepare an entirely new one in line with the chancellor's comments and wishes. 'Mr Easton declined to vary his design in any way; and asked that it be either accepted as it stood, or rejected by the donor, in which case he proposed to use it for another client in a northern Diocese'[58] (thus far undiscovered). With some reluctance Viscount Ebrington was persuaded to abandon Easton's design, and Christopher Webb took over the commission.

Easton's last commission discovered so far is for a set of five heraldic windows in the Hall of the Worshipful Company of Clothworkers, done in 1963. In the final years of Easton's life the cancer caused him greater trouble, he hobbled and had to resort to a walking stick. Though perhaps a little lonely, he showed no signs of bitterness regarding his illness and still retained his 'thigh slapping' sense of humour.

A friend at the time felt Easton regarded himself as having had a rewarding and fulfilled life. He moved into a hotel in Soho Square, and as the cancer took greater hold he was finally admitted to the Edward VII Hospital. Those who visited or whom he telephoned in his last days still found him in good spirits.[59] Hugh Easton died on 15 August 1965. Obituaries were carried in newspapers and magazines but unfortunately the *BSMGP Journal* only managed a brief announcement in 1967.

His memorial service was held in the Henry VII Chapel in Westminster Abbey before his Battle of Britain window.[60] Such was the privacy of Easton's life and his ability to keep parts of it 'in water tight compartments', that some of the guests were unaware of his friendships with others.[61] 'Ever the mystery man', as one of his friends described him.[62] Easton's ashes were interred in the family plot at St Giles, Bradford on Tone, where two years later a memorial window designed by Gerald Coles was dedicated to him.

Easton's great friend the Reverend D. H. Booth, former vicar of Stepney and then Archdeacon of Lewes wrote an obituary in the Stepney Parish magazine.

> It is difficult for me to express at all adequately my feelings about Hugh – he was one of my oldest and closest friends and Godfather to my son David. I knew him first as a struggling artist, trying to achieve recognition; never with the ultimate purpose of financial gain, but always with the desire of the better fulfilment of the God-given vocation which was his. This meant that satisfaction with his work was unknown to him at this stage – or any other in his life. He suffered from a divine fretting – a deep urge for the better realisation of his skill. He was, and he remained, permanently unsatisfied, and this surely must be the hallmark of every true artist.
>
> In Stepney he gave of his best, and I shall never forget that moment of unveiling of the East Window with the floodlights behind. From the vast congregation there was drawn a spontaneous cry of sheer admiration and wonder as the lights went up and revealed that great Christus in glory above the stupidities of man shown in the panorama of bombed out Stepney – there put that none may forget not only the majesty of God, but the poverty of man.
>
> This and the other windows are there for all men to see... . The work of an artist who combined great technical skill with a deep spiritual perception and love of his fellow men.
>
> This was Hugh Easton – the man – a man prodigal of himself – his friendship, his affection, his time and his material wealth. There are few, if any, who know the full extend of Hugh's sheer goodness to those in any sort of trouble – even the kind of trouble that deprived them of the sympathy of their fellow men. This, and I can only hint at the fullness of it, was combined with a great gaiety and joy in living. He was no "do-gooder," he was a full-blooded, warm hearted man with only one sheer hate – the hatred of affectation either in art or human relations. He was quick to spot any sort of insincerity and he gave it short shrift.
>
> The knowledge that Hugh's great chuckle and warm understanding will be no more for his friends has meant that a part of life has died for us, but every one of us has been enriched by this noble man who lived life so fully and well. "To love abundantly is to live abundantly." It is better that a man's works than another man's words should praise him.[63]

This article represents a minute amount of the information I have on Hugh Easton, however if any reader can offer information, particularly regarding commissions pre-1936 and post-1959 and details of Easton as a person, I would be most grateful.

ACKNOWLEDGEMENTS

I would like to acknowledge the assistance of those people named in the endnotes with whom I have spoken or corresponded, particularly the late Dr and Mrs Easton for their interest during the early years of my research, and their grandson Stephen Wallace for his continued interest. Also my thanks go to Alf Fisher and Sep Waugh for their help in identifying faces in FIG. 9, and to Peter Summerfield at Rolls Royce, Nicholas Ritchie and John Edwards at Wellington College, Stephen Bucknall and Jonathan Jarvis.

NOTES

Every effort has been made to obtain permission to quote material.

[1] Nikolaus Pevsner, *Durham. Buildings of England* (Harmondsworth: Penguin, 1983), 196.

[2] Nikolaus Pevsner, *Berkshire. Buildings of England* (Harmondsworth: Penguin, 1966), 262.

[3] Birkin Haward, 'Stowlangtoft' in *Nineteenth Century Suffolk Stained Glass* (Woodbridge: The Boydell Press, 1989), Gazetteer.

[4] Birkin Haward, 'Elveden' in *Nineteenth Century Suffolk Stained Glass* (Woodbridge: The Boydell Press, 1989), Gazetteer.

[5] Correspondence with Mr & Mrs J. Easton, Stephen Wallace and Wellington College.

[6] Correspondence with Wellington College.

[7] Correspondence with Mr J. Easton; see also Eileen Roberts, 'Christopher Webb and Orchard House Studio', *The Journal of Stained Glass* vol. 25 (2001): 80.

[8] They were certainly acquainted by 1931 as Easton's note books refer to visits and correspondence.

[9] Information from *Spaldings Street Directory*, in 'The Cambridge Collection', Cambridge City Library.

[10] From *Romsey Abbey Magazine*, quoted in conversation with Mrs Judy Walker.

[11] Correspondence from Mr K. Richardson with information from Surrey Record office. *Barn Church Magazine* (June 1950).

[12] Simon O'Corra, 'W. Frank Knight O.B.E. (1885-1972): Ecclesiastical Artist Craftsman', *Ecclesiology Today* 27 (January 2002): 22-24.

[13] T. D. S. Bayley M.A., *Pebmarsh Church* (Oxford: Oxford University Press, 1946), 33, 34, 47.

[14] Nikolaus Pevsner, *Essex. Buildings of England* (Harmondsworth: Penguin 1965), 313.

[15] Unsigned letter of 14 January 1935, Diocese of Newcastle, Faculty 1294, in the collection of Northumberland Archives Service.

[16] 'Memorial Window in Durham Cathedral', *The Times* (20 April 1936), 11.

[17] 'Cathedral Window Memorial to Fourth Earl Fortescue', *Western Times* (11 October 1935).

[18] Conversation with Mr J. Easton.

[19] Theodore Fyfe, 'Recent Stained Glass in Cambridge and Burwell', *The Cambridge Review* (1 May 1936): 349-50.

[20] Theodore Fyfe, *Who Was Who 1941-1950* (London: Adam & Charles Black, 1952): 415.

[21] Conversation with Mrs Susan Hughes-Onslow.

[22] Correspondence with Sir Carol Mather.

[23] Incorrectly identified as Easton's first commission in *Dictionary of National Biography* (Oxford: Oxford University Press 1981), 320-21.

[24] Eric Milner-White, 'New Glass in Clare College Chapel', *The Cambridge Review* (15 May 1936): 382.

[25] Nikolaus Pevsner, *Cambridge. Buildings of England* (Harmondsworth: Penguin 1970), 60.

[26] *Halifax Daily Courier and Guardian* (5 May 1937), 6.

[27] 'British Gift Unveiled', *The Times* (23 May 1938), 13.

[28] Both commissions were secured for Easton by Stephen Dykes Bower. Correspondence with Fr Anthony Symondson S.J.

[29] Major Guy Cassie, 'Glimpses of Modern Continental Windows on a Return Journey from Holiday', *Journal of the BSMGP*, Vol. 12, No. 1 (1955-6): 59.

[30] 'City Companies Gift to School', *The Times* (20 October 1938), 9. The window was destroyed by fire in 1993.

[31] 'Royal Visit to Winchester', *The Times* (4 July 1939), 11.

[32] Correspondence with Mrs Judith Scott.

[33] Conversation with Mrs Susan Hughes-Onslow.

[34] Correspondence with Mr S. Wallace.

[35] 'Obituary Mr Hugh Easton', *The Times* (16 August 1965), 10.

[36] From correspondence with Mr Stephen Wallace.

[37] 'Where The Battle of Britain Glows Forever in Memorial Glass', *The Illustrated London News* (12 July 1947): 44-45.

[38] 'Battle of Britain Memorial', *The Times* (11 July 1947), 7.

[39] 'Memorial in Westminster Abbey to The Battle of Britain', *The Builder* (11 July 1947), 32.

[40] Fr Anthony Symondson S.J., 'John Betjeman and the Cult of J. N. Comper' *The Thirties Society Journal* 7 (1991): 3-6.

[41] Letter from J. N. Comper to J. Betjeman (10 May 1947). Private Collection.

[42] Letter from J. Betjeman to J. N. Comper (26 August 1947). Private Collection.

[43] Symondson, *op. cit.*, p. 8.

[44] Letter from J. Betjeman to J. N. Comper (18 November 1948). Private Collection.

[45] Correspondence with Fr Anthony Symondson S.J.

[46] Correspondence with Mr Peter Ryall.

[47] Letter from W. Lappin to Lord Tedder (6 October 1948), in the archives held by Rolls Royce Heritage Trust.

[48] Brochure produced by Rolls Royce to commemorate the unveiling on 11 January 1949.

[49] Rolls Royce internal minutes, 25 October 1948, in the archives held by Rolls Royce Heritage Trust.

[50] Letter from W. Lappin to Hugh Easton (12 January 1949) in the archives held by Rolls Royce Heritage Trust.

[51] Letter from Hugh Easton to W. Lappin (13 January 1949) in the archives held by Rolls Royce Heritage Trust.

[52] Hawes and Harris's workshop was at Park Stables, Harpenden, where they glazed the windows of Christopher Webb, Ernest Heasman and Francis Skeat.

[53] E. Liddal Armitage, *Stained Glass; History, Technology and Practice* (London: Leonard Hill, 1959), 188-89.

[54] 'New Stained Glass Window', *Manchester Guardian* (20 June 1959)

[55] *ibid.*

[56] Correspondence with Sir Carol Mather.

[57] Letter from W. I. Croome (16 March 1963) in the archives of The Diocese of Gloucester.

[58] Letter from W. I. Croome (16 May 1964) in the archives of The Diocese of Gloucester.

[59] Personal reminiscences of Mr John Christian and Sir Carol Mather.

[60] On 24 September 1965.

[61] Conversation with Mr John Christian.

[62] Correspondence with Sir Carol Mather.

[63] *Step Ahoy* (1965), 8

Caroline Swash

Gerdur Helgadóttir (1928-1975);
stained glass by a sculptor

Gerdur Helgadóttir deserves to be better known. Originally an accomplished sculptor, she worked in Paris and was fully involved in the avant-garde scene during one of the most intellectually exciting periods of the last century. She then turned to stained glass (FIG. 1), making fine windows for churches in Iceland and Germany before dying tragically young. After her death, her panels of glass, preparatory work and sculpture were gathered together and housed in a building specially designed for them, the Kópavogur Art Museum (FIGS. 2, 8).

Iceland's independence from Denmark, finally established in 1944, had an enormous effect on the outlook of its artists. In earlier days under Danish rule, the automatic route for training in all the art and craft disciplines were the universities and colleges in Scandinavian countries. The sound construction and high quality of architecture, sculpture, painting and weaving in Iceland bear witness to the importance of this contact. However, once the 1939-45 War was over, a few of the most lively young artists went further afield. The painter and glass artist, Nina Tryggvadóttir, for example, studied first with Asgrímur Jónsson in Reykjavík before going to Copenhagen and then to New York where, among others, she was taught by Hans Richter, Hans Hofmann and Fernand Leger. She subsequently made her name with subtle abstract paintings, exhibiting work during the 1940s with the New Art Circle.

Gerdur began her studies in sculpture at the School of Art in Reykjavík learning to carve the heavy grey stone of the local quarries. At nineteen she went to Italy where, at the Academy of Fine Art in Florence, the careful study of the human body remained fundamental to all that mattered in sculpture. Impatient at the limited expectations of this institution, she moved to Paris in 1949 and became a student of Ossip Zadkine at l'Academie de la Grande-Chaumière, learning new methods in carving and modelling that had evolved from Cubism.

Paris at this time was still the centre of the avant-garde. Young artists longing for a visual language to express their desire for change turned to ideas first promulgated there during the 1920s. 'Concrete-Abstract' art was particularly attractive, with its insistence on the importance of basic principles. These were outlined by the painter Vasarely in his 'Notes for a Manifesto' written in the form of an introduction to the *Le Mouvement* exhibition at the Gallery Denise René in April 1955. Here Vasarely referred to 'Pure Composition', which he felt should consist of abstract elements used either to indicate a sense of space or even the illusion

FIG. 1: *(Overleaf) Untitled* (1969), stained glass panel by Gerdur Helgadóttir in the collection of the Kópavogur Art Museum. Copyright Kópavogur Art Museum.

FIG. 2: Interior of the Kópavogur Art Museum, showing works by Gerdur Helgadóttir on display. Photograph by Caroline Swash.

of movement. Colour was expected to find a new role, either as coloured light or as coloured form. Together these were intended to create what he called 'la nouvelle beauté plastique mouvante et émouvante'.

Gerdur, then in her early twenties, responded to these ideas with enthusiasm. She abandoned her post-Cubist models and worked instead with iron; bending and forging the metal to create strong, simple, rather architectural shapes (FIG. 3). Her progress surprised the French critics. They referred to 'the rapid evolution' of her work as the solid forms gave way to light geometric pieces, some with symbolic overtones and a few with glass inclusions. She worked astonishingly fast. In 1952, for example, she had solo shows in Paris and Reykjavík and contributed to the prestigious group exhibitions *Divergences* and the *Salon de la Jeune Sculpture* in Paris and *Art Islandais* in Brussels. She was still only twenty-four. The following year she won a prize for her submission to the international sculpture competition 'The Unknown Political Prisoner' at the Tate Gallery, London.

During the 1950s and 60s, her sculpture was enthusiastically reviewed by the critics and she appears to have been regarded as one of the most promising young artists working in Paris at the time, her name linked with Calder, Herbin, Pevsner, Gonzalez, Tashiri and Jacobsen. An article written by Michel Ragon for *Cimaise revue de l'art actuel*[1] gives us some idea of her working life. Ragon wrote of her as small, fairhaired, blue-eyed, and very young and likened her studio to a garage scattered about with tools for cutting metal, cluttered with enormous bottles of oxyacetylene gas. Dressed in blue overalls and wearing her protective goggles, Ragon felt she resembled 'un personage de science-fiction'.

Despite critical success, the postwar years were lean ones financially and with few sales from her Paris exhibitions Gerdur looked about for another source of income. Having already used glass in her sculpture she wondered whether money could be earned from making windows for the new churches being built in Iceland and elsewhere in postwar Europe. She went briefly to the studio of Jean Barillet to learn the craft of stained glass before responding to her father's suggestion to compete for a series of windows for the newly-refurbished Church of Skalholt in Iceland. She won the competition in 1958 and elected to make the stained glass windows with the Oidtmann Studios at Linnich. Fritz Oidtmann and his brother Ludovicus (FIG. 4, PLATE 1, p. 9) allowed Gerdur to build the windows as she chose. Accustomed to total control in her sculpture, she had to find an equivalent relationship with this new architectural medium.

Since the windows were for a sacred space, Gerdur read widely, searching for core images and key colour to convey the essential spiritual importance of the new glass for Skalholt. That she thought of the windows as upright sculpture seems probable, since a sense of solidity is so much a feature of the series. Once the colour disposition had been worked out in sketch form, Gerdur drew and painted the cartoons herself, establishing the exact width of each lead and the space for visible glass. Indeed these great drawings in black ink and watercolour on continuous cartridge paper reveal so clearly her background in metalwork; the knots and twists of the lines have a powerful inner rhythm entirely absent from the formal pattern-making of much contemporaneous abstract work in France and Germany.[2]

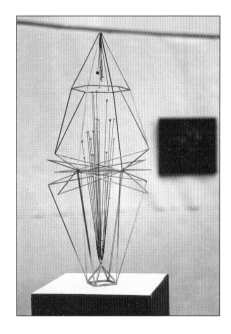

FIG. 3:
Dew (1956), iron wire sculpture by Gerdur Helgadóttir. Copyright Kópavogur Art Museum.

The link with Oidtmann Studios proved to be a profitable one for Gerdur. Churches were being built in an architectural language that firmly rejected the past and she won several competitions arranged to find suitable artists for these new buildings. Her best work in Germany can be seen at St Antonius Abbas Church, Herkenrath (1962) and the Evangelical Churches of Rüttenscheid, Essen (1964), Billebrinkhöhe, Essen (1964) and Melanchton Church, Dusseldorf (1966). For all these buildings Gerdur created windows that softened and complemented the austere style of the new architecture. Commissions for windows in Icelandic churches were also executed at the Oidtmann studios: these included the subtle series in Hallgrimur Petursson's Memorial Church (1956/1965) and the astonishing clover leaf arches of Kópavogur Church (1962). She also used slab glass for an effective sculptural doorway at the Evangelical Church, Kempen (1971). Here the combination of low relief and brilliant colour presaged what was to be the final stage of her work in sculpture (FIG. 5).

In 1960 she married a young French painter Jean Leduc, buying a farmhouse 'Cheval Mort' at Avrainville, 30Km south of Paris, to provide room for both their studios. Together they created the decoration in 1962 for Saint Pierre le Piel in Cantal, France; Leduc designing the glass and Gerdur making a complex metal casing

FIG. 4:
(From L-R) Ludovicus Oidtmann, Gerdur Helgadóttir and Fritz Oidtmann working on the Skalholt windows at Linnich, Germany in 1959. Copyright Kópavogur Art Museum.

for the Tabernacle (FIG. 6). Similar sculptural commissions followed, including a cross for the Cathedral of Aachen in an unusual combination of iron and gold.

Following the breakdown of her marriage, she travelled to Egypt in 1966 and on her return to France was inspired to create a series of magnificent standing sculptures which combined cast concrete with glass inserts in an entirely original way. As well as these upright works she continued to fashion new forms in terracotta, plaster and bronze. Indeed, she was working in metal on a series of wall pieces for a Grammar School and a Bank in Iceland (FIG. 7) during the last few debilitating months of her life. She died aged 47.

Her cartoons, drawings, sculpture tools and ephemera were collected from her studios by her friend Elin Palmadóttir and her sister Unnur and taken home to Iceland. Here the enlightened town of Kópavogur, recognising the remarkable talent of this young artist, commissioned an Art Museum from the architect Benjamin Magnússon. In 1994 this fine and spacious building was opened to the public (FIG. 8). In honour of her achievement in so many techniques, the museum is called *Gerdarsafn*.

FIG. 5:
Slab glass and concrete doorway by Gerdur Helgadóttir at Kempen, Germany (1971). Copyright Kópavogur Art Museum.

FIG. 6:
St Pierre le Peil, Cantal, France, bronze ornamentation for the Tabernacle by Gerdur Helgadóttir and stained glass by her husband Jean Leduc (1962). Copyright Kópavogur Art Museum.

The website for the Kópavogur Art Museum is www.gerdarsafn.is (see English version at www.gerdarsafn.is/e_nn/index_museum.html). The site gives details of ongoing exhibitions and opening times and also provides a list of places where Gerdur's stained glass windows and mosaics can be seen. Check for updated news of the Glass Conference to be held at the Museum in April 2005.

Photographs reproduced with kind permission of Kópavogur Art Museum.

FIG. 7: *Meeting* (1969), cement and glass sculpture by Gerdur Helgadóttir. Copyright Kópavogur Art Museum.

NOTES

[1] Michel Ragon, 'Gerdur', *Cimaise Revue de l'art actuel*, no 5 (April 1954): 16-17.

[2] Contemporaries working in a similar way include Maria Katzgrau in Germany and Jean Bazaine, Maria Elena Viera da Silva and Brigitte Simon in France.

LIST OF CHURCHES WITH GLASS BY GERDUR HELGADÓTTIR

ICELAND
Chapel, Grund Nursing Home (1956)
Hallgrimur Petursson's Memorial Church (1956)
Skalholt Church (1959)
Kópavogur Church (1962)
Nes Church, Reykjavík (1966)
Olafsvik Church (1975)

FIG. 8: Exterior view of the Kópavogur Art Museum, with Kópavogur Church in the background. Copyright Kópavogur Art Museum.

GERMANY
Catholic Church, Monschau (1961)
St Antonius Abbas Church, Herkenrath (1962)
Evangelical Church, Rüttenscheid, Essen (1964)
Evangelical Church, Billebrinkhöhe, Essen (1964)
Evangelical Melanchton Church, Düsseldorf (1966)
Evangelical Church, Kempen (1971)

Research and
Methodology

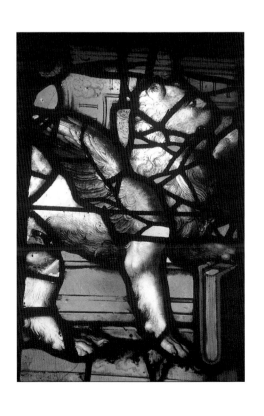

Mary Callé

Winchester Cathedral medieval glass in Australia

PLATE 2: *(overleaf)*
Lion of St Mark
and Ox of St Luke,
Caboolture,
Flemish?
Photos M. J. Callé.

FIG. 1:
'Goldilocks', detail
of West window,
Winchester
Cathedral. Photo
Christopher Wilson.

The great West window of Winchester Cathedral would, if laid flat, cover two thirds of a lawn tennis court. Its forty-four lights contain fragments of medieval glass from several glazing programmes spanning 200 years from 1330 to 1530, together with some more modern insertions. Winchester's medieval glass suffered both at the hands of the puritan Bishop Horne in the sixteenth century and from the vandalism of the Civil War. The fragments that remained, probably hanging in the leads, were gathered up and placed in the West window as a mosaic following the restoration of Charles II. Less that ten percent of Winchester's medieval glass remains. Some re-ordering of the fragments has taken place since that time, most notably by John le Couteur[1] in the early 1920s, who re-arranged some of the fragments. More recently the whole window was cleaned and re-leaded by Chapel Studios in 1994. Following this I undertook to decipher the fragments for the benefit of the Guild of Voluntary Guides, and my findings were published in *Winchester Cathedral Record*, Vol. 69 (2000). One head in particular intrigued me: a beautiful head with golden ringlets and downcast eyes.[2] Le Couteur attributed it to the sixteenth century. It did not fit any known scheme and I nicknamed it 'Goldilocks' (FIG. 1). Where did it come from?

My attention had been drawn to a 1934 article in the *Hampshire Chronicle*, which referred to an item published in *The Times* of 2 October 1934. I followed this lead in July 2002 and found a report that the Reverend John Ward had acquired medieval glass from Winchester Cathedral's Lady Chapel for his newly-founded Abbey Folk Park Museum at New Barnet, Hertfordshire. A second article, including a photograph of Ward surveying part of his purchase, was published in *The Times* on 25 January 1935 (FIG. 3). Ward had acquired some twenty-six panels of glass following the final closure of Charles Eamer Kempe's studios in 1934. The majority of these comprised panels made up of glass fragments removed from the Lady Chapel at the end of nineteenth century when Kempe had inserted three new windows.

The Abbey Folk Park Museum was attached to Ward's non-denominational religious community. It closed at the

FIG. 2:
The northeast
window at
Caboolture. Note
the 'Goldilocks'
angels at the foot
and the 'Angel in
Exile' above.
Photo M. J. Callé.

FIG. 3:
Father Ward
surveying his
purchases. Only
the left-hand
section was
published in *The
Times*. Copyright
Archive, Abbey
Museum of Art
and Archaeology,
Caboolture.

beginning of World War II for safety reasons and, for other reasons too complex to detail here, never reopened in New Barnet. Andrew Mussel, former archivist at Barnet Council, directed me to the Museum of Art and Archaeology at Caboolture, Queensland, Australia, which he understood was the successor to Abbey Folk Park. The story of the community, its move to Australia and the re-founding of the museum at Caboolture is long and involved – suffice it to say that the contents of Abbey Folk Park Museum were not unpacked in Australia until 1986. My contact with the museum resulted in the discovery that 'Goldilocks' had several 'sisters' (FIG. 2) in Caboolture!

In 1486 Elizabeth of York, Henry Tudor's Queen, came to Winchester for the birth of her first child. He was born in the Prior's dwelling, now the Deanery, and christened Arthur. As a thank offering for her safe delivery, Elizabeth made a substantial donation to the Cathedral Priory of St Swithun in Winchester. This may well have been used to pay for the Tudor extension and embellishment of the Cathedral Lady Chapel, including the glazing of the windows. Thanks to a diary written by a Lieutenant Hammond[2] in 1635 before the Cromwellian destruction, we know that the medieval Lady Chapel windows contained scenes from the Nativity on the south side, the story of the Revelation on the north side and a Jesse Tree in the East window.

In April 2003 I visited Caboolture in Queensland where the survivors of Father Ward's community have built a museum and a church which houses an extraordinary collection of stained glass from a variety of sources, but much of it identified by Ward as coming from Winchester. Photographs do not do justice to

FIG. 5: *(next page)*
Detail: Lion
'beast' and angel
with 'eagle' face.
Photo M. J. Callé.

the beauty and quality of these fragments. Five 'Goldilocks' lookalikes are surrounded by brilliant blue glass including stars and must be angels from the Nativity scene. The lead lines indicate that they originated in the trefoil heads of windows in the Cathedral Lady Chapel. A single dramatic star, obviously the Star of Bethlehem, and a lion 'beast' fitting the Revelation story can also be seen (FIG. 4). The lion is an extraordinary creature, and without the benefit of Hammond's description had been thought to be a haloed winged monkey. Careful observation, however, showed it to be a composite image and that the animal was actually a lion with a tufted mane (FIG. 5). The face of an angel adjacent to the lion revealed a clever insertion of an alien fragment. This appears to be part of the head of an eagle, another of the beasts in the Revelation story. Over the altar in the Caboolture church (FIG. 6), two branches of a Jesse tree have been fitted together to make a hexafoil (interestingly, Kempe copied this pattern for his Cathedral Lady Chapel East window). The quality of the work throughout and the royal connection noted above suggests that the workshop of the King's Glazier, William Neve, may have been involved.

Among other items which survive in the church, are a magnificent angel with huge wings, now nicknamed 'Angel in Exile' (SEE FIG. 2), and the strongly painted head of a Scourger (FIG. 7). The angel may represent the angel of the Annunciation or the angel announcing Christ's birth to the shepherds. However, three independent comments made to the author suggest that this angel is of a slightly later date and shows a strong Flemish style, thus questioning the assumption that it was part of the original Lady Chapel scheme. However, its Winchester origin is not in question. A photograph of the Lady Chapel taken c.1885 (FIG. 8) shows the lower register of

FIG. 4:
The southeast window at Caboolture. Note star, lion 'beast' and another 'Goldilocks' head. Photo M. J. Callé.

FIG. 6:
Jesse tree hexafoil
above East
window,
Caboolture.
Photo M. J. Callé.

the East window. The 'Angel in Exile' is clearly visible at the head of the southernmost light. Small fragments now in the Cathedral's West window match the pattern of this angel's robe. 'Goldilocks' lookalikes may also be seen in the heads of the other lights.

The very powerful Scourger[3] head (FIG. 7), which Ward identified as coming from Winchester, is set in a separate window panel. This head does not fit into Hammond's description of the Lady Chapel windows. The work is of very high quality. The style resembles early 16th-century work, which may be compared with that of the King's Glazier, Barnard Flower, and his team at King's College,

FIG. 7:
Head of
'Scourger',
Caboolture.
Photo M. J. Callé.

Cambridge. Richard Fox, Bishop of Winchester from 1501-29, had oversight of this project on behalf of Henry VII. He was also responsible for a major building programme in the Cathedral Presbytery and for the glazing of the Presbytery aisles. Few fragments remain of this glass, but they are also of superior quality. It is not unreasonable to suggest that Fox employed the same glaziers for his work at Winchester and that the Scourger may be part of this scheme.

The Museum of Art and Archaeology at Caboolture now holds Father Ward's archive, including his copious hand-written notes about the collection. Among the papers is the photograph of Ward viewing his purchases, of which only part was published in *The Times*. The unpublished right half of the photograph (SEE FIG. 3), shows four panels not seen in Australia today. They include a dove of the Holy Spirit, probably from an Annunciation scene and a seraph head, dating from c.1450, whose companions can still be seen in the Cathedral presbytery clerestory (FIG. 9). The Mother of the Caboolture community, who grew up within the Abbey Folk Park community, told me that these panels were not unpacked in Australia and that she believes that they were sold before Ward left England – possibly to the photographer, Michael Scott, who took *The Times* photograph and was known to have helped Ward financially. Has anyone seen or heard of this glass?

The windows at Caboolture also contain, *inter alia*, a number of heads (FIG. 10), some heraldic glass yet to be identified, the figure of a Kempe-Tower king dated 1921 seated under a Winchester medieval canopy, and panels that Ward claimed were from Herckenrode Abbey, the source of important late medieval Netherlandish glazing – now at Lichfield Cathedral and other locations in this country. This claim was refuted by the Venerable Hugh Bright, Archdeacon of Stafford, in a letter to *The Times* dated 17 October 1934. Two small panels in Caboolture show the Lion of St Mark and the Ox of St Luke (SEE PLATE 2, p. 67), which are similar to glass in windows that Kempe restored in Lichfield Cathedral, however these images bear no comparison to the Herckenrode glass there.

It is always satisfying to be able to solve a mystery. The knowledge that 'Goldilocks' was part of the medieval glazing in the Lady Chapel and the discovery of a picture showing the 'Angel in Exile' *in situ* c.1885 (FIG. 8), has opened up a whole new area for further research. The remaining glass in the church at Caboolture also needs further investigation. This work has been started by Dr Geoff Down but may falter through lack of funding. Last, but not least, the missing panels (SEE FIG. 3) need to be tracked down.

FIG. 8: Winchester Cathedral Lady Chapel c.1885. Glass now in Caboolture can be seen in the heads of the lower register of lights. Photograph © Winchester City Museum Service.

FIG. 9:
Seraphim,
Winchester
Cathedral
Presbytery
Clerestory.
Photograph by
John Crook.

ACKNOWLEDGEMENTS

The church at Caboolture houses a collection important to the history of stained glass. It is an active church and I am greatly indebted to the Museum Director, Michael Strong, and his assistant, Edith Cuffe, for their hospitality, support and for access to Father Ward's archive.

I must also thank Dr Geoff Down, the stained glass historian funded by Queensland University to undertake the cataloguing of the windows, for his stimulating observations. None of this work would have been possible without the photographic skills of my husband, Michael J. Callé.

NOTES

[1] J. D. Le Couteur, *Ancient Glass in Winchester* (Winchester: Warren & Sons, 1920), together with his subsequent paper read to The Archaeological Society meeting in Winchester in July, 1924.

[2] *Corpus Vitrearum* Ref. 5e; *Le Couteur* Ref. Light 31.

[3] British Library MS. Lansdowne, 213. See also R. N. Quirk, 'A Tour of the Cathedral Before the Civil War', *Winchester Cathedral Record* 22 (1953): pp. 9-15, where the items relating to the Cathedral have been extracted.

[4] Edward Tasker in *Encyclopaedia of Medieval Church Art* (London: Batsford, 1993) states that images of a scourger in glass are rare. He lists only two, one at Great Malvern Priory and the other at Fairford. Neither of these resembles the head at Caboolture.

FIG. 10:
Other heads
at Caboolture.
Photo M. J. Callé.

J. W. F. Harriman

A reappraisal of the English Civil War window in Farndon Church, Cheshire

The small, painted glass memorial window depicting Royalist soldiers and weapons of the English Civil War in St Chad's Church in Farndon, Cheshire, is often referred to in books on 17th-century warfare (FIG. 1). The images within the window are also regularly cited by military historians as important primary source material for weapons, accoutrements and clothing utilised during the English Civil War 1642-1651. The subject matter of the window is unusual within the canon of British stained and painted glass – indeed in the writer's experience it is unique.

A varied range of methodologies can be applied to stained glass, art historical and otherwise. This paper demonstrates how stained glass itself can be used to illuminate other disciplines, revealing important historical data not always available elsewhere. In this instance, close study of a particularly unusual window yields detailed information on the weaponry of the Civil War era.

The paper has two further purposes. Firstly, it will adduce evidence to show that, in the main, the design of the window is not the original work of its artist but is drawn instead from three early 17th-century European printed works. Secondly, by exposing the window to a wider specialist audience, it is hoped that others learned in the field of painted glass may subject it to further analysis to examine its technical aspects and identify a putative artist or school.

History

A review of the literature[1] shows that the Farndon window routinely featured in the reports of visits of local antiquarian societies between 1893 and 1961. It was also the subject of an article in *The Journal of the Society of Army Historical Research* in 1926,[2] which identified an early 17th-century source for several of the figures. This prompted me to examine further contemporary source material to see if other elements could be tied to specific works. There is also a 19th-century engraving of the window (FIG. 3, p. 78), after a drawing by the Very Reverend Hugh Cholmondley, Dean of Chester (1772-1815), which appeared in *The History of the County Palatine of Chester* by George Ormerod.[3] Significantly, the engraving incorporates a number of minor errors of detail. A print of the engraving which is in the collection of the Grosvenor Museum in Chester was also overpainted with watercolours at some time. These are garish by comparison with the subtle enamel colours used in the original window. Although a familiar image to English Civil War historians, widely disseminated in the form of coloured postcards and plates in books, the distortion of both the colour and content in the 19th-century print serves as a reminder to researchers of the dangers of relying on later copies rather than on original material.

The Farndon window appears to have been commissioned by William Barnston of Churton, near Chester, who is depicted in it as a Royalist army officer. It is natural that he wished to raise a memorial to his and his comrades' loyalty to King Charles I in his unsuccessful attempt to raise the siege of Chester in September 1645. The church itself suffered much in the Civil War. It was used as a garrison and was burnt during the siege of Holt Castle in 1645. The journals of two local antiquarian societies reported that the impact marks of bullets could be seen in the door and elsewhere.[4] Barnston died in 1664 and his will of 31 August 1663 requests that he be buried in St Chad's. He also bequeathed a sum of forty shillings 'towards the

FIG. 1:
Civil War
Window, St
Chad's Church,
Farndon,
Cheshire.
Photograph by
Peter Cormack.

repairing of Farne [*sic*] Church having done well therein already'. It has been suggested that this may be an oblique reference to the window which had already been commissioned and installed.[5] This is a credible proposal and on that basis, it is reasonable to conclude that the window was made and placed in the church between the Restoration of Charles II in May 1660 and the drafting of Barnston's will at the end of August 1663. It seems unlikely that Barnston would have been rash enough to put up such a public advertisement to his Royalist past during the

Commonwealth period. It may be that Barnston's motives in commissioning the window were not entirely altruistic – perhaps he hoped that the new King might extend his favour to one of his late father's supporters.

Ormerod states that by the early nineteenth century the window was in an extreme state of decay and that it had been rescued and repaired at the expense of Dean Cholmondley. Later churchmen were not so well disposed to it and in 1869 the then incumbent of Farndon, the Rev. B. W. Johnstone, objected to the window, considering that its subject matter was inappropriate in a place of worship.[6] It was removed by Major Barnston and preserved at Crewe Hill, the seat of the Barnston family. By 1893, there were moves to have the window reinstated in the church[7] and this was ultimately achieved in 1896 by Henry Barnston and the Rev. L. E. Owen.[8]

The window is quite small, measuring only 18" across and 28½" high (46cm x 73cm). It is made up of four central panels surrounded by twenty smaller rectangular panels leaded together and depicts individual officers and generic soldier types of the Civil War. The central panels combine to form a scene illustrating the field of war, showing a senior officer emerging from his tent with the full panoply of weapons and armour used by Infantry soldiers laid out on the ground before him (FIG. 2). The arms displayed on the tent identify the officer as Sir Francis Gamul who raised a Regiment of Foote (Infantry) for the King. Gamul is shown pointing at the weapons and armour. A standard artistic convention drawing the viewer's attention to a particular aspect of a picture, in this case it emphasises that Gamul took up arms in support of his King.

Weapons

The uppermost weapon is a matchlock musket, the standard Infantry firearm from c.1520 to c. 1700. Of simple construction with a barrel of some 48", it fired a lead ball of about ¾" diameter which weighed about 1¼ oz. Its ignition system was provided by a length of smouldering cord known as 'match', made by soaking a length of cord in a saturated solution of saltpetre (sodium or potassium nitrate). As most muskets weighed at least 10lb, they were provided with a forked rest, illustrated here with its wrist strap. As the Civil War progressed, muskets became lighter and the use of the rest declined. In any case, a type of lighter and smaller musket known as a 'Caliver' was used without a rest. Towards the end of the conflict, matchlock muskets began to be superseded by early flintlocks which struck their own sparks to ignite their powder charges. Contemporary drillbooks show some forty or so 'postures' for the management of muskets. The loading

FIG. 2:
Detail of central panels.
Photograph by Peter Cormack.

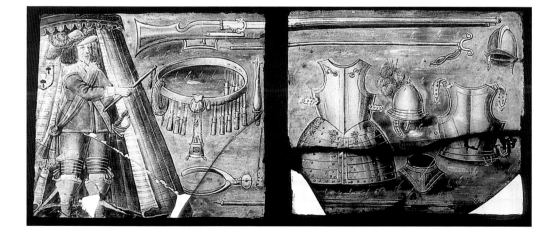

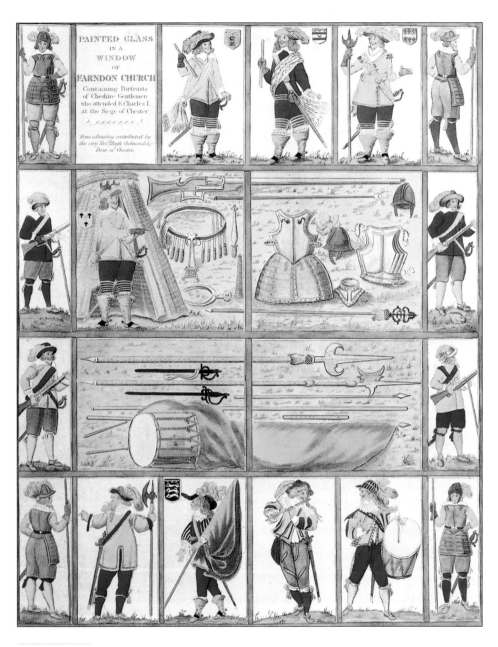

FIG. 3:
Early 19th-century
engraving (with
watercolour) of
Farndon window,
after drawing
by the Very
Reverend Hugh
Cholmondley,
(1772-1815).
© Grosvenor
Museum, Chester.

process was complicated and potentially hazardous with burning match and loose gunpowder in close proximity. The soldier needed to load his musket quickly and safely without thinking about it during battle. Infantry firepower was based on volleys from close-knit formations which required a high level of co-ordination. The large number of drill movements for the musket led to the assumption that it had a slow rate of fire with each shot separated from the next by a matter of minutes. However, this is not so as experiments by myself and others have shown that a loading regime based on the drill books of the period can produce a rate of fire of at least one shot per minute.

The musketeer needed his ammunition to hand when in action and most used bandoleer equipment, shown here below the musket. This consisted of a broad leather belt with a small bullet pouch attached to it. A number of wooden or tin containers (normally twelve) were suspended from the belt by strings, which led to the bandoleer equipment being somewhat irreverently dubbed 'The Twelve Apostles' by 19th-century commentators. Each container or 'charge' held a pre-measured quantity of coarse gunpowder for the propellant charge. This was protected from spillage, the weather and stray sparks by a top attached to the suspension string to prevent its becoming lost. A small flask for fine priming gunpowder was suspended from the bullet bag. The small pear-shaped object depicted to the right of the bullet pouch is probably a metal oil bottle. A coil of match is depicted wrapped around the left side of the belt. Three tools necessary for the management of the musket are also shown. To the immediate right of the bandoleer equipment is a scraper, used for the bore of the musket. The combustion of gunpowder is inefficient with only 60% of the material being transformed into gas, and the remaining 40% forming a thick black solid known as fouling. This is also hygroscopic and is soon transformed into corrosive acid by atmospheric water. A fouled barrel becomes difficult to load after a few shots and scrapers were provided to remove fouling when the gun was cleaned after action.

FIG. 4:
Detail of upper central panel, showing pikeman's armour. Photograph by Peter Cormack.

The Gun Makers' Rates established by a Royal Select Committee in 1631[9] set out the prices for firearms and ancillary equipment: 'For a new musket with mould, worm and scouwrer 15/6d' (the worm was a corkscrew-like tool attached to the ramrod for drawing out a charge which was wet or which could not be otherwise ignited). It is clear from the Gun Makers' Rates that barrel scourers were standard issue tools for muskets. However, I am not aware of any surviving specimen. The tapered object pierced with holes is a match cover, probably made from wood. This protected the glowing end of the burning match from rain or wind. It may have also reduced the match's visibility at night. A body of musketeers would be revealed by their glowing matches, as would the position of a sentry. The pincer-shaped article is a bullet mould. As there was no standardisation of bore sizes during the seventeenth century, muskets were provided with moulds so that the soldier could cast his own bullets if the official supply failed. Molten lead was poured into the cavity in the top of the mould – this solidified rapidly and the finished bullet could be removed when the mould was opened.

Armour

The pikeman's armour is shown to the left of the musketeer's equipment (FIG. 4), and comprises breastplate, backplate, gorget (for the throat) and tassets (protective plates covering the thighs and groin). Two helmets are illustrated, one with a prominent peak and central comb, the other with a narrow brim and a small finial on its top. The right of the backplate is fitted with a small U-shaped handle – and was used in conjunction with the S-shaped hook to allow the soldier to suspend his helmet from his armour during the march. This was not a new idea. The archaeological record has produced a number of Roman helmets with similar features.[10]

Considerable attention to detail is evident throughout the depiction of the armour. The shoulder straps which held the backplate to the breastplate are carefully drawn, as are the hooks on the breastplate that secured them. Unusually, two small straps which join the back and breastplate below the armholes are also shown (as far as I am aware, there are no extant sets of pikeman's armour with this feature). The piece of armour between the back and breastplates is a gorget which protected the throat. It was also worn on its own as a badge of rank by officers. This practice continued after the Civil War, although by the 1680s the gorget was no more than a stylised representation of the original piece of armour. It remained one of the distinguishing marks of a commissioned officer well into the nineteenth century, and today the vestiges of the gorget remain in the form of the red or white coloured tabs worn on the collars of the uniforms of, respectively, senior army officers and officer cadets.

Displayed just below the armour, the pole with the curiously shaped openwork finial is a leading staff. Although the detail of the finial is lost as this area of glass is missing from the window, it is illustrated in some detail in the 19th-century engraving, and given it is generally an accurate reproduction it is reasonable to assume this was like the original. Leading staffs were carried by infantry officers both as a badge of office and to indicate their position to their men. When a unit manoeuvred, the officer would raise his leading staff so that his men could follow. I am unaware of any example surviving. It seems likely that they went out of use early in the Civil War as officers found it more advantageous to carry a polearm instead.

FIG. 5:
Detail showing
Drummer and
Fifer. Photograph
by Peter
Cormack.

The lower central panels illustrate three polearms. The uppermost is a partisan polearm, characterised by its long double-edged point and curved side blades. Below this is a halberd, which was both a weapon and badge of rank for Serjeants. A multi-purpose polearm which combined a spear point with an axe blade and a cutting hook, it was also used to 'dress' the ranks to ensure that the men formed the straight lines fundamental to the linear battle tactics of the period. Both the halberd and partisan are shown as having pointed butts and their shafts are covered with round-headed nails to improve purchase. The tassels were intended to prevent rainwater or blood flowing down the shaft and making it slippery. It is unlikely, however, that they would have proved durable in the field and with the expediencies of war they soon fell into disuse. The pike lies immediately below the halberd, and is shown in two pieces merely by way of artistic convention to indicate its considerable length, which varied between fifteen to eighteen feet.

FIG. 6:
Engraving of a
Drummer of the
Gardes Françaises
by Abraham
Bosse (1635).

The pike was the direct descendant of the Macedonian long spear or *sarrissa* used by heavy infantry during the 2nd century B.C. in the close-knit formation known as a phalanx.[11] The Swiss developed its tactical use during the sixteenth century and were adept at producing large bodies of highly-drilled pikemen who were the most effective infantry shock troops of their day. Nonetheless, pike formations were vulnerable to missile attack and broken ground often caused disorder within their ranks. Once they began to lose their cohesion and their defensive perimeter had been penetrated, pikeman were easily dealt with as the great length of their weapons prevented any effective self-defence.[12] By the Civil War, the pike's importance was waning in favour of the musket. Pikes were mainly used to protect the musketeers whilst they reloaded although bodies of pikemen still confronted each other in giant scrimmages known as 'Push of Pikes'. For convenience, many shortened their pikes, although this was frowned on by authorities. An officer serving in Ireland commented bitterly: 'Some that were not strong enough in the British Army for his pike in a windy day would cut off a foot and some two foot of their pikes which is a damned thing to be suffered'.[13]

The two swords laid out between the polearms are typical of the cheap munition quality sidearms supplied early in the Civil War. The top one is shown in its scabbard with a carrying strap known as a baldrick. The hilts are of a type known to modern scholars as 'swept hilts', comprising a number of interlaced bars to protect the hand. Swords were commonly referred to as 'tucks' – an English corruption of the French *estoc*. It seems that, like pikes, swords were also abused by soldiers, as General Monk recounts: 'for if you arm your men with Swords, half the Swords you have in your army amongst your common men, will upon the first March you make be broken with cutting boughs'.[14]

The bottom portion of the lower panels is devoted to the flag, known as an 'ensign' or 'colour', the fife and the large wooden drum with its two sticks. Every company in an infantry regiment carried a colour. Measuring about 6½ foot square and often made of silk embroidered or painted with a variety of devices, they embodied the collective pride or *esprit de corps* of the unit that bore them and served as a rallying point in battle. The ensign in the Farndon window is a tawny colour throughout without any device upon it, indicating it was the Colonel's flag. Other officers' flags bore devices to declare their seniority within the Regiment.

Another accoutrement was the fife which provided music for both battle and on the march. Fifers were not included in the official establishment of infantry companies and were paid for by the Captain out of his own pocket, although two drummers were provided for within the establishment of a company. They were mature men rather than boys (although this changed by the late eighteenth and nineteenth centuries). Drums were large and heavy and were played under the arm rather than suspended from a waistbelt. Their wooden shells were often decorated with brass-headed nails – these are clearly seen on the drum in the Farndon window. The drum gave orders and signals for manoeuvre as well as the cadence on the march, and drummers needed to be a cut above the average soldier as they were often used to carry messages to the enemy. An observant individual could bring back useful intelligence as well as the reply.

Officers and Soldiers

The upper row of the surrounding panels begins at the left with the figure of a pikeman, hand on hip (and is matched by another on the opposite diagonal). The second panel is largely missing and has been replaced with plain glazing upon which has been scratched the inscription: 'THIS WINDOW BEING IN A DECAYED STATE WAS FRAMED ANEW BY HUGH CHOLMONDELEY DEAN OF CHESTER 1808'. A tiny fragment of original glass is preserved in the upper right-hand corner. This has some ornamental detail remaining and what might be the corner of an heraldic shield. Although impossible to say what was on the portion now lost, it would be logical to assume it might have depicted another Cheshire Royalist Officer. Alternatively, it could have borne an inscription about the donor and the date it was made. The third panel shows Richard Grosvenor (2nd Baronet from 1645), who raised the *posse comitatus*[15] in Cheshire in 1644 and was High Sheriff of the county. He is shown in typical civilian clothes of the 1640s, with his military status indicated by the large sash draped over his left shoulder and stiffly knotted and the commander's baton in his right hand. His arms appear in the upper right corner, as do those of all of the officer figures. Next to him is Sir William Mainwaring who was killed at the siege of Chester. He is similarly attired and also carries a baton. Barnston himself appears next. Dressed for battle in a buffcoat[16] and gorget with his sash wound tightly round his waist, he carries a partisan polearm as both a weapon and a badge of office.

Down both sides of the window are four panels depicting the two basic types of infantrymen, pikemen and musketeers. Although each soldier differs in minor details, there are two views of each type. The pikemen are fully armoured with plumed helmets, back and breastplates and tassets, and are shown in the drillbook position of 'Order your Pike'. This position was the basis for some thirty drill movements necessary to create cohesion through unity of action in a pike formation. In the upper left and lower right corners of the window the pikemen are shown full frontal whilst those in the opposite corners are depicted from the right rear. Of the four musketeers, two are pictured with forked rests for their muskets and are in the drillbook position of 'Hold your Musket on the Rest'. Those without rests are in the position 'Hold your Piece Well'.

Within the side rows, the four figures in panels along the bottom edge are, from left to right, a Serjeant, an Ensign with colour, a Fifer and a Drummer. The Serjeant is shown rear view carrying his halberd. Serjeants were often relatively well-to-do men and this individual is portrayed with a plumed hat, a lace collar and long coat trimmed with lace. The Ensign was the most junior rank of infantry officer and was charged with carrying and protecting the colour. The arms delineated above identify him as Thomas Berrington, a Chester attorney.[17] The musicians are wonderfully animated and wear short doublets, lace collars and

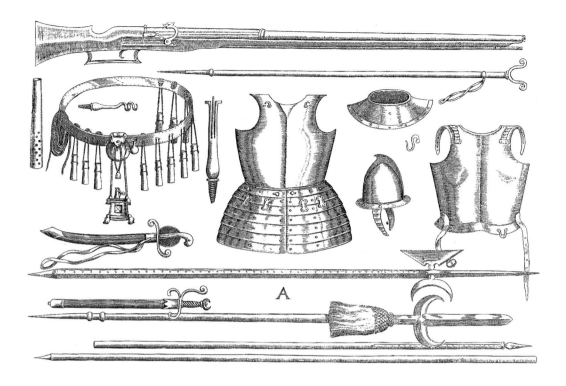

plumed headgear (FIG. 5). The Drummer wears a cap called a *montero* which was a popular alternative to the broad-brimmed felt hat. His large drum is carried under the left arm on a strap. The Fifer has fashionably slashed breeches, which allowed their coloured lining to show through.

FIG. 7: Engraving of infantry weapons from Johann Jacobi von Wallhausen, *Kriegskuntz zu Fuss* (1615).

Iconographic sources

In his article in *The Journal of the Society of Army Historical Research*, Colonel Field states that the original source for three of the four figures in the panels of the lower edge is the work of the French artist Abraham Bosse (1602-1676).[18] The Serjeant is described as 'Officer d'Infanterie 1643'. The Ensign is derived from 'Porte Drapeau des Gardes Françaises 1635'. Field describes the original having a different features and hair and wearing a cuirass (upper body armour consisting of back and breastplates). This is not shown in the Farndon window. The Drummer is almost identical to the picture 'Tambour des Gardes Françaises 1635' (FIG. 6). It seems likely that the Fifer comes from the same source.

The revelation that three figures were not the original work of the artist prompted me to further investigate other contemporary graphic sources such as drill books and military manuals. This approach was rewarded by an identical match of some of the weapons in a German book on infantry warfare by J. J. Wallhausen, first published in 1615.[19] One of the engraved plates shows infantry weapons identical to the musket, bandoleer equipment, scourer, match guard and musket rest depicted in the Farndon window (FIG. 7). The worm in Wallhausen is omitted in the Farndon window, but the musket and its accoutrements are direct copies. Some similarities between the armour in Wallhausen and the Farndon window are evident but the resemblance is generally only superficial, as the Farndon window has two helmets and the gorget is completely different. However, the backplate in Wallhausen includes the loop and hook for carrying the helmet which is also found in the Farndon window.

In addition, the pike and partisan in Wallhausen are similar to Farndon, but the two swords and the halberd are wholly different. The bullet mould does not appear in Walhausen. In fact I do not know of any other contemporary image of a bullet mould. On this small point alone, the Farndon window is highly important in the study of firearms and their accessories as it contains what may well be the earliest representation of a bullet mould for a military firearm.

The figures of pikemen and musketeers are very like those which appear in the 1637 book, *Principles of the Art Militaire* by Captain Henry Hexham.[20] The engravings, by an artist named N. C. Goodnight, appear to be inspired by the wonderful plates in the seminal drill book of the period, *The Exercise of Armes* by Jacob de Gheyn (FIGS. 8 & 9).[21] First published in the Netherlands in 1607, many other editions were produced as well as pirate copies, making de Gheyn's drill common throughout Europe. It would therefore have been logical for Hexham to instruct his illustrator to base the plates in his new book on those which had been familiar to soldiers for the previous three decades.

The use of existing graphic representations of soldiers and their equipment by the artist who painted the Farndon window is easily explained. In 1660 or thereabouts, William Barnston wanted to record and honour the service of his fellow Cheshire men in the Civil War some fifteen or so years earlier. It is likely that the artist was unfamiliar with both the military fashion of the 1640s and also with the infantry arms and accoutrements of that period. Either Barnston provided the images from Wallhausen, Bosse and probably Hexham, or the artist had access to them elsewhere. These images formed the working reference material which would have allowed the artist and his patron to settle upon a format which was the blueprint for the window. The only original elements that the artist would need to produce were illustrations of Sir Francis Gamul, the three senior officers and a few military items, such as the drum and the ensign. Doubtless Barnston would have been able to advise on those matters.

Although drawn from several sources, the design of the window integrates the various images with considerable panache – and the glass is painted and stained with skill and sensitivity. The delicate colouring, in predominantly light blue, russet, yellow and green enamels, is particularly appealing.

As an example of secular painted glass within an ecclesiastical context, the Farndon window is something of an enigma. Apart from its depiction of the bullet mould, it cannot be considered primary source material for the uniforms and weapons of the Civil War as it is a pastiche taken from two and possibly three extant 17th-century military manuals. Ultimately, it is a wonderful work of art which forms a fitting memorial to the Cheshire Royalists who fought in the conflict described by the great Parliamentary General Sir William Waller as 'this war without an enemy'. Its small scale and detailed imagery give it a special charm amongst the long tradition of military memorials in English parish churches.

ACKNOWLEDGEMENTS

Sandra Coley for proposing this article to me and for her research in the library of the Society of Antiquaries of London

Peter Cormack, FSA for taking the photographs of the Farndon window

Andrew Cormack, FSA for drawing my attention to the article on the window in the *Journal of the Society for Army Historical Research*

Anne Hubbard for proofreading various drafts

NOTES

[1] Conducted on my behalf by the Editor of this journal, Sandra Coley, in the Library of the Society of Antiquaries. As well as references below, see Maurice H. Ridgway, 'Coloured Window Glass in Cheshire, 1550-1850', *Journal of the Chester and N. Wales Architectural, Archaeological and Historical Society*, Vol. 49 (1961): 15, pl. IV.

[2] Colonel C. Field, 'Army Uniforms in a Stained Glass Window in Farndon Church, Cheshire – *temp*. Charles I', *Journal of the Society of Army Historical Research*, Vol. V (1926): 174-77.

[3] Revised by Thomas Helsby (London: G. Routledge, 1882).

[4] *Journal of the Architectural, Archaeological and Historic Society for the County and the City of Chester and North Wales*, NS Vol. XII (1906): 75; *Archaeologia Cambrensis*, 6th series, Vol. 10 (1910): 198-99.

[5] *Archaeologia Cambrensis*, Vol. XC (1935): 336.

[6] Reported in the *Transactions of Lancashire and Cheshire Antiquarian Society*, Vol. XI (1893): 151; *Notes and Queries*, Vol. CLI (July-Dec. 1926): 290.

[7] *Ibid.*

[8] Field, *op. cit.*, 175.

[9] Reproduced in *The Age of Firearms* by Robert Held (New York: Bonanza Books, 1978), 87.

[10] Principally found on Imperial Gallic and Italic helmets of the later 1st Century AD. See *The Armour of Imperial Rome* by H. Russell Robinson (London: Arms and Armour Press, 1975), 48, 60 & 68.

[11] See *The Roman Army* by Peter Connolly (London: Macdonald Educational, 1975), 8-17.

[12] At Flodden in 1513, the English army inflicted huge casualties on a Scots army composed mainly of badly trained pikemen. Salvoes of English arrows combined with poor cohesion and discipline during manoeuvre caused the pike blocks to disintegrate leaving the hapless Scots easy victims to English billmen.

[13] Quoted in *Soldiers of the English Civil War – Infantry* by Keith Roberts (London: Osprey, 1989), 63.

[14] *Ibid.*, 22.

[15] A body of men over the age of fifteen raised by the Sheriff of a county to suppress a riot or for other purposes.

[16] A coat of thick leather worn either as armour in its own right or in conjunction with other armour.

[17] Mentioned in Raymond Richards, *Old Cheshire Churches: A Survey of Their History, Fabric and Furniture, with Records of the Older Monuments* (London: B. T. Batsford, [1947]), 155.

[18] These figures are reproduced in J. Quicherat, *Histoire du Costume en France* (Paris: Hachette, 1877).

[19] Johann Jacobi von Wallhausen, *Kriegskuntz zu Fuss* (1615), facsimile reprint (Graz: Academische Druck, 1971).

[20] Originally conceived as a manual for English soldiers in the Netherlands but reprinted during the English Civil War.

[21] Facsimile reprint edition, David Blackmore, ed. (London: Greenhill Books, 1986).

FIG. 8:
Engraving of a pikeman from
The Exercise of Arms by Jacob de Gheyn (1607).

FIG. 9:
Engraving of a musketeer from
The Exercise of Arms by Jacob de Gheyn (1607).

Tony Benyon

British glass painters, designers and draughtsmen in 1881 and 1901: CD and on-line research

The British 1881 Census CD-ROM, on a set of 25 discs, covers all of the counties of England, Scotland and Wales and offers a facility for making sequential searches from house to house. A recent search of census websites revealed numerous commercially-produced CD-ROMs that contain transcribed census information of specific counties and towns. 19th-century trade directories of various towns and cities from a range of dates are also available.

The 1901 Census for England and Wales is now available on-line and freely supplies names, towns and occupations of individuals but does not provide a complete list of the occupants of each household or supply a full address unless a fee is paid. The Scottish 1901 Census is also on-line on a separate website, but no information is freely available (so no stereotyping there, then!).

A variety of factors involving the setting up of the 1901 Census on-line has resulted in a flawed and clumsy resource. True to form, on the day the site was launched it immediately crashed and was out of action for almost a year. Transcription errors abound with annoying or hilarious consequences – due one supposes to the fact it was first transcribed by prisoners in British jails and then finished on the Indian subcontinent. Importantly, the 1901 Census website, unlike the 1881 Census CD-ROM, only responds to precise names and not to misspellings, leading to carpet-chewing frustration.

A Study Combining Genealogical Websites and Census Material to Examine Family Connections Between Glass Manufacturers and Glass Painters

Genealogical websites are potentially useful research tools providing information that would be otherwise difficult to obtain. The Kayll family, for example, has its own website which is well researched. In combination with other family history websites, in particular the Church of Latter-day Saints' site and by using the 1881 Census CD-ROMs it is possible to trace the movements of one of the leading 19th-century glass-making families.

John Hartley, a Durham man, married Margaret Stevenson, the daughter of William Stevenson and Margaret Kayll (the eldest daughter of James Kayll from the Isle of Man, whose grandson John James Kayll became a partner in Hartley Wood) in 1802 at Monkwearmouth, Durham. The couple moved to Dumbarton in Scotland where their son, James Hartley, was born in 1811.

John Hartley moved south to Nailsea, Bristol in 1812 where he began working with Robert Lucas Chance. In 1827 he moved north to W. E. Chance's glass manufactory at Oldbury, and after he died in 1833 his sons James and John were taken into partnership by W. E. Chance in 1834 when the firm became Chance and Hartley.

In 1836 James and John left Smethwick and moved to Sunderland, where they founded a firm of glass manufacturers (John James Kayll Senior became a partner), which continued until its closure in 1894. A year before the closure of the glassworks, James Hartley, the grandson of the founder, had gone into partnership with Alfred Wood, late of W. E. Chance, at the Portobello Lane Works.

John James Kayll Jr's relationship with glass manufacturing had also ended and he moved south to Leeds where he entered into partnership, making stained glass with Edwin Reed, late of Albert and Charles Powell, who had themselves moved north from London.

Glass merchants and manufacturers are important to the development of British stained glass design. Combining census material with information available on genealogy websites can occasionally contribute towards a greater understanding of their historical relationship.

Searches of three towns for glass painters in the 1881 Census, with reference to the 1901 Census

A systematic door-to-door search was made of Windsor, Warwick and Lancaster in 1881

Windsor glass painters in the 1881 Census

Several years ago, I encountered the remains of the Royal Windsor Stained Glass Company in the form of several panels of stained glass in a garden shed in the grounds of the old works. A number of bicycles, a hand-pushed lawnmower and assorted gardening tools were piled up against them – not a UKIC-approved storage system. The glass was exceedingly dull, most of the colour had been achieved with stain and coloured enamels, but a legend existed that on the closure of the works the glass painters had left to work for Morris & Co in Merton (see *Royal Windsor Stained Glass Manufactory* by Gordon Cullingham). The firm eventually ran into financial difficulties and it is not difficult to see why. Monsieur Henri Henry, a single man and 'Director of the Royal Tapestry Wks & Artists' – which included stained glass – lived in New Windsor with his mother and seven servants, including a footman and a butler while his less flamboyant workforce huddled together around the workshop in Old Windsor. The senior glass painters were all French and the apprentices were either the children of the French glass painters or the sons of local workmen and women. The 1901 Census revealed that all of the French glass painters had vanished, presumably back to France, and only one of the English apprentices, who was living in South Manchester, had remained in the craft.

Warwick glass painters in the 1881 Census

A search of Warwick in 1881 revealed a reduced stained glass work force to that which had operated in 1851 (see *Journal of Stained Glass*, Vol. XXIV). The probable stained glass workforce is listed as follows:

Frank Holt a 'Master Glass Painter & Decorator employing 22 men and 6 boys' had taken over from his father-in-law William Holland, who had employed 96 men in 1851, although the majority of them manufactured hats not stained glass. In 1901 Holt simply described his occupation as a 'Decorator'.

Peter Fischer was living in the home of Frank Holt and working as his 'apprentice'. He later emigrated to Australia, where he continued to work as a glass painter.

Teresa Norman, an 'Artist' in 1881, was listed in 1901 as a 'House Keeper' living in Warwick. She may or may not have worked for Holt in 1881 as he described his employees as 'men and boys' (see above).

Richard Lambert, a 'Tile and Glass Painter', was living in Cherry Street where Clement Heaton had lived in 1851. He was born in York and had worked in Newcastle prior to 1881, but by 1901 he was living in London working as a 'Trainer [*sic*] glass painter'.

James Montgomery a 'Fret Lead Glazier' was born in Birmingham and just prior to 1881 he had worked in Smethwick. In 1901 he was living in Leicester and working as a 'Fret head [*sic*] glazier', which one can only hope is a transcription error.

George Jack, listed as a Scottish born 'Artist' in 1881, had moved to Handsworth in Staffordshire by 1901 where he was working as a 'Decorator'.

The remaining workforce of Frank Holt, totalling 28, must have been made up from the assorted glaziers and plumber glaziers to be found in Warwick at this time. I checked all of these glaziers and plumbers in the 1901 census and failed to find any who had a connection with stained glass.

N.B. It is possible to plot the geographic movements of the probable workforce listed above by checking the dates and locations of their children's birth.

Lancaster glass painters in the 1881 Census

A systematic search of Lancaster revealed a number of craftsmen who are known to have worked for Shrigley and Hunt. Arthur Hunt was born in Hertford and trained in London and his workforce was made up of men who had travelled from as far away as Cornwall, as in the case of Edward Prest. Arthur Berridge, his foreman, was born in London. In 1881 Edward Prest was involved with the designs of Carl Almquist, a designer influenced by the aesthetic movement. In 1901 Prest was living in Hampstead, London and working as a stained glass artist and in 1915 he was an 'expert witness' in the case of Albert Wolmark's 'abstract' window for St Mary's, Slough.

William Tipping and his son Joseph appear as 'Artists' living in Lancaster in 1881 and by 1901 they have moved to Acton in London where they are working as 'Stained Glass Artists'. William was born in Prescot, Lancashire and may have trained at Pilkington under Ralph Bolton Edmundson. A son, Joseph, was born in Birmingham, where William may have moved to work for Hardman. To complicate matters, in 1901 William Tipping, a glass painter born in London in 1865 (who was not listed in the 1881 census), was also living in Acton. William Tipping Senior may well have moved to London, where Junior was born, from Birmingham before moving north to Lancaster.

National List of Glass Painters, Designers and Draughtsmen from 1881 Census, with Notes from 1901 Census

Birth	Name	Occupation	Address	Place of Birth	Notes
1865	ABBOTT James H.	Plumber & Glazier	Lancashire Lancaster 24 Penny St	Lancashire Lancaster	Son of William Abbott. In 1901 Census an 'Artist In Stainer Glass' living in Lancaster
1838	ABBOTT William	Plumbers & Glazier	Lancashire Lancaster 24 Penny St	Lancashire Lancaster	Established Abbott & Co. 1860
1849	ADAM James	Glass Stainer Employing 6 Men 3 Boys	Scotland Lanark Govan 101 Aitkenhead Rd	Scotland Lanark Maryhill	
1848	ADAM Stephen	Glass Stainer Master Employing 18 Men	Scotland Lanark East Kilbride Peel Park	Scotland Edinburgh Bonnington	Connected with Cottier and later with Ballantine
1869	AIKMAN William	Scholar	Scotland Linlithgow Whitburn East Whitburn	Scotland Edinburgh	Apprenticed to Ballantine 1890-92. In 1892 joined J P & Sons as a painter
1835	ANDERSON Robert Rowand	Architect	Scotland Edinburgh Colinton Burnshot Park Allermuir Ho	Scotland Edinburgh Liberton	Designed some SG
1862	ASSHENTON Ralph	Student	Cambridgeshire Cambridge	Lancashire Downham Hall	Brother of Richard Asshenton. Made some SG
1864	ASSHENTON Richard	Student	Berkshire Eaton	Lancashire Downham Clitheroe	Brother of Ralph Asshenton. Was ordained & made some SG
1829	ASTLEY John	Color Glass & Lead Merchant (Paint)	Warwickshire Coventry St Michael 4 Broad St	Warwickshire Coventry	Stepson of T Cash oil & colour manufacturer
1862	ATKINSON Albert	Artist In Stained Glass	Northumberland Elswick 6 Victoria St	Yorkshire Ripon	In 1901 Census an 'Artist' living in Newcastle. Brother of Fred Atkinson. Worked for Wailes & Strang
1865	ATKINSON Fred	Artist In Stained Glass	Northumberland Elswick 6 Victoria St	Yorkshire Ripon	In 1901 Census a 'Stained Glass Artist' living in Newcastle. Brother of Albert & William. Worked for Wailes & Strang & took over Henry Barnett's firm
1854	ATKINSON William	Artist In Stained Glass	Northumberland Elswick 6 Victoria St	Yorkshire Ripon	Designer for HM Barnett. Bother of Fred
1873	BAGULEY Clement	Scholar	Northumberland Newcastle on Tyne 16 North Ter	Northumberland Newcastle On Tyne	In 1901 Census 'Artist Stained Glass Art Teacher' living in Coxlodge, Northumberland. Son of George Baguley

Birth	Name	Occupation	Address	Place of Birth	Notes
1834	BAGULEY George J.	Artist In Stained Glass (Merchant)	Northumberland Newcastle on Tyne 16 North Ter	Durham	In 1901 Census an 'Artist In Glass' living in Newcastle but provides Dublin Ireland as his birthplace. Father of John G & Clement Baguley. Designed for Wailes. Started own firm in 1867
1859	BAGULEY John G.	Artist In Stained Glass (Merchant)	Northumberland Newcastle on Tyne 16 North Ter	Northumberland Newcastle On Tyne	In 1901 Census a 'Glass Painter' living in Newcastle. Son of George J Baguley
1864	BAKER Edward Thos.	Glass Painters Apprentice	Stafford Harborne High Park Road	Stafford Smethwick	In 1901 Census a 'Tin Plate Worker' living in Birmingham
1841	BALLANTINE Alexander	Glass Stainer Artist	Scotland Edinburgh Colinton Deanhaugh House	Scotland Edinburgh	Son of James Ballantine Senior
1850	BALLANTINE James	Painter & Decorator Master Employing 12 Men	Scotland Edinburgh St Cuthberts Warrender Lodge	Scotland Edinburgh	Son of James Ballantine Senior
1833	BARNET Henry M. [BARNETT]	Artist In Stained Glass	Northumberland Tynemouth 9 Percy Gardens	Yorkshire York City	Son of Mark, Grandson of John Joseph. Worked for Wailes. Own business later taken over by Atkinson Bros
1845	BARNETT William C.	Stained Glass Artist Employing 6 Men	Scotland Edinburgh South Leith 101 Constitution St	Scotland England	Staying in sister's home. Barnett & Son, Leith founded by father Francis. Grandson of John Joseph
1800	BEER Elizabeth	Painter on Glass Employing 5 Men	Devon Exeter 41 Bartholomew Street	Devon Teignmouth	Widow of Robert Beer
1837	BEER Lucy	Artist on Glass (Mf)	Devon Exeter 41 Bartholomew Street	Devon Teignmouth	Daughter of Robert & Elizabeth Beer & partner of Robert Driffield
1847	BELL Frederick H.	Artist In Stained Glass (Painter)	Gloucestershire Westbury-on-Trym 5 Clevedon Ter	Gloucestershire Bristol	Son of Joseph Bell of Bristol. Business later taken over by Arnold Robinson
1810	BELL Joseph	Artist in stained glass employ 8 men + 2 boys (Glass MF)	Gloucestershire Augustine College Green Bristol St Southy House	Staffordshire Stoke-on-Trent	Of Joseph Bell & Son, Bristol – founded in 1840. Taken over by Arnold Robinson
1862	BELL Robert	Student of Arts	Scotland Lanark Glasgow 60 Gt. Western Rd	Scotland Kirkcudbright Carsphairn	Robert Anning Bell. Professor of Art at Royal College and designed SG
1827	BELL Thos.	Glass Stainers (Manuf)	Northumberland Newcastle-on-Tyne St Andrew 44 Percy St	Northumberland Newcastle-on-Tyne	

Birth	Name	Occupation	Address	Place of Birth	Notes
1867	BELLRINGER William	Stained Glass Workers Apptce (Manf)	Devon Exeter Allhallows-on-the-Walls Rackfield Place	Cornwall Truro	In 1901 Census 'Glazier Paint' living in Croydon. Trained with Frederick Drake
1863	BENNETT Albert	Artistic Decorator	Lancashire Chorlton on Medlock 9 Gore St	Lancashire Manchester	In 1901 Census a 'Decorating Artist' living in Blackpool. Brother of Reuben & Harold
1859	BENNETT Harold B.	Artistic Decorator	Lancashire Chorlton on Medlock 9 Gore St	Lancashire Ashton Under Lyne	In 1901 Census a 'Manager For Decoration & Painting' living in Stretford. Brother of Reuben & Albert Bennet. Son of Anthony Bennett, a Varnish & Brush merchant
1840	BENNET John C.M.	House Painter Master Employing 74 Men 17 Boys	Scotland Lanark Govan 171 Gt Western Rd	Scotland Lanark Glasgow	Father of John B. H. Bennet born 1871 of Bennet, JB & Sons
1849	BENNETT Reuben	Artistic Decorator (Painter)	Lancashire Chorlton on Medlock 9 Gore St	Lancashire Ashton Under Lyne	In 1901 Census a 'Church Decorator' living in Burbage Entire, Derbyshire. Arthur Orr & WH Cotton designed for him
1825	BILL George	Artist in stained glass	Warwickshire Birmingham Aston Wills St 26	Warwickshire Birmingham	In 1901 Census an 'Artist In Stain Glass' living in Smethwick, aged 76. Appears in 1851 Census as a 'Glass Painter Stainer' living in Birmingham
1853	BLACK James	Glass Stainer	Scotland Lanark Barony 45 Dorset Street	Scotland Lanark Glasgow	
1868	BOON James H.	Apprentice To Glass Stainer	Lancashire Manchester Helera Barlow St	Lancashire Salford	In 1901 Census a 'Stac [sic]... Glass Cutter' living in South Manchester
1851	BORRIDGE Arthur [Berridge – error in transcription]	Foreman Glass Painter (Mf)	Lancashire Lancaster 50 Windermere Rd	London	In 1901 Census a 'Glass Painter' living in Poulton Bare & Torrisholme, Lancashire
1845	BOURNE Swaine	Artist In Stained Glass MF	Warwickshire Edgbaston 174 Hagley Rd	Warwickshire Kingsbury	In 1901 Census an 'Artist In Stained Glass' living in Edgbaston, Warwick. Frederick Louis Tait was chief designer in 1890s
1829	BRASON John	Stainer In Glass Works	Northumberland Elswick 105 Sycamore St	Gateshead Durham	Not found in 1901 Census
1850	BRAY Robert E.	Artist Industrial Stain Glass Ecclesiastical Decorative	Lancashire Lancaster 79 Ullswater Rd	London Mary Le Bone	

Birth	Name	Occupation	Address	Place of Birth	Notes
1875	BRETT Jasper	Scholar	Surrey Wandsworth No 6 Keswick Road	Surrey Putney	In 1901 Census a 'Stained Glass…' living in Wandsworth. Apprenticeship with CW Whall. Son of artist John Brett
1872	BRICKDALE Mary E.F.	Scholar	Surrey Croydon Beulah Hill (Birchamp Villa)	Surrey Upper Norwood	Eleanor Fortesque Brickdale. Designs executed by Burlison & Grylls
1863	BRITTAIN Thos	Glass Stainer	Lancashire Chorlton on Medlock 9 Gore St	Warwickshire Birmingham	Not found in 1901 Census. Living in the same house as Albert Broadbent in 1881 Census
1865	BROADBENT Albert	Glass Stainer	Warwickshire Birmingham Warwick No 2 Bk 69 Garbett St	Warwickshire Birmingham	In the 1901 Census a 'Glass Stainer' living in Birmingham. In 1881 lodging with the mother of Thos. Brittain
1852	BROOKS Ralph	Artist (Painter)	Lancashire Moss Side 81 Raby Street	Lancashire Salford	Boarding with Vout in 1881. Not found in 1901 Census
1831	BROWN Christopher	Draughtsman In (Stained Glass)	Northumberland Newcastle-on-Tyne St Andrew 3 Spital Tongues	Northumberland Newcastle On Tyne	Not found in 1901 Census
1866	BRUIXAND Joseph	Apprentice Glass Staining (Mftr)	Berkshire Old Windsor 3 Lorne Villas	France Rouen	Worked at the Royal Stained Glass Works, Old Windsor
1866	BUCKMAN Percy	Scholar	Dorset Sherborne Kings School Church Lane	Dorset Bradford Abbas	In 1901 Census an 'Artist' living in Fulham. On list for SG at Lytchett Minster, Dorset (NADFAS)
1861	BULFIELD Alfred P.	Glass And Tile Painter Mf	Lancashire Lancaster 3 Spring Bank	Lancashire Lancaster	In 1901 Census a 'Decorator & Painter' living in Eaton & Bulfield, Lancaster
1863	BURGESS William	Fret Lead Glazier	London 87 Church St	London Marylebone	In 1901 Census a 'Stained Glass Artist Winder' living in St Pancras
1849	BURNELL John	Stain Glass Glazier	London 50 Cornwall Rd	Hertford Watford	In 1901 Census a 'Stained Glass Cutter' living in Willesden. Possibly the 'Mr Burnell' who ran the workshop of WF Dixon. MH
1852	BURROW John	Artist in Stained Glass	Westmorland Haverbrack Sandside Station	London St Pancras	Son of Frederick & cousin of Harry Burrow
1816	BURROW Fredrick	Artist on Stained Glass	Westmorland Haverbrack Sandside Station	Westmorland Haverbrack	Father of John Burrow. Brother of Edward & uncle of artist Harry Burrow

Birth	Name	Occupation	Address	Place of Birth	Notes
1857	CAKEBREAD George H.	Accountant Coal Exporter	Wales Glamorgan Cardiff St John 14 Edward Terrace	Middlesex Clapton	In 1901 Census a 'Builders Merchant' living in Stoke Newington. Partner of Arthur Robey in Cakebread & Robey
1832	CALDWELL Samuel	Artist on Glass	Kent Canterbury Archbishops Palace 52 Palace St	Kent Canterbury	Father of Samuel Caldwell
1862	CALDWELL Samuel	Glazier	Kent Canterbury Archbishops Palace 52 Palace St	Kent Canterbury	In 1901 Census a 'Stained Glass Artist' living in Canterbury. Son of Samuel Caldwell and nephew of George Austin
1850	CALETON Lawrie	Glass Cutter & Painter	Stafford Harborne High Park Terr	Stafford Handsworth	
1860	CAMM Alfred	Draftsman in Glass	Staffordshire Harborne Sherland Road	Staffordshire Smethwick	In 1901 Census a 'Stained Glass Artist' living in Smethwick. Son of Thomas Camm
1875	CAMM Florence	Scholar	Stafford Harborne Sycamore Road	Staffordshire Smethwick	In 1901 Census an 'Art Student & Teacher' living in Smethwick. Studied under Henry Payne
1844	CAMM Henry C.	Artist on Glass	Staffordshire Harborne Broomfield	Staffordshire West Bromwich	In 1901 Census an 'Artist In Staines [sic] Glass' living in Smethwick
1855	CAMM James F.P.	Designer & Draughtsman on Stained Glass	Staffordshire Harborne Broomfield	Staffordshire Smethwick	
1842	CAMM John M.	Artist on Glass	Staffordshire Harborne Broomfield	Staffordshire West Bromwich	In 1901 Census an 'Artist On Glass' living in Smethwick
1813	CAMM Thomas	Fret Lead Glazier	Staffordshire Harborne Sherland Road	Staffordshire Drayton	Father of Alfred Camm
1839	CAMM Thomas W.	Artist in Stained Glass 19 Men & 13 Boys	Staffordshire Harborne Sycamore Road	Staffordshire Smethwick	In 1901 Census a 'Stained Glass Artist' living in Smethwick. Father of Florence, Robert & Walter Herbert Camm. Worked for Chance under Sebastian Evans
1856	CAMPBELL John	Artist Portrait Painter	Durham Gateshead 4 Bloomfield Terrace	Durham Gateshead Northd Ovingham	In 1901 Census an 'Artist Portrait Painter' living in Gateshead. Apprenticed to Wailes. Son of John Thomson Campbell of Edinburgh who designed for Wailes from c. 1840
1821	CASOLANI Henry	Artist Historical Painter	Lancashire Eccleston in Prescot Wood St	Malta Valletta	Designed SG for J P & Sons & William Gardner in Lancashire

Birth	Name	Occupation	Address	Place of Birth	Notes
1868	CASTELL George	Apprentice Cutter Glazier	London 25 Hadley St	London St Pancras	In 1901 Census a 'Stained Glass' living in Islington. Brother of Thomas Castell
1866	CASTELL Thomas	Apprentice Figure Painter	London 25 Hadley St	London St Pancras	In 1901 Census a 'Glass Painter' living in St Pancras. Brother of George Castell
1844	CHANCE William	Glass Manufacturer Employing 43 Men 23 Boys	Warwickshire Edgbaston Augustus Rd	Warwickshire B Ham	Manufacturer of Chance Antique glass & Norman Slabs, etc.
1862	COLLINGWOOD John G.	Glass Stainer	Durham Gateshead Blacksmiths Bk	Durham Gateshead	In 1901 Census a 'Stand glass Lead worker' [sic] living in Gateshead
1840	CONNELL William	Artist in Stained Glass & China (Earth Man)	Durham Gateshead 33 Buck Lane	Dublin Ireland	In 1901 Census a 'Stained Glass Artist' living in Gateshead
1862	CONSTABLE William E.	Assistant In Glass Staining	Cambridgeshire Cambridge St Andrew the Less 4 College Ter	Warwickshire Warwick	In 1901 Census a 'Stained Glass Artist' living in Canterbury. Son of William H. Constable
1832	CONSTABLE William H.	Artist In Stained Glass Emply. 4 Men	Cambridgeshire Cambridge St Andrew the Less 4 College Ter	Suffolk Bury S. Edmunds	Took over W.J. Bolton's workshop
1855	COOPER Allan	Glass Painter	Stafford Harborne 26 Helena St	Oxfordshire Heyford	
1844	COTTERELL John	Manager At Stained Glass Works	Stafford Harborne 243 St Pauls Rd	York Leeds	
1864	CRABBE William	Artist (Stain Glass)	Kent Charlton Next Woolwich 34 Maryon Rd	Scotland	In 1901 Census a 'Glass Painter' living in Islington. Worked for Morris & Co (Sewter, p. 101)
1815	CULLYER William F.	Ornamental Painter	Norfolk Norwich St Giles Cow Hill Red Cow	Norfolk Norwich	(BH Norfolk SG, p. 233)
1813	CUNNINGHAM Peter	Painter On Stained Glass (No Occ)	Northumberland Newcastle Elswick Union Workhouse	Ireland Monaghan Co Castle Blakney	In 1901 Census an 'Inmate Handicap Imbecile' in Newcastle
1844	CUTLER Ephraim	Glass Merchant	Warwickshire Edgbaston 5 George Road	Staffordshire West Bromwich	Partner of W Pearce in making SG & son of glass dealer Soloman Cutler.
1811	CUTLER Soloman	Glass Dealer	Warwickshire Aston Rose Villa	Staffordshire West Bromwich	Father of Ephraim
1852	DACRE George	Lead & Glass Merchant	Lancashire Manchester 10 Peel Terrace	Lancashire Manchester	

Birth	Name	Occupation	Address	Place of Birth	Notes
1828	DANKS John Ed.	Glass Painter (Unemployed)	Staffordshire Harborne Vicarage Rd	Warwickshire Edgbaston Kings Norton	In 1851 Census a 'Glass painter' living in Birmingham
1833	DAVIS John [DAVIES]	Glass Stainer	Shropshire Shrewsbury 73 Wyle Cop St	Shropshire Wem	William Done & John Davies trained under D. Evans
1866	DAVIS Alfred E.	Artist On Glass	Durham Gateshead 30 Snowball Ter	Stafford Smethwick	In 1901 Census a 'Glass Painter' living in Handsworth, Stafford. Son of William F Davis, a Die Sinker (glass) moulder
1863	DAVISON William	Glass Stainer	Staffordshire Harborne Church St	Staffordshire Harborn	
1825	DAY Henry	Painter decorator	Suffolk Ipswich St Margaret Cemetery Rd 2 Fern Villa	Suffolk Ipswich	(BH Suffolk SG, p. 274)
1826	DEAR George	Manager of Stained Glass & Art Tile Work Mf	Lancashire Lancaster High St Cottage	Sussex Brighton	Worked for S&H
1849	DIXON John Herbert	Stain Glass Artist	Devon Yarnscombe Vicarage House	Oxfordshire Oxford	Not in 1901 Census
1865	DONE Harry	Glass Stainer & C	Shropshire Shrewsbury 65 Wyle Cop	Shropshire	In 1901 Census a 'House Painter & Paper Hanger'. Son of William Done
1834	DONE Willm.	Glass Stainer & C	Shropshire Shrewsbury 65 Wyle Cop	Shropshire	In 1901 Census a 'Glass Stainer Embosser' living in Birmingham. Father of Harry Done. Trained under David Evans
1856	DOVE Henry R.	Glass & Tile Painter	Lancashire Lancaster 26 Sun Street	London St Pancras	Not in 1901 Census
1838	DRAKE Frederick	Glass Painter Employing 5 Men & 1 Boy	Devon East Teignmouth 1 Triangle Place	Devon Teignmouth	Father of Maurice Drake & cousin of Lucy Beer
1876	DRAKE Maurice	[Not provided]	Devon East Teignmouth 1 Triangle Place	Devon Teignmouth	In 1901 Census a 'Glass Painter' living in Exeter. Son of Frederick
1880	DRAKE Wilfred	[Not provided]	Devon East Teignmouth 1 Triangle Place	Devon Teignmouth	In 1901 Census a 'Glass Painter' living in Exeter Son of Frederick
1849	DRIFFIELD Robert M	Artist On Glass (Painter 3/7)	Devon Exeter Bartholomew Street	London	With Holland of Warwick and C& B before moving to Exeter to work with Beers
1863	DRUMMOND Henry G	Draughtsman Staned Glass	Durham Gateshead 52 Redheugh Ter	Scotland Edingburgh	Shares in the Gateshead Stained Glass Company incorporated on 7 Sept. 1887. Not found in 1901 Census

Birth	Name	Occupation	Address	Place of Birth	Notes
1838	DU MORNET Jules DRUET DU MORNET	Artiste in Stained Glass	Berkshire Old Windsor 1 Leopold Villas	France Nantes Loire Infr	Worked at the Royal Stained Glass Works, Old Windsor
1840	DUNCAN John	Artist & Glass Painter	Northumberland Newcastle-on-Tyne St Andrew 44 Percy St	Northumberland Newcastle On Tyne	In 1901 Census an Artist & Naturalist living in Whitley, Northumberland. Son & Brother of taxidermists
1829	DUNN John	Glass Stainor & Paintor Employing 41 Men 38 Boys & 4 Girls	Northumberland Newcastle-on-Tyne St John 32 Clayton St	Northumberland Wark	Not found in 1901 Census
1817	DUNN Gabriel	Glass Painter Unemployed	Warwickshire Birmingham 7 Nursery Terrace	Warwickshire Birmingham	Not found in 1901 Census
1864	DUNN Thomas F.	Glass Stainer	Northumberland 7 Dunn St	Not Known	Not identified in 1901 Census
1841	DURAND Leopold	Stained Glass Worker	Berkshire Old Windsor 1 Gothic Villas	France Nantes Loire Inferiure	Worked at the Royal Stained Glass Works, Old Windsor
1819	DURY Tony	Artist Painter	Lancashire Liverpool 3 Bold Place	France	Worked some time in Warwick
1859	EARTHY Charles J	Glass Painter	Staffordshire Harborne Broomfield	Lancashire Liverpool	Listed in Reading from at least 1899-1924. MH
1861	EATON Ernest	Painter Stained Glass & Tile Mnf	Lancashire Lancaster 28 Castle Hill	Cheshire Crewe	Eaton & Bulfield, Lancaster
1865	EAVES E. William	Glazier	Lancashire Lancaster 47 Lune Road	Lancashire Liverpool	In 1901 Census an 'Ecclesiastical Glass Cutter'. Later designed for Shrigley & Hunt. Son of Glazier W Eaves
1820	ECCLESTON Henry	Glass stainer Employing 3 Men 3 Boys	Warwick Birmingham 261 Camden St	Shropshire Shrewsbury	Not found in 1901 Census. c.1845 worked for Holland of Warwick where he married daughter of glass painter WJH Bigland. In 1851 lived in Oldbury. In 1881 boarding with William Hadley. MH
1864	EDEN Frederick Charles	Scholar	Berkshire Sandhurst Wellington College	Sussex Brighton	In 1901 Census an 'Architect' living in St George, Hanover Sq. Designed SG
1832	EDMUNDSON J.	Glass Warehouseman (Manuf)	Lancashire Chorlton On Medlock 5 Bremner St	Northumberland Leamington	Listed on Pilkington's 1849 payroll. Father of Glass Stainer Noah. Relative of Ralph Bolton Edmundson of Newburn Northumberland (b.1808-d.1864). In 1846 Ralph started up Pilkington's SG department & in 1854 started own business, which closed in 1890

Birth	Name	Occupation	Address	Place of Birth	Notes
1855	EDMUNDSON Noah W.	Glass Stainer	Lancashire Chorlton On Medlock 5 Bremner St	Lancashire Manchester	Son of J Edmundson. Continued the business of Ralph B Edmundson until 1890s
1833	EDMUNDSON William	Glass Stainer	Lancashire Eccleston In Prescot 167 Westfield St	Lancashire St Helens	In 1901 Census Glass painter living in St Helens. Possibly a relative of Ralph B Edmundson. Listed on Pilkington's 1849 payroll
1845	EDWARDS Alfred H.	Glass Cutter	Scotland Lanark Barony 85 Taylor St	Scotland England	
1860	EDWARDS Thomas	Glass Stainer	Scotland Lanark Barony 26 Findlay St	Scotland Lanark Glasgow	
1864	EVANS George S.	Stained Glass Manufacr	Staffordshire Harborne Stafford 169 Oldbury Rd	Staffordshire Smethwick	In 1901 Census a 'Manufacturers Clerk' living in Smethwick. Son of Samuel Evans
1827	EVANS James	Glass Stainer (Manuf)	Lancashire Liverpool 3 Stafford St	Warwickshire Wolverhampton	Not in 1901 Census
1865	EVANS Joseph K.	Stained Glass Manufacr	Staffordshire Harborne 169 Oldbury Rd	Staffordshire Smethwick	In 1901 Census 'Manager Trained Glass Business'. Son of Samuel Evans
1843	EVANS Samuel	Stained Glass Manufacr Employg 14 Men & 25 Boys	Staffordshire Harborne 169 Oldbury Rd	Lancashire Liverpool	1901 Census a 'Stained Glass Manufacturer' living in Smethwick. Father of Joseph & George Evans
1827	EVANS William	Retired Glass Painter	Shropshire Shrewsbury Holy Cross 134 Abbey Foregate		Son of David. Brother of Charles (1828-1864). Joined the firm in 1861
1857	FANTHAM Elizabeth	Glass Stainer	Stafford Harborne 60 Bridge St	Stafford Smethwick	
1866	FERGUSON William L.	Apprentice Artist (Painter)	Northumberland Newcastle-on-Tyne St Andrew 1 St James Street	Scotland	Living near to Wailes / Strang workshop and may have worked for them.
1861	FISCHER Peter Auguste	Glass Painter	Warwickshire Warwick 9 Oil Mill Lane	London	Living with & working for Frank Holt. Emigrated to Australia
1864	FISHER James	Glass Stainer	Northumberland Newcastle-on-Tyne St Andrew 9 Princess Street	Durham Sunderland	In the 1901 Census a 'Glass Painter' living in Fulham
1828	FISK Edward	Plumber & Glazier	Suffolk Yoxford Great St	Suffolk Yoxford	(BH Suffolk SG, p. 272)

Birth	Name	Occupation	Address	Place of Birth	Notes
1815	FORREST James A.	Stained Glass Maufacturer	Cheshire Claughton With Grange 5 Charlesville	Scotland	Partner of James Bromley until 1857. Early pioneer of photography
1849	FORREST James C.	Glass Merchant (Dealer)	Cheshire Tranmere 17 Kingsland Rd	Cheshire Birkenhead	In 1901 Census a 'Glass Merchant' living in Birkenhead. Son of James A Forrest
1863	FORSYTH James C.	Glass Stainer	Scotland Lanark Barony 13 Belgrave St	Scotland Lanark Glasgow	
1858	FOULGER Howson R.	Clerk	Surrey Sutton Carshalton Rd Manor Park House		Not in 1901 Census. Designed at least one SG window
1844	FOURACRE John Thos.	Decorator & Artist In Stained Glass Employing 20 Men 6 Boys	Devon Plymouth 21 S D Place	Devon Stonehouse	In 1901 Census a 'Stained Glass Maker' living in Plymouth. Son of John born 1819 in 1851 Census, a Painter / Plumber who employed 1 Man 1 Boy, Devonport
1857	FRAMPTON Edward	Artist (Painter)	Surrey Penge Aldwythohme	Kent Fordwich	In 1901 Census an 'Artist in Stained Glass' living in Sutton Surrey & born in 1849. (JBSMGP, vol XI, No 2, obit). Living with his parents-in-law in 1881
1862	GARDNER Albert	Glass Painter	Lancashire Eccleston In Prescot 32 Croppers Hill	Lancashire St Helens	In 1901 Census a 'Dent & Staine [sic] Glassman' Son of William Gardener & brother of William
1857	GARDENER Charles W.	Artist In Stained Glass	Durham Gateshead 72 Redheugh Rd	Newcastle On Tyne	In 1901 Census a 'Artist On Stained Class' living in Westgate, Newcastle
1869	GARDNER Harold	Scholar	Lancashire Eccleston in Prescot 121 Boundary Road	Lancashire St Helens	In 1901 Census a 'Glass Stainer' living in Birkenhead. Son of Thos. Gardner
1831	GARDNER James	Glass Stainer	Lancashire Windle 25 Westfield St	Lancashire Manchester	In 1881 Census a 'Glass bender' Brother of Benjamin Gardner
1843	GARDNER Thos	Designer	Lancashire Eccleston in Prescot 121 Boundary Road	Lancashire Manchester	In 1901 Census a 'Draughts Man' living in St Helens. Father of Harold & Frederick & Herbert, all lead light workers
1861	GARDNER William	Glass Painter	Lancashire Eccleston In Prescot 32 Croppers Hill	Lancashire St Helens	In 1901 Census a 'Glass Burner' living in Eccleston, Prescot. Son of William Gardener & brother of Albert
1823	GARDNER William	Master Glass Painter Employing 11 Men 3 Boys 1 Woman	Lancashire Eccleston In Prescot 32 Croppers Hill	Lancashire Manchester	Managed Pilkington Bros. Ornamental Glass Dept & took it over in 1872

Birth	Name	Occupation	Address	Place of Birth	Notes
1830	GASCOYNE Alexander	Decorator Emp 10 Men 2 Boys	Nottinghamshire Nottingham St Mary Alexander Park Leland Home	Nottinghamshire Nottingham	Not in 1901 Census
1878	GASCOYNE Alexder	[not provided]	Nottinghamshire Nottingham St Mary 13 Lower Talbot St	Nottinghamshire Hawksworth	In 1901 Census 'no occupation' & living in Nottingham. Studied at Nottingham Art College & on continent. Son of George F Gascoyne
1853	GASCOYNE George F.	Painter Emp 8 Men & 2 B	Nottinghamshire Nottingham St Mary 13 Lower Talbot St	Nottinghamshire Nottingham	In 1901 Census an 'Artist In Stained Glass' living in Nottingham. Father of Alexander Gascoyne
1866	GAULD David B.	Scholar	Scotland Lanark Barony 122 Berkeley St	Scotland Lanark Glasgow	Designed for J & W Guthrie. Noted painter, one of the 'Glasgow Boys'
1870	GERE Charles M.	Scholar	Gloucestershire Gloucester Littleworth No 14 Brunswick Sqr.	Gloucestershire Gloucester	Designed some SG. Brother-in-law of Henry Payne
1866	GILSON Arthur	Scholar	Surrey Croydon Uppr Addiscbe Rd	Middlesex London	In 1901 Census a 'Glass & Colour Merchant' living in Croydon
1879	GILSON Bernard	Scholar	Surrey Croydon Uppr Addiscbe Rd	Surrey Croydon	In 1901 Census a 'Lead Glazier Paint' living in Croydon
1865	GILSON Chas. J.	Apptce To Leaded Window Manufacturer	Surrey Croydon Uppr Addiscbe Rd	Middlesex Highbury	Croydon. Son of Robert Gilson
1872	GILSON Hy. P [Percy]	Scholar	Surrey Croydon Uppr Addiscbe Rd	Surrey Croydon	In 1901 Census a 'Glass & Colour Merchant' living in Croydon
1834	GILSON Robt. A.	Glass And Color Merchant	Surrey Croydon Uppr Addiscbe Rd	Sussex Seaford	Partner in Britten & Gilson
1865	GILSON Robt. C.	Apptce To Leaded Window Manufacturer	Surrey Croydon Uppr Addiscbe Rd	Middlesex Highbury	Partner in Britten & Gilson
1876	GINNETT Louis J.	Scholar	Warwickshire Leamington Priors 63 Clarendon St	Warwick Leamington	In 1901 Census an 'Art Student' living in Preston, Sussex. In 1881 living in lodgings while his parents performed with horses in Devon. Studied in London & Paris. Designed some SG, e.g. Royal Masonic School, Rickmansworth
1847	GOODMAN William H.	Glass Painter	Staffordshire Harborne 77 Cape Hill	Worcestershire Worcester	Not found in 1901 Census

Birth	Name	Occupation	Address	Place of Birth	Notes
1848	GOW Charles	Glass Stainers Master	Scotland Glasgow Lanark 240A New City Rd	Scotland Lanark Glasgow	Apprenticed to John Cairney, cartoonist with Daniel Cottier c.1866. In 1883 in partnership with Hugh McCulloch. 1891 emigrated to Australia to work again for Daniel Cottier
1831	GOW John	Glass Merchant Stained Glass Cutter	Northumberland Westgate	Northumberland Newcastle On Tyne	Not found in 1901 Census
1809	GRANT Joseph	Painter General	Suffolk Ipswich St Margaret Freehold Terrace Caldwell Hall Rd 5	Norfolk Costessey	(BH Norfolk SG, p.229). Listed as a Glass Stainer in many 1836-1865 directories
1846	GRANT William	Coach Painter	Suffolk Ipswich St Margaret Freehold Terrace Caldwell Hall Rd 5	Norfolk Costessey	(BH Norfolk SG, p.229). Son of Joseph Grant & listed as a Glass Painter in 1861 Census
1852	GRIFFITH Wm. [Spelled Griffiths in 1901 Census]	Glass Painter	Staffordshire Harborn 91 Church Rd	Worcestershire Dudley	In 1901 Census an 'Artist In Stained Glass' living in Headingley, Yorkshire
1862	GRIFFITHS Arthur	Artist in Stained Glass	Staffordshire Harborne 83 Reynold St	Staffordshire Bilston	In 1901 Census a 'Designer & Painter Of Church Windows' living in St Pancras
1856	GRISDALE William	Glass & Tile Painter (MF)	Lancashire Lancaster 2 Alfred St	Lancashire Allithwaite	In 1901 Census William Grisdale a 'Stained Lass [sic] Artist' born 1836 in South Wales Risca [...] and living in Kendal, Westmorland. Same person?
1875	GUTHRIE John G.	[none provided]	Scotland Lanark Barony 385 Sauchiehall St	Scotland Lanark Barony	John Gordon Guthrie. Son of William Guthrie. Emigrated to USA & worked with Henry Wynd Young and then independently from 1920s
1852	GUTHRIE William	Painter Master Employ 35 Men	Scotland Lanark Barony 385 Sauchiehall St	Scotland Glasgow Lanark	Began making stained glass c. 1886
1851	HADLEY William	Manager (Glass Staining)	Warwick Birmingham 261 Camden St	Warwick Birmingham	Landlord of William Ecclestone. In 1901 Census no occupation provided & living in Birmingham
1843	HALL John Wesley	Glass & Colour Merchant Employing 60 Men & 28 Boys	Gloucestershire Clifton Clifton Hill "Callender House"	London	In 1901 Census a 'Magistrate Glass Lead Paints' living in Westbury On Trym, Glos.
1845	HANCOCK Edward	Color Manufacturer D P	Worcestershire Worcester Claines No 10 Ombersley Rd	Derbyshire Derby	Manufacturer of 'Hancock's' glass paints, stains & enamels

Birth	Name	Occupation	Address	Place of Birth	Notes
1859	HANNING Jane	Glass Stainer	Durham Gateshead 27 East St	Durham So Shields	Not found in 1901 Census
1847	HARDY Paul	Stained Glass Worker	Berkshire Old Windsor Lord Nelson Inn	France Rouen	Worked at the Royal Stained Glass Works, Old Windsor in 1881 Census
1865	HARGREAVES Frederick	Glass Painter	Lancashire Lancaster High St Nursery Garden Cottage	Lancashire Lancaster	In 1901 Census a 'Stained Glass Painter' living in Lancaster
1858	HARRISON Samuel	Glass Stainer York St Maurice 1 Park Crescent	Yorkshire	Yorkshire York	In 1901 Census an 'Artist In Stained Glass' living in Headingley, Yorks. Later S Harrison & Sons, Hull
1811	HARTLEY James J.P.	Retired Glass Mfctrer	Durham Bishopwearmouth Ashbrook Hall	Scotland	Father of John. Moved from Dumbarton to Nailsea then Birmingham. Worked with Chance
1843	HARTLEY John	Glass Manuf & County Magistrate	Durham Bishopwearmouth 1 Mowbray Villas	Durham Sunderland	Son of James of the 'Wear Glassworks'
1848	HARVEY John I.	Glass Painter (Mf)	Warwickshire Birmingham 63 Lr Hurst St	Gloucestershire Dursley	In 1901 Census a 'Stain Glass Artist' living in Kings Norton. Worked for Hardman
1858	HENRY Geo.	Draughtsman	Scotland Lanark Glasgow 4 Binnie Place	Scotland Ayr Irvine	Designed for J & W Guthrie. Painter, one of the 'Glasgow Boys'
1847	HENRY Henri C. J.	Director of the Royal Tapestry Wks & Artists	Berkshire New Windsor Queensmead	France (Naturalized British Subject)	Head of the Royal Stained Glass Works, Old Windsor in 1881 Census
1830	HERDMAN Robert	Artist Portrait And History	Scotland Edinburgh St Cuthberts 12 Bruntsfield Cresc	Scotland Perth Rattray	Designed for Ballantine
1841	HILL John	Glass Painter	Warwickshire Birmingham Melbourne Terr Brougham St 6	Warwickshire Birmingham	In 1901 Census a 'Glass Painter' living in Aston Manor
1865	HILLER G. Henry	Apprentice To General Draper	Lancashire Withington Athelney Stanley Rd	Lancashire Manchester	In 1901 Census a 'Stained Glass And Decorative Artist' living in Chorlton Cum Hardy
1806	HINKLEY Francis	Glass Painter Handicap: Deaf & Dumb	Warwickshire Aston 144 Victoria Road	Warwickshire Birmingham	In 1851 Census a 'Glass Painter' living in Birmingham
1834	HINKLEY Francis	Artist (Artzn)	Warwickshire Aston 144 Victoria Road	Warwickshire Birmingham	In 1851 Census a 'Glass Painter' living in Aston

Birth	Name	Occupation	Address	Place of Birth	Notes
1855	HODGSON Thomas G.	Lead And Glass Merchant Plumber & C	Yorkshire York St Michael Le Belfry 26 Stonegate	Yorkshire York	Not found in 1901 Census
1821	HODGSON William	Decorative Painter	Northumberland Westgate 214 Stanhope St	Durham Jarrow	Not found in 1901 Census
1853	HOLLOWAY Arthur	Stained Glass Artist (Manul)	Lancashire Liverpool Toxteth Park 8 Cawdor Street	Staffordshire West Bromwich	Not in 1901 Census. Possible relative of Isaac & Enoch Holloway
1804	HOLLAND William	Income From Property	Warwickshire Leamington Priors Spencer St	Lancashire Manchester	Founder of Holland of Warwick
1828	HOLLOWAY Enoch	Glass Merchant	Cheshire Cheadle Hulme Claremont Smith Green	Staffordshire West Bromwich	Son of Isaac Holloway and possibly the brother of Isaac JR
1840	HOLLOWAY Isaac	Glass Dealer	Lancashire Toxteth Park 76 Berkley St	Staffordshire West Bromwich	In 1901 Census a 'Stained Glass Manuf' living in Liverpool
1870	HOLLOWAY John	Scholar	Lancashire Toxteth Park 76 Berkley St	Lancashire Liverpool	In 1901 Census a 'Stained Glass Manufacturer' living in Southport, Lancashire. Son of Liverpool glass dealer Isaac Holloway
1843	HOLT Frank	Master Glass Painter & Decorator Employg [sic] 22 Men & 6 Boys	Warwickshire Warwick 9 Oil Mill Lane	Worcestershire Worcester	In 1901 Census a 'Decorator' living in St Nicholas Warwick. Took over from William Holland of Warwick
1845	HOOPER Frederick	Glass Stainer	Scotland Lanark Barony 21 Alexander St	Scotland Lanark Glasgow	Of Hooper & Edwards
1865	HORNELL [sic, HORNEL] Edward A.	Artist Painting	Scotland Edinburgh St Cuthberts 58 Pilrig Model Buildings	Australia Near Melbourne Victoria	Designs made by Guthrie. Painter, one of the 'Glasgow Boys'
1834	HORWOOD Edwin	Glass Painter 2 Men 2 Boys	Somerset Frome 4 South Parade	Somerset Mells	Brother of Mark Horwood
1840	HORWOOD Mark	Glass Painter	Somerset Frome 1 New Cottages at End of Butts	Somerset Mells	Brother of Edwin Horwood
1849	HUNT Arthur	Stained Glass & Art Tile Painter Shrigley & Hunt Empl 40 Persons	Lancashire Lancaster 22 West Place	Hertford Hoddesdon	In 1901 Census a 'Stained Glaes [sic] Window Manufac' living in Lancaster. Founder of Shrigley & Hunt

Birth	Name	Occupation	Address	Place of Birth	Notes
1862	HURLEY John H.	Glass Painter	Stafford Harborne 22 Feeder St	Stafford Smethwick	Not found in 1901 Census
1867	HUTCHINSON Gerald Pemberton	Scholar	Warwickshire Rugby 24 Hillmorton Rd	Warwickshire Rugby	In 1901 Census 'An Artist In … Glass' living in Chislehurst Kent. Employed by J P & Sons
1867	HUTCHINSON John Thomas	Glass Stainer	Durham NK Gateshead East St	Durham Gateshead	In 1901 Census a 'Glass Cutter & Tet [sic] Head Worker' living in Newcastle
1855	HYMERS Henry	Glass Stainer	Northumberland Westgate 49 Villa Place	Northumberland Newcastle Upon Tyne St Andrews	Visiting this address. Not found in 1901 Census
1849	JEWITT Edward H.	Artistic Principally in Stained Glass & Mural Decorations	Lancashire Lancaster 8 Albert Terrace	Oxfordshire Headington	In 1901 an 'Artis [sic] Painter' living in Slyne With Hest Lancs. Employed by S&H from 1876 as second chief designer based in Lancaster. Bill Waters
1862	JONES Francis Clement	Glass Painter	Warwickshire Birmingham Aston 37 Brougham St	Warwickshire Birmingham	Not found in 1901 Census
1838	JONES James	Master Glass Stainer Employs 6 Men 2 Boys	Lancashire Beswick Oriol Villa	Surrey Lambeth	Not found in 1901 Census. Lived in St Pancras, Manchester & Longsight Lancashire
1865	JONES James	Glass Stainer	Lancashire Beswick Oriol Villa	Lancashire Manchester	Not found in 1901 Census. Son of James
1822	KAYLL John Jas.	Glass Manufacturer J P Alderman Borough	Durham Monkwearmouth 20 Roker Terrace	Isle of Man	Father of John Jas. Kayll Relative of James Hartley & partner in Hartley & Kayll
1851	KAYLL John Jas.	Glass Manufacturer	Durham Monkwearmouth 20 Roker Terrace	Durham Sunderland	Not found in 1901 Census. Son of John Jas. Kayll. Later of Kayll & Edwin Reed, Leeds
1839	KEIR James	Glass Stainer	Scotland Lanark Barony 91 Kent Rd	Scotland Ayr	
1826	KEIR William	Glass Stainer 12 Men 7 Boys	Scotland Lanark Barony 8 Derby St	Scotland Ayr Irvine	Son of David Keir
1856	KEIR William Junr	Glass Stainer	Scotland Lanark Barony 6 Cleveland St	Scotland Lanark Glasgow	
1838	KEMPE Charles Eamer MA Oxon.	Artist	Sussex Lindfield Old Place	Sussex Ovingdean	In 1901 Census a 'Constractional [sic] Artist' living in Lindfield

Birth	Name	Occupation	Address	Place of Birth	Notes
1854	KERR Charles	Artist in Stain Glass	Staffordshire Harborne 100 Coopers Lane	Bedfordshire Bedford	Not found in 1901 Census
1861	KIND George	Artist Glass Painter	Lincoln Brant Broughton The Rectory High Street	London	In 1901 Census 'A Farmer' living in Peterborough. In 1881 staying at the home of Frederick H. Sutton
1851	KING George A.	Decorative Artist Painter	Norfolk Heigham 35 Distillery Street	Norfolk Norwich	In 1901 Census a 'Decorator Artist' living in Norfolk
1831	KING Thomas C.R.	Lead & Glass Merchant	Norfolk Norwich St George Tombland 57 Prince Of Wales Rd	Norfolk Norwich	In 1901 Census a 'Geals [sic] Merchant' living in Norwich
1839	KNOWLES John Ward	Glass Painter Employing 4 Men And One Boy	Yorkshire York St Michael Le Belfry 23 Stonegate	Yorkshire York	In 1901 Census an 'Artist In Stained Glass' living in York. Apprenticed to Clayton & Bell
1820	KNOX John	Glazier Employing 6 Men 2 Boys	Scotland Lanark Glasgow 26 Robertson	Scotland Lanark Glasgow	
1844	LAIDLER Geoe. Gavin	House Painter	Northumberland Newcastle On Tyne St Andrew 14 St Thomas Crescent	Northumberland Newcastle On Tyne	In 1901 Census a 'House Decorator' living in Jesmond. Worked with and executed the designs of Thomas Ralph Spence, and J Edgar Mitchell. Shares in Gateshead Stained Glass Company incorporated on 7 Sept. 1887
1862	LAIDMAN John Mitford	Glass Painter	Durham Gateshead 56 Melbourne St	Northumberland Newcastle	In 1901census a 'Glass Painter' living in Tottenham. Working for Powell &Sons (Whitefriars Glass, p. 188)
1844	LAMBERT Richard B.	Glass & China Painter	Warwickshire Warwick St Nicholas 20 Cherry St	Yorkshire York	In 1901 Census a 'Trainer Glass Painter' [sic] living in St Pancras
1852	LAPPER George	Glass Painter & Organist	Staffordshire Harborne 62 Raglan Rd (The Hawthorns)	Warwickshire Bham	In 1901 Census 'Artist Station [sic] Glass' in Smethwick
1855	LATHAM Edmund R.	Glass Decorator	Lancashire Liverpool 9 Roe St	Lancashire Liverpool	In 1901 Census a 'Glass Decorator' living in Liverpool. Son of Edmond Latham of Liverpool. Brother of William
1861	LATHAM William A.	Glass Decorator	Lancashire Liverpool 9 Roe St	Lancashire Liverpool	In 1901 Census a 'Glass Decorator' living in Liverpool. Son of Edmond Latham of Liverpool & brother of Edmund

Birth	Name	Occupation	Address	Place of Birth	Notes
1868	LAURENSON Albert	Errand Boy	Surrey Camberwell 17 Sturdy Rd	Surrey Peckham	In 1901 Census a 'Glass Painter' working for J P & Sons (*Whitefriars Glass*, p. 188) Brother of John Laurenson
1857	LAURENSON John	Glass Painter (21-4)	Surrey Camberwell 17 Sturdy Rd	Surrey Peckham	Not found in 1901 Census. Brother of Albert Laurenson
1865	LEACH Barnet M.	Apprentice Art Worker	Cambridgeshire Cambridge St Andrew the Less 35 To 37 City Road	Cambridgeshire Cambridge	In 1901 Census an 'Artist Stained Glass' living in Cambridge
1837	LEACH Frederick R.	Designer & Art Worker Employ 28 Men 2 Women & 6 Boys	Cambridgeshire Cambridge St Andrew the Less 35 To 37 City Road	Cambridgeshire Cambridge	Not in 1901 Census. Father of Barnet Leach
1861	LEAVENS Norman W.	Painter Stained Glass & Tile Mnf	Lancashire Lancaster 28 Castle Hill	Yorkshire Snaith	In 1901 Census a 'Retired Glass Painter' living in Scarborough. Worked for S&H
1807	LILLY William	Painter Master Employing 2 Men	Suffolk Wrentham High Street	Suffolk Wrentham	(*BH Suffolk SG*, p. 271)
1866	LISTER Chas. W.	Glass Stainer	Durham Gateshead 25 Hartington Street	Northumberland Newcastle	Not found in 1901 Census. Son of Charles Lister, a 'Glassmaker'
1857	LOWNDES Mary	[not provided]	Huntingdon Tetworth Tetworth Hall	Wiltshire Poole Keynes	Visiting her Grandmother Mary Kaye. Co-founder of Lowndes & Drury. In 1901 Census a 'Designer ... Glass Painter' living in Chelsea
1862	LUCAS Edward G.H.	Artist	Surrey Croydon 87 Church St	Surrey Croydon	In 1901 Census an 'Artist' living in Croydon. Glass painter to Comper
1851	LUSH Silas	Artist on Glass	Staffordshire Harborne Sherland Road	London	In 1901 Census an 'Artist Stainer Glass' living in Harrow. Painted for C&B
1864	MANN John [Harrington]	Student of Arts	Scotland Renfrew Queenslea Cathcart	Scotland Lanark Glasgow	Designed for J & W Guthrie
1842	MARSH Arthur H. [Hardwick]	Artist Painting	Lancashire Moss Side 107 Cecil St	Lancashire Manchester	In 1901 Census an 'Artist Painter' living in Newcastle. Produced designs for Sowerby
1845	MARTIN Joseph	Glass Stainer Unemployed	Staffordshire Harborn A New Street	Staffordshire Hanley	Not found in 1901 Census
1861	MATHEWS Harry	Artist Glass Painter (Mf)	Lancashire Lancaster 78 Church St	Yorkshire Laycock	Not found in 1901 Census. Worked for S&H

Birth	Name	Occupation	Address	Place of Birth	Notes
1851	MAYES Alfred	Glass Painter	Staffordshire Harborne 36 Church Rd (Lane)	Gloucestershire Eastington	Not found in 1901 Census
1821	McAUTHER Alex	Glass Stainer	Durham Gateshead 4 Penshaw Str	Scotland	Not found in 1901 Census
1869	McINTOSH [sic, MACKINTOSH] Charles Rennie	Scholar	Scotland Lanark Barony 2 Firpark Ter	Scotland Lanark Glasgow	
1869	MEATYARD [sic, METEYARD] Sidney H [Harold]	Scholar	Stafford Kingswinford Audnam	Stafford Kingswinford	In 1901 Census 'Meteyard Sidney Harold' an 'Art Master Municipal School' living in Kings Norton. Associated with Bromsgrove Guild, painter and illustrator, etc.
1851	MEIN Fraser	Artist In Stained Glass (Manuf)	Northumberland Westgate 206 Stanhope St	Northumberland Newcastle On Tyne	In 1901 Census a 'Tobacconists Assistant' living in Westgate. Son of James. Brother of William & John Mein
1819	MEIN James	Glass Stainer	Northumberland Elswick 10 Lefroy St	Scotland	Worked for W Wailes. Father of Fraser, John, William & James born 1847 who does not appear in 1881 Census, but in 1901 is an 'Artist in Stainid Class' [sic] living in Battersea
1845	MEIN John	Glass Stainer	Northumberland Ash Street Benwell	Northumberland Newcastle	Son of James. Brother of Fraser & William Mein
1858	MEIN William	Glass Stainer	Northumberland Elswick 10 Lefroy St	Northumberland Newcastle	Son of James. Brother of John & Fraser Mein
1866	MELVILLE John	Glass Figure Painter	Scotland Lanark Glasgow 172 Graeme St	Scotland Lanark Glasgow	Worked for Meikle & CW Whall. Partner of Oscar Paterson in 1911 went to America in 1913 (SSG MD)
1851	MILLER Alfred P	Decorative Artist	Surrey Lambeth 32 Wellington Rd	Surrey Lambeth	In 1901 Census a 'Designer Of Decortative' [sic] living in Wandsworth
1858	MILLER Frederick	Artist China Painting & Stained Glass	London 44 Devonshire St	Middlesex Marylebone	In 1901 Census an 'Artist Writer' living in Keston, Kent. Author of 'The Training of a Craftsman'
1845	MILLER Joseph	Glass Stainer	Lanark Woodside Road 9 Groveside Place	England	Born in Newcastle worked for Bennet in Edinburgh and Stephen Adam in Glasgow from 1877 (SSG MD)

Birth	Name	Occupation	Address	Place of Birth	Notes
1860	MILLER Robert	Glass Painter	Northumberland Elswick 2 Dobson St	Northumberland Newcastle	Not found in 1901 Census
1859	MONTGOMERY Joseph	Glass Painter Out Of employ	Staffordshire Harborn 177 Oldbury Rd	Staffordshire Smethwick	In 1901 Census a 'Glass Writer' living in Camberwell
1822	MORGAN William	Artist Painter	Warwickshire Birmingham 178 Gt King St	Warwickshire Birmingham	In 1851 Census a 'Glass Painter' living in Birmingham
1854	MUNRO James	Glass Painter	Scotland Barony Lanark 7 Gayfield St	Scotland Lanark Glasgow	
1850	NEALE Arthur	Glass Painter	Stafford 104 St Pauls Rd Harborne	Stafford Smethwick	Living with his father John Neale, a 'Retired Manager Glass Works'
1861	NEWILL Mary J.	Art Student	Shropshire Wellington The Vineyard	Shropshire Admaston	Designed some SG
1866	NEWTON Edward	Glass Stainer Apprentice	Gateshead Durham 22 Stanley Street	Durham Gateshead	In 1901 Census a 'Warehouse manager' living in Gateshead
1850	NICHOL David	Glass Stainer	Northumberland Elswick 11 Suffolk St	Ireland Antrim	In 1901 Census a 'Foreman Gas Stoker' living in Elswick
1863	PALIN William	Figure Painter on Pottery	Stafford Burslem 54 Lyndhurst St	Stafford Hanley	In 1901 Census an 'Artist Painter' living in Willesden. Made some SG (NADFAS)
1852	PAPE William	Glass Merchant Employing 8 Hands	Yorkshire Headingley Cum Burley 6 Regent Park Terrace	Yorkshire Thimbleby	In 1901 Census a 'Glan [sic] Merchant' living in Potternewton, Yorks. Business established in 1876. Made SG
1852	PARKES William	Glass Painter	Staffordshire Harborn Oldbury Rd Boot Shop	Staffordshire Stafford	Not in 1901 Census
1863	PATERSON Oscar	Designer Glass	Scotland Lanark Govan 118 Ardgowan Str	Scotland Lanark Glasgow	Partner of Harry Thomson & assisted by John Stark Melville
1868	PAYNE Henry	Errand Boy	Gloucestershire Cheltenham 17 Normal Terrace	Warwickshire Birmingham	Instructed in SG by CW Whall. Influential lecturer at Birmingham Municipal School of Art
1849	PEARCE William	Glass & Lead Merchant	Warwickshire Solihull Lode Lane	Warwickshire Birmingham	Later firm amalgamated with Ephraim Cutler. Son of William Pearce 'glass lead merchant employing 4'
1857	PEARCE Walter J.	House Decorator	Kent Lewisham No 8 Clyde Terr	Sussex Brighton	in 1901 Census a 'Stained Glass Artist' living in Didsbury, Lancashire

Birth	Name	Occupation	Address	Place of Birth	Notes
1864	PEARSON Ellen	Painter On Glass	Warwickshire Birmingham 14 Back Bartholomew Row	Warwickshire Birmingham	Not in 1901 Census. Daughter of a Birmingham chairmaker
1863	PEGRAM Henry A.	Art Student	London 320 Euston Rd	London St Pancras	In 1901 Census an 'Artist'. Designed for J P & Sons, best known as sculptor
1857	PEMBERTON Benjamin	Glass Painter	Stafford Harborne 375 Green Lane	Stafford Smethwick	Living with his brother-in-law T Hackett, a brewery worker. Not in 1901 Census
1871	PENWARDEN Ernest	Scholar	Surrey Newington 71 Mina Rd	Surrey Walworth	In 1901 Census a 'Draughtsman Stained...' living in Camberwell. Brother of John Penwarden. Worked for J P & Sons (*Whitefriars Glass*, p. 188)
1823	PERKS William	Glass & Lead Merchant Emply 23 Men & 7 Boys	Warwickshire Edgbaston Sir Harrys Rd The Shrubbery	Warwickshire Birmingham	Son of William a 'glass merchant' Supplier to Hardman
1880	PIPPIT Gabriel J.	[not provided]	Warwickshire Solihull Lode Lane	Warwickshire Solihull	In 1901 Census an 'Art Student' living in Solihull. Worked with brother Michael for Paul Woodroffe. Son of Joseph Pippet. PC
1841	PIPPIT Joseph A.	Designer	Warwickshire Solihull Lode Lane	Somerset Nettlebridge	In 1901 Census an 'Artist Ecclisiostical' [*sic*] living in Solihull. Neighbour of W Pearce. Worked for Hardmans
1870	PIPPET Oswald	Student	Stafford Cotton Cotton Hall	Warwick Solihull	In 1901 Census an 'Artist Ecclisiostical' [*sic*] living in Solihull. Son of Joseph Pippet
1875	PIPPET Raphael	Scholar	Warwick Solihull Lode Lane	Warwick Solihull	In 1901 Census 'Artist' living in Solihull. Son of Joseph Pippet
1860	PITT Henry H	Agent (Glassworks)	Durham Lamesley 5 Chowdean Terrace	Warwick Birmingham	Shares in Gateshead Stained Glass Company when incorporated on 7 Sept. 1887
1849	PORTEOUS Thos	Glazier In Stained Glass Works	Northumberland Elswick 75 Hawes St	York York	Not found in 1901 Census
1842	POWELL Albert	Artist Designer Manufacturer of Stained Glass	Yorkshire Potter Newton Spencer Ter 15 Louis St	London	Brother of Charles, trained with Ballantine of Edinburgh?
1875	POWELL Andrew	Scholar	Cambridgeshire Cambridge 40 Perowne St.	Cambridgeshire Cambridge	In 1901 Census 'Ecclesiastical decorator' living in Lincolnshire. Son of William & brother of Lewis born 1882. In 1901 an 'Apprentice to church...' living in Horninglow, Stafford

Birth	Name	Occupation	Address	Place of Birth	Notes
1812	POWELL Arthur	J P for Surrey and Merchant	Surrey Dorking Milton Heath	London	Partner in J P & Sons 1812-1894. Brother of Nathaniel
1845	POWELL Arthur C.	(Manuf) In A Glass Merchant	Surrey Dorking Butter Hill	Sussex Malling	Partner in J P & Sons. Son of Arthur Powell
1841	POWELL Charles J.	Artist in Stained Glass	Yorkshire Potter Newton 33 Leopold St	London [Pentonville]	In 1901 Census an 'Artist In Shiened [sic] Glass' living in Potter Newton. Trained with Holland of Warwick. Brother of Albert
1862	POWELL Dunstan J.	Artist in Stained Glass	Warwickshire Edgbaston 252 Hagley Rd	Warwickshire Birmingham	Son of John Hardman Powell
1862	POWELL Ellen E.	Glass Stainer	Stafford Harborne 9 Stone St	Stafford Smethwick	Sister of Sarah Powell
1853	POWELL Harry J.	Manufacturing Clerk Glass Works ... Oxford	Essex Loughton High Road (White House)	Essex Walthamstow	In 1901 Census a 'Glass Manufacturer' living in Camberwell. Partner in J P & Sons
1799	POWELL Henry	Glass Cutter & C (Manuf)	Cambridgeshire Cambridge St Andrew the Less 108 Newmarket Road	Yorkshire York	A possible relative of Charles Powell
1848	POWELL James Crofts	Glass Manufacturer	Surrey Dorking Milton Heath	Middlesex Clapton	Partner in J P & Sons. Son of Arthur Powell
1849	POWELL John H	Stained Glass Painter (Manuf)	Middlesex London 4 Somerset St	Northumberland Newcastle On Tyne	In 1901 Census an 'Artist On Stained Glass' living in Southgate, Middlesex
1828	POWELL John H. [Hardman]	Artist in Stained Glass	Warwickshire Edgbaston 252 Hagley Rd	Warwickshire Birmingham	In 1901 Census a 'Retired Artist' living in Canton, Glamorganshire. Took over from his father-in-law John Hardman
1814	POWELL Nathanuel [Nathaniel]	Glass Manufacturer	Essex Chigwell Powells	Middlesex Hackney	Partner in J P & Sons. Brother of Arthur
1864	POWELL Sarah A.	Glass Stainer	Stafford Harborne 9 Stone St	Stafford Smethwick	In 1901 Census 'no occupation' living in Smethwick. Sister of Ellen Powell
1851	POWELL William	Painter	Cambridgeshire Cambridge 40 Perowne St.	Cambridgeshire Cambridge	In 1901 Census a 'Stain Glass Painter & C' [sic] living in St Nicholas Lincolnshire. Father of Andrew, born 1875 an 'Ecclesiastical Decorator' & Lewis born 1882 'Apprentice To Church'. Uncle of Christopher Powell of Camden

Birth	Name	Occupation	Address	Place of Birth	Notes
1856	PRENDERGAST James	Glass Cutter (Manuf)	Lancashire Liverpool 184 Ct Roscoe Lane	Lancashire Liverpool	In 1901 Census a 'Glazier Paint' [sic] living in Liverpool
1858	PREST Edward J.	Draughtsman & General Assistant Stained Glass Works Mfu	Lancashire Lancaster 9 Ullswater Rd	Cornwall Lewanwick	In 1901 Census an 'Artist In Stained Glass' living in Hampstead. Worked for S&H. Independent in the early 20thC. Expert witness in Wolmark's 'abstract' window trial at Slough. MH
1856	PREST Lucy	Asst Stained Glass Works Mf.	Lancashire Lancaster	London Camden Town 9 Ullswater Road	Wife of Edward worked for S&H
1826	PRINCE Edwin	Glass Painter Retired	Norfolk Overstrand Londs [sic]	Derbyshire Derby	A Derby china painter who moved to London in 1848 and then to William Wailes in Newcastle to work as a glass painter. He stayed there for over 20 years. NM
1855	PRYNNE Edward	Artist (Painter)	Worcestershire Worcester House Adjoining Manor House Grafton Manor	Devon Plymouth	In 1901 Census an 'Artist' living in Ealing. Worked with Percy Bacon and JJ Jennings
1858	RAMSEY Robert	Glass Stainer	Northumberland Westgate 42 Elswick Street	Northumberland Newcastle On Tyne	In 1901 Census a 'Glass Stainer' living in Hanover Sq. London
1861	REED Edwin	Glass Printer	Yorkshire Potter Newton Lodge Quarries Ho	Yorkshire Moortown	In 1901 Census an 'Artist In Stained Glass' living in Potter Newton. Worked for A Powell & later partner of John J Kayll
1879	REED Edwin	[no occupation provided]	Northumberland Elswick 61 Westmorland	Northumberland Newcastle On Tyne	Son of Joseph Reed In 1901 Census a 'Glass Stainer' living in Jesmond.
1837	REED Joseph	Glass Merchant	Northumberland Elswick 61 Westmorland	Northumberland Newcastle On Tyne	In 1901 Census a 'Glass Merchant' living in Jesmond. Father of Edwin Reed
1877	REES Charles	No Occ	London 66 Lambs Conduit St	London Herts	In 1901 Census an 'Artist On Glass' living in East Barnet. Son of George & brother of George Rees Working for J P & Sons (*Whitefriars Glass*, p. 188)
1862	REES George	No Occ	London 66 Lambs Conduit St	London Clerkenwell	In 1901 Census a 'Glass Painter' living in Friern Barnet. Son of George & brother of Charles Rees Working for J P & Sons (*Whitefriars Glass*, p. 188)
1868	REID James [Eadie]	Scholar	Scotland Forfar Dundee 7 Hill Street	Scotland Forfar Dundee	In 1901 Census an 'Artist' living in Southwick Durham. Designed SG 1903-1926 for Gateshead Stained Glass Co. NM

Birth	Name	Occupation	Address	Place of Birth	Notes
1855	RICH Edwin	Artist (P N)	Lancashire Lancaster 19 Borrowdale Rd	Warwickshire Rugby	Worked for S&H and apprenticed at 16 to H B & B.
1836	ROBERTSON William John	Glass Painter	Durham Gateshead 44 Albert St	Northumberland Newcastle	In 1901 Census a 'Joiner Carp' living in Benwell. Father of William John Robertson
1863	ROBERTSON William John	Glass Painter	Durham Gateshead 44 Albert St	Northumberland Newcastle	Not found in 1901 Census
1867	ROBSON William J.	Glass Stainers Assistant	Durham Gateshead 21 Greensfield St	Durham Gateshead	In 1901 Census a 'Cabman' living in Newcastle
1828	ROSSITER Charles	Artist Painter And Art Master	Rutland Uppingham High Street	Middlesex Westminster	SG designs made by W G Saunders
1865	ROWAT Jessie	Scholar	Scotland Renfrew Abbey Rosehill Cottage	Scotland Renfrew Paisley	Married Fra Newbery. Studied at Glasgow School of Art. Designed SG
1862	ROWLAND James	Glass Painter	Stafford Harborne 145 St Pauls Rd	Stafford West Bromwich	Son of Richard Rowland a 'Glass cutter' & brother of Samuel Rowland a 'Glass leader' & John Rowland a 'Glass leader's assistant'
1854	ROWLANDS John	Glass Stainer Employing 6 Men & 6 Boys	Cheshire Heswall Heswall Cum Oldfield	Lancashire Liverpool	Visiting this address. Business based in Liverpool. In 1901 Census a 'Glass Merchant' living in Hoylake, Cheshire
1819	RUSKIN John	Author	Lancashire Brantwood Hawkshead Monk Coniston Skelwith	London	Designed some SG
1866	SADLER Thomas	Glass Painter	Durham Whickham	Durham Whickham	Shares in the Gateshead Stained Glass Company incorporated on 7 Sept. 1887
1874	SALISBURY Francis O.	Scholar	Hertford Harpenden Great House	Hertford Harpenden	In 1901 Census an 'Artist Sculp' living in St Albans. Began by working for brother Henry H Salisbury. Designed some SG
1839	SALISBURY Henry	Plumber Decorator & Ironmonger	Hertford Harpenden Great House	Buckingham North Crawley	Father of Francis & Henry Salisbury
1864	SALISBURY Henry H.	Apprentice Decorator	Hertford Harpenden Great House	Hertford Harpenden	Brother of Francis O Salisbury. In 1901 census an 'Artist on Stained Glass' living in Hampstead, London
1846	SANDERS Joseph	Artist (Painter)	Warwick Aston Alexandra Terrace Brougham St 3	Warwick Birmingham	In 1901 Census an 'Artist In Stained Glass' living in Aston Manor

Birth	Name	Occupation	Address	Place of Birth	Notes
1843	SAVAGE Thomas	Glass Painter	Stafford Harborne Pt H 84 Baldwin St	Worcester Suckley	In 1901 Census a 'Glass Painter' living in Smethwick
1812	SCOTT John	Retired Glass Stainer Alderman	Rickergate Cumberland 1 Scotts Lane	Cumberland Carlisle	Son of John Scott of Carlisle. Closed business in 1870s
1845	SCOTT Thomas J.	Decorative Painter And Artist	Norfolk Heigham No 1 Heigham Rd	Cambridgeshire Carlton Colville	John King's nephew & chief designer of J & J King, Norwich
1866	SEARLE William	Glass Stainer (Apprentice) (MF)	Berkshire New Windsor Sussex Place 1 Kings Road	Berkshire Windsor	In 1901 Census a 'Stained Glass Maker' living in South Manchester. Worked at the Royal Stained Glass Works, Old Windsor
1815	SEWARD Abraham	Magistrate Commission Councillor Poor Law Guardian	Lancashire Lancaster 12 West Place	Lancashire Lancaster	1815-1904. Son of Abraham Seward founder of business.
1837	SHAW Joshua	Glass Stainer	Durham Gateshead 58 Abbey Street	York Mexboro	Not found in 1901 Census
1864	SHIRLEY Thomas	Glass Artist	Staffordshire Stafford 315 Oldbury Rd (Post Office)	Staffordshire Smethwick	In 1901 Census a 'Glass Cutter' living in Stafford
1840	SIMPSON Edward H.	Decorator	Middlesex Laleham	London Oxford St.	Son of William Butler Simpson
1866	SKILBECK Clement O	Art Student	London Middlesex 16 Buckland Cres	Middlesex St James Clapham	In 1901 Census an 'Artist Painter & Designer' living in St Marylebone. Windows made at Lowndes & Drury, Fulham Glasshouse
1872	SLEIGH Bernard	Scholar	Warwickshire Edgbaston 88 Pershore Rd	Warwickshire B'Ham	In 1901 Census an 'Artist Painter & Wood Engineer' [sic] in Yardley. Designed some SG
1859	SMALL Alexander	Glass Painter	Northumberland Westgate 161 Stone Street	Northumberland Newcastle On Tyne	Son of Peter & brother of David Small. Articled to Wailes & Strang in 1873. Became a furniture salesman. Died 1899 NM
1831	SMALL David	Glass Stainer Employs 11 Men 4 Boys	Scotland Edinburgh South Leith 8 Murano Pl	Scotland Edinburgh	Worked some time with Stephen Adam
1857	SMALL David	Lead Worker & Glass Cutter	Northumberland Westgate 161 Stone Street	Northumberland Newcastle On Tyne	Son of Peter Small & brother of Alexander. In 1901 Census a 'Glass Cutter' living in Westgate
1832	SMALL Peter	Glass Painter (Manuf)	Northumberland Westgate 161 Stone Street	Scotland	Father of David & Alexander Small. Possible brother of David who worked with Stephen Adam

Birth	Name	Occupation	Address	Place of Birth	Notes
1859	SMITH Herbert A.	Glass Painter	Stafford Harborne 155 St Pauls Rd	Stafford Smethwick	Brother of Arthur L Smith, a 'Fret Lead Glazier'
1851	SMITH Thomas	Glass Painter	Staffordshire Harborn Sherland Road	Staffordshire Smethwick	In 1901 Census an 'Artist On Glass' living in Smethwick
1863	SNELL William D	Painter In Decorative Design	Devon St Andrew Plymouth 7 Cobourg Lane	Devon Plymouth	In 1901 Census a 'Designing Main Glass Decorator' living in East Stonehouse, Devon. Worked for & later 'conducted' the Fouracre & Watson studio
1849	SOMERSET Charles	Artist In Stained Glass	Durham Gateshead 38 North Tyne St	Northumberland Newcastle	In 1901 Census a 'Seret [sic] Lead worker' living in St Pancras, London. Son of William Somerset & brother of Joseph
1846	SOMERSET Joseph	Glass Stainer	Durham Gateshead 49 Lincoln Street	Northumberland Newcastle	In 1901 Census a 'Stained Glass Worker' living in Jesmond. Son of William, brother of Charles. Father of Ernest, a glass cutter in 1901 living in Jesmond
1822	SOMERSET William	Artist In Stained Glass	Northumberland Elswick 375 Westgate Road	York York	Not in 1901 Census. Father of Joseph & Charles Somerset
1856	SOWERBY George	Glass Manufacturer Master	Durham 9 Vernon Trce Gateshead	Durham Chester Le St	Of Sowerby Glass. Brother of John
1850	SOWERBY John George	Glass Manufacturer	Durham Gateshead Ravenshill	Durham Gateshead	In 1901 Census an 'Artist' in Sebergham Cumberland. Of Sowerby Glass. Brother of George
1862	SPARREN James (Junr)	Artist In Stained Glass	Northumberland Tynemouth 9 Percy Gardens	Yorkshire Rippon City	Nephew of Henry Barnett. Working for & living with him
1846	SPENCE Ralph	Artist (Painter)	Northumberland Newcastle On Tyne St Andrew 49 Alexandra Place	Yorkshire Richmond	Founded 'The Gateshead Stained Glass Co.' in 1879 with JG Sowerby and acted as their principal designer
1859	STACEY George	Glass Painter	London 3 Northampton Street	London Islington	In 1901 Census a 'Glass Artist' living in Islington, c.1905 went to New Zealand. CF
1868	STANBROOK Harry	Appren To Glass ...iting (Maf)	Berkshire New Windsor Adelaide Sq "Cambria Villa"	Berkshire N Windsor	Worked at the Royal Stained Glass Works, Old Windsor in 1881 Census. In 1901 Census a 'Professor Of Music'
1857	STEEL Charles Edwd.	Glass Merchants Clerk	Yorkshire Leeds 5 Exmouth St	Yorkshire Leeds	In 1901 Census a 'Glass Merchant' living in Headingley Cum Burley. Established own firm in 1898 became Tudor Studio Leeds Father of John R, Joseph H & Edward Steel

Birth	Name	Occupation	Address	Place of Birth	Notes
1859	STEWART John Tytler	Decorator	Scotland Lanark Barony 110 Ingleby Drive	Scotland Fife Leslie	Designer for Meikle & Sons
1842	STICKS George B.	Artist	Northumberland Westgate 200 Westgate Rd	Northumberland Newcastle St Johns	Father of George E Sticks & son of James Sticks. Worked for William Wailes
1863	STICKS George E.	Artist	Northumberland Westgate 200 Westgate Rd	Northumberland Newcastle St Johns	In 1901 Census an 'Artist' in Northumberland. Son of George B Sticks & grandson of James Sticks. Worked for William Wailes
1812	STICKS James	Draughtsman Glass Manufact	Northumberland Westgate 46 Villa Place	Scotland Edinburgh	Designed for William Wailes
1879	STRACHAN Alexander	none	Scotland Aberdeen St Nicholas 4 Jute Street	Scotland Aberdeen	Worked with brother Douglas at start of their careers. Designed & made his own SG and taught at Edinburgh College of Art
1876	STRACHAN Robert D. (Douglas)	Scholar	Scotland Aberdeen St Nicholas 4 Jute Street	Scotland Aberdeen	Brother of Alexander. Studied SG in England where he was influenced by CW Whall. Scotland's most prolific and brilliant 20th century SG designer
1836	STRANG Thomas R.	Artist In Stained Glass Employing 30 Men 4 Boys 1 Apprentice & 1 Girl	Northumberland Newcastle On Tyne 9 Bath Lane St John House	Scotland Lanark Glasgow	Thomas Rankine Strang (1835-1877). Son-in-law of William Wailes and partner
1867	STRANG William W.	Scholar	Northumberland Newcastle On Tyne 9 Bath Lane St John House	Northumberland Newcastle On Tyne	In 1901 Census a 'Glass Stainer' living in Elswick. Strang ran the firm of Wailes & Strang after his father's death until its closure in 1914
1824	SUMMERS Charles	Glazier & Glass Merchant Employing 7 Men & 2 Boys	Scotland Lanark Glasgow 4 Sydney St	Scotland Lanark Glasgow	Not found in 1901 Census
1833	SUTTON Frederick H. [Heathcote]	Rector of Brant Broughton	Lincoln Brant Broughton High Street The Rectory	Norfolk Syndford Hall	Designed & made SG
1869	TAIT Frederick Louis	Scholar	Durham Gateshead 27 Tent Street	Durham Gateshead	In 1901 Census 'No occupation' living in Birmingham. Designer for Swaine Bourne. From 1912 worked at Bogardus Wickens in Vancouver
1831	TAYLOR Martha A.	Glass Stainer	Stafford Harborne 137 Oldbury Rd	Worcester Dudley	Mother of Sarah Taylor. Husband worked as a labourer At Chandelier Works

Birth	Name	Occupation	Address	Place of Birth	Notes
1854	TAYLOR Sarah A.	Glass Stainer	Stafford Harborne 137 Oldbury Rd	Stafford Smethwick	Daughter of Martha Taylor
1861	TIPPING Joseph	Artist	Lancashire Lancaster 1 South Regents St	Warwick Birmingham	Son of William Tipping. In 1901 Census a 'Stained Glass Artist' living in Acton, London
1832	TIPPING William	Artist	Lancashire Lancaster 1 South Regents S	Lancashire Prescot	Father of Joseph Tipping. In 1901 Census a 'Stained Glass Artist' living in Acton, London
1865	TROTMAN Bernard H.	Glass Painter (Apprentice)	Stafford Harborne Broomfield	Stafford Smethwick	In 1901 Census an 'Art Teacher' in Birmingham
1869	TURNER Charles F.	Scholar	Lancashire Lancaster 69 Damside St	Lancashire Lancaster	In 1901 Census a 'Stained Glass Artist' living in Lancaster. Worked for S&H
1813	TURNER Reubin	Artist At Stain Glass Wks	Northumberland Elswick 9 East Parade	Derby Ridgway	Handicap: Deaf & Dumb. Not found in 1901 Census
1863	UPTON Albert	Glass Painter	Stafford Harborne Jockey Street	Stafford Smethwick	In 1901 Census an 'Artist Stained Glass' living in Smethwick
1822	VOUT William S.	Glass Dealer	Lancashire Moss Side 81 Raby Street	London	Father of William Samuel Vout
1848	VOUT William S.	Glass Silverer & Carpet Planner (C & Gilder)	Lancashire Stretford 9 Clifton Street	London	Son of William Samuel Vout of 87 Chapman St. Hulme, Manchester
1832	WARRINGTON James	Artist In Stained Glass	Cheshire Little Budworth Out Office	London	Son of William Warrington. Visiting this address
1843	WATSON Henry	Glass Stainer	Devon Stonehouse East 28 Chapel St	Northumberland Newcastle on Tyne	Partner of John Fouracre. In 1901 Census a 'Retired Stained Glass Painter' living in Meopham, Kent
1863	WATSON Robt.T.	Church Window Decorator (Painter)	Northumberland Newcastle On Tyne St Andrew 15 Leazes Crescent	Northumberland Newcastle On Tyne	Not found in 1901 Census
1812	WEST-COPE Charles	Royal Academician (Artist P)	Berkshire Cookham No 11 Crawford Rise	Yorkshire Leeds	Designs made by LB & W and JP & S
1864	WEYER William	Stain Glass Artist	Norfolk Norwich St Paul Bull Close	Norfolk Norwich	1864-1942 (*BH Norfolk SG* p. 211). In 1901 Census no occupation given
1864	WILSON Charles	Student Of Arts	Scotland Edinburgh St Georges 19 Palmerston Place	Scotland Lanark Glasgow	

Birth	Name	Occupation	Address	Place of Birth	Notes
1854	WOOD Alfred	Managing Clerk Glass Wks	Worcester Oldbury Mark Street	Warwick Birmingham	In 1901 Census a 'Glass Manufacturer' living in Sunderland. Partner in Hartley Wood from 1894 after leaving Chance Bros.
1850	WOOD John J.	Fret Lead Glazier	London 11 Grove St	London Middlesex M Bone	In 1901 Census a 'Stained glass artist' living in Paddington. His son Herbert Wood, born 1881 was a 'Stain [sic] glass artist' in 1901
1875	WOODROFFE Paul V.	Scholar	Somerset Bathwick 1 Arlington Villa	Madura Madras Presidency	In 1901 Census an 'Artist Painter Sculp' living in Hammersmith. Instructed in SG by CW Whall
1827	WRIGHT Henry	Lead & Glass Merchant	Hampshire Southampton All Sts 70 Bedford Place	Norfolk Sholesham	Father of Henry, Edward & Geo – Lead & Glass Merchant Assts.
1839	WYLIE John	Artist Glass Stainer	Northumberland Elswick 18 Norfolk St	Scotland Glasgow	Not in 1901 Census
1854	YATES Thomas H.	Glass Painter	Staffordshire Harborne 272 St Pauls Rd	Staffordshire West Bromwich	In 1901 Census a 'Stained glass artist' living in Smethwick
1868	YOUNG Daniel	Apprentice Glass Stainer	Scotland Lanark Barony 40 Elderslie St	Scotland Renfrew Govan	Brother of Henry Young
1881	YOUNG Henry	[none provided]	Scotland Lanark Barony 40 Elderslie St	Scotland Lanark Barony	Brother of Daniel Young. The only Henry Young to fit the profile of Henry Wynd Young. In 1915 he formed a partnership with the American George Owen Bonawit in New York & worked with J Gordon Guthrie

- The 1881 Census material on CD-ROM covers all of the counties in Scotland, England and Wales. The Church of Latter-day Saints transcribed it in 1999.

- Errors, which occurred in the process of transcription from the original census form to CD-ROM, have been retained.

- Census forms list the ages of the glass painters, which I have transferred into years, i.e. for the age 25, read date of birth 1876 or the previous year 1875.

Abbreviations:

BG	=	Burlison & Grylls
BS	=	British Subject
CB	=	Clayton & Bell
HB&B	=	Heaton Butler & Bayne
JP&S	=	James Powell & Sons, Whitefriars
LB&W	=	Lavers, Barraud & Westlake

MH   =   Information from Martin Harrison
NM   =   Information from Neil Moat
PC   =   Information from Peter Cormack
SG   =   Stained glass

BH Norfolk SG   =   *Nineteenth Century Norfolk Stained Glass* by Birkin Haward

BH Suffolk SG   =   *Nineteenth Century Suffolk Stained Glass* by Birkin Haward

NADFAS   =   *Stained Glass Marks & Monograms*, compiler Joyce Little
            and edited by Margaret Washbourn and Angela Goedicke

Sewter   =   *The Stained Glass of William Morris and his Circle* by A.
            Charles Sewter

SSG MD   =   *Scotland's Stained Glass; Making the Colours Sing* by
            Michael Donnelly

Whitefriars Glass =   *Whitefriars Glass: James Powell & Sons of London* by
            Wendy Evans, Catherine Ross and Alex Werner

Conclusion

Searching through the 1881 Census and comparing information from the 1901 Census reveal a continuing movement of stained glass craftsmen throughout the nineteenth century, with glass painters flowing from Scotland to Newcastle to Lancashire to the Midlands and on to London. Newcastle in particular appears to have been a major supplier of glass painters and draughtsmen. The training in the Art College and local studios was of a high standard and London firms such as James Powell & Sons made much use of the skills of these workers. Henry Watson, the partner of John Fouracre of Plymouth, came from Newcastle, as did Ralph Bolton Edmundson, who founded the stained glass workshop at Pilkington's, and James Fisher, who left Newcastle to establish a studio in Fulham. William Wailes is known to have attracted Scottish painters to his stained glass works in Newcastle and the firms of Atkinson and Barnett originated in Yorkshire, bringing their influence and ideas to the city. However, Wailes had died by 1881 and Atkinson and Barnett were no longer in expansion, so many of the newly-trained apprentices and graduates would have needed to seek work elsewhere. A study of Gateshead shows that many artisans employed in the manufacture of stained glass in 1881 were in quite different occupations by 1901.

The frequency of 19th-century London glass painters moving business premises can be partly explained by the facility provided by independent kiln men to fire glass, especially in the capital, making it unnecessary for individual glass painters to keep building new kilns or to acquire the extra space necessary for a kiln. Peter Cormack informs me that Morris & Co seem not to have had a kiln at their Queen Square premises, nor at Merton for some years, and that their glass was fired in Camden Town.

Shortage of work may have been the cause of many glass painters having to move about the country, but poaching appears to have been common practice. Clayton & Bell, for example, trained many craftsmen and designers who left to start up their own businesses in various parts of the country, taking with them some of Clayton & Bell's other workers.

It is obvious that the stained glass world was a small one in the nineteenth century and that many glass painters and glaziers knew each other, because of the fluidity of the workforce and because of the establishment of unions that created greater communication between the shop floors of different workshops throughout the country.

Compiling lists from census material is not a precise science. The search for Edward Frampton illustrates how difficult dates can be. The 1881 Census provides a birth date of 1857 but the 1901 Census offers a birth date of 1849. His obituary in the *BSMGP Journal* (Vol. XI, no. 2, 1952-3), suggests his dates as being 1845-1928. In the 1881 Census he is listed as born in Fordwich, but in the 1901 Census his birthplace is given as Woolwich. Frampton's illegitimacy may have resulted in his not knowing the precise location of his own birth, but the inconsistency of the dates is inexplicable.

Names can also fluctuate alarmingly. A search for William Francis Dixon in the 1881 Census led to the home of his father, Henry John Dixon, the Vicar of Yarnscombe in Devon, where a John Herbert Dixon, a stained glass artist born in Oxford and aged 32, was staying. William Francis Dixon and John Dixon both share the same parents, the same birth date, the same birthplace and the same occupation. Was John, a previously unknown stained glass artist, the twin brother of William, or was the census form filled in after a long lunch at the 'Yarnscombe Arms'?

ERRATUM NOTE
Access to the 1901 Census has proved the article in the last *Journal* (Vol. XXV, pp. 109-118) contained some errors. I falsely claimed that Alfred Bouchette designed canopy work for Clayton & Bell. It was more likely to have been his brother, Martin Bouchette, born 1861 and listed as 'Artist Stained Glass', who did not have the decency to appear anywhere in the 1881 Census. The other absentee from the 1881 Census was James Mein, born in 1847, the son of the Scottish-born glass painter also called James Mein, who was born in 1819 and moved to Newcastle to work for William Wailes. In 1901 James Mein Junior, whom I had mistaken for his father, was living in Battersea and working as an 'Artist Stainid Class' [*sic*].

ACKNOWLEDGEMENTS
My main thanks go to Martin Harrison, also to Peter Cormack, to Dr Michael Kerney and to Neil Moat for his help with Newcastle and Gateshead glass painters.

Contemporary
Practice

Ruth Kersley Greisman

ETZ CHAIM 'Tree of Life': Eleven windows for the Jewish Free School Synagogue 2002

This project was commissioned in February 2002 by Dame Ruth Robins, Head Teacher of the Jewish Free School in London. The school and synagogue were designed by architect Jane Lock-Smith of Terence O'Rourke plc. My brief to create eleven windows for the new circular synagogue presented a considerable design challenge: to convey the school's long and illustrious history within a contemporary architectural context.

History

The Jews Free School, now known as JFS School, is probably the oldest Jewish school in the world still in existence. In 1656 when Jews were re-admitted to England there was a Jewish population of about 400 in London. The first school, the Talmud Torah (religious school) of the Great Synagogue was founded in 1732 in Duke's Place, Aldgate, East London and admitted twenty-one orphaned German Jewish boys. Girls were admitted in 1822 when the school's first permanent home opened in Bell Lane. The new school was divided into three separate departments: the original Talmud Torah, a Boy's school and a Girl's school. By 1900 it had become the largest school in Europe with four thousand pupils.

Conditions have changed immensely over its two hundred and seventy-year history: the majority of pupils from the nineteenth and early twentieth centuries were immigrants escaping persecution in eastern Europe (my own grandparents were part of this wave). At JFS, pupils were taught English and how to become citizens of their newly-adopted country whilst maintaining strong religious values. The bombing of the East End of London and a shift of the Jewish population to the suburbs finally took its toll and falling rolls led to its temporary closure at the end of the Second World War. The school building was destroyed during an air raid in 1941 whilst the students were evacuated to Ely.

In 1958, a new centrally-located Jewish Free School opened in Camden Town to provide a religious and secular education for Jewish children throughout London. With the rapid expansion of the school it outgrew the Camden Road site and some ten years ago an alternative site was identified in Kingsbury, London Borough of Brent. Work on the new school began in 1998. The new JFS opened at the start of the academic year in 2002 and is now one of the top comprehensive schools in this country.

The school was fortunate to have Dame Ruth Robins as the prime mover in securing the new school site and masterminding its development: her determination, persuasive skills and sheer hard work ensured its successful completion. My initial visits to the site in 2001 required the wearing of hard hat and boots; the synagogue at this time was open to the sky and filled with scaffolding and building debris. Still, that first impression was one of spaciousness, with its monumental height and a mezzanine which promised superb viewing of the glass.

Concept

I was given a free hand in the design and felt immediately that the long narrow window openings were suggestive of trees. By chance I came across a 'Tree Cathedral' during a walk on Dunstable Downs and this left a great impression. It was created by Edmund Blyth in 1931 and planted as a memorial to friends lost in the Great War. I have always loved trees and explored this theme many times in different works (FIG. 1). What I now discovered was a range of references to trees within Jewish tradition and writings. In Kabbalistic teaching the tree represents a model for human behaviour: roots denote the fulfilment of good deeds and branches denote wisdom or intellectual pursuit and the two remain inextricably linked.

FIG. 1:
Tree of Life 1992.
Photograph by
Don Lawson.

> *The true meaning of life is to plant trees, under whose shade you do not expect to sit.*
> Nelson Henderson

This quotation echoes the famous Babylonian Talmudic story of Honi who asks the man planting a carob tree why he bothers to plant it if it takes seventy years to bear fruit. The man replies: 'I found this world provided with carob trees and as my forebears planted them for me, so will I plant for my offspring'. To plant a tree is to make a statement of hope and a commitment to the future: Abraham planted a tamarisk tree in Beersheba as an affirmation of his faith and today *Tu B'shvat*, the Jewish festival of trees, is marked by tree planting ceremonies in Israel.

> *A carob tree*
> *A fig tree*
> *An almond tree*
> *I stop my tears not easily*

Trees are also testaments to our past. While creating these designs I saw the film *Divided We Fall* set in wartime Czechoslovakia and I recall a poignant and haunting song from it: *'Ich shtey unter a bokserboym'* (I stood beneath a carob tree) written by the Yiddish poet Zhame Telesin. The destruction of European Jewry is only hinted at through allusions to trees, as memories of a vanished world.

The transience of our lives is portrayed in Window 8: 'Man is like a breath; his days are like a passing shadow' (Psalms 144:4). This theme again is echoed in the words of the Mishnah 'would that life were like the shadow cast by a tree, but it is like the shadow of a bird in flight'.

Design

My primary consideration in designing these windows was to attract and inspire the students who would be using the Synagogue for study and prayer. My initial designs (FIG. 2) were created in the heart of the countryside and took the form of collages and watercolours, which I repeatedly refined and reassembled to achieve the desired level of harmony and balance. The eleven lights form a semicircle, and are intended to be viewed from right to left as in the Hebrew language (FIG. 3). Passages from biblical texts were abbreviated to act as titles and to guide the viewer through my non-figurative imagery, which may at first seem inaccessible. The texts were taken from the *Tehilim* (*Psalms*), the *Mishnah* (part of the *Talmud*) and *Proverbs*. For the calligraphy, I chose a variation of the 'David' script based on the more free-flowing

'Dead Sea Scrolls' script. The 'David' script was also used for the school's motto: 'oreh ver yakar' (light and honour) which appears elsewhere in the school.

The windows viewed from right to left:

Heavens like a curtain	(Window 1)	104:2	*Psalms*
Clothed with glory	(Window 2)	104:1	*Psalms*
On the wings of the wind	(Window 3)	104:3	*Psalms*
And it took deep root	(Window 4)	80:10	*Psalms*
Planted by streams of water	(Window 5)	1:3	*Psalms*
A Tree of Life	(Window 6)	3:18	*Proverbs*
Like a cedar of Lebanon	(Window 7)	92:13	*Psalms*
Passing shadows	(Window 8)		*Aboth* iii:22
Like the palm tree	(Window 9)	92:13	*Psalms*
Full of sap and freshness	(Window 10)	92:15	*Psalms*
And all the trees shall sing	(Window 11)	96:12	*Psalms*

The windows are set over a metre apart but all are connected and sustained by the waters of Paradise, represented by blue glass at the base of each light. The water is a metaphor for spiritual nourishment and the trees personify a higher level of existence: 'He is like a tree planted by streams of water which yields its fruit in season whose foliage never fades and whatever it produces thrives' (Window 5).

The righteous are likened to a leafy olive tree (Window 10), firmly planted in the soil and flourishing, withstanding storms: 'even if all the winds of the world come and blow upon it, it cannot be stirred from its place' unlike the wicked man who is easily uprooted. The reference to an olive tree also has association with the olive leaf in the beak of the dove who returned to Noah after the storms of the Flood had subsided.

FIG. 2:
Detail of design
collage, 2001.

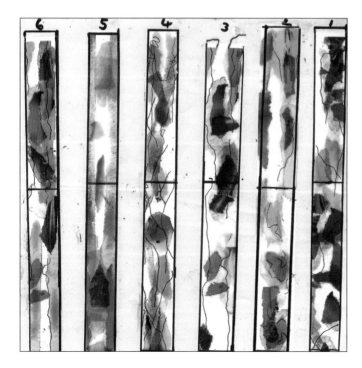

Colour

Colour was determined in part by the compass aspect of each window, by my response to the texts and more specifically by the position of the windows in relation to each other.

Every colour ought to encourage prayer.
Marc Chagall

Blue purple is referred to in the *Talmud* as the colour of heaven, and is a constant reminder to the Jew of G-d and his commandments. The Hebrew word *tekhelet* was the name of the dye used for one of the threads of the *tallit* (prayer shawl) and was purported to be derived from the *chilazon*, a sea creature which was believed to

FIG. 3:
Interior of JFS
Synagogue, 2002,
showing seven of
the eleven
windows.
Photograph by
Rosalind
Schogger.

surface only once every seventy years. A detail from the base of Window 1 shown here (FIG. 4) demonstrates the effect of layering and acid-etching to resemble thin layers of gauze or tulle. This is explored further in the next window where the acid etching resembles a microscopic view of cloth fibres (FIG. 8). This is the only panel with golden glass: the Hebrew word for glory *hadar* is also the name of the tree which bears the yellow citron fruit, one of the four species of plant used to celebrate *Succot* (FIG. 6).

By contrast, the large areas of clear sandblasted glass punctuated by smaller passages of colour in the third window, '*On the wings of the wind*' (FIG. 7), suggest the invisible air currents which permeate our atmosphere. The deeply-etched amber glass of window 4 (FIG. 10) appears more vivid in its position next to the almost monochrome effect of Window 3. The earth colours and root-like lines illustrate 'And it took deep root'. Joseph is compared to a fruitful vine which later became a symbol of Israel, appearing on the coins of the Maccabees and grapes (the fruit of the vine) are depicted overhanging the Temple.

Admired for its stature, the palm tree can grow up to thirty metres and is known to sometimes live for two hundred years and still produce fruit. Although an ancient people, the Jewish people are like the palm tree, retaining their vigour because their youth is constantly being renewed. Here in Window 9 (FIG. 5), a screen-printed resist simulates my original collage: the bark of the palm tree is synonymous with the bricks of the *Kotel* (the Western Wall of the Temple in Jerusalem).

The final panel (FIG. 9), with its south-westerly aspect bathed in afternoon and evening sunlight was designed to be the most uplifting. Inspired by a passage read on fast days which refers directly to the return from exile in Babylon, it is both a call for repentance and a promise of salvation: 'shout for joy, O mountains, O forests with all your trees!'. The words can be interpreted in two ways: that people will feel nature joining them in their expression of joy or, that a transformation will occur in nature itself: the barren mountains and hills will be filled with plentiful vegetation and trees will abound with fruit.

FIG. 4:
Detail window 1,
*Heavens Like a
Curtain*

FIG. 5:
Detail
window 9,
*Like the
Palm Tree*

FIG. 6:
Detail window 2,
Clothed with Glory

FIG. 7:
Detail window 3,
On the Wings of the Wind

FIG. 8:
Detail window 2,
*Clothed
with Glory*

FIG. 9:
Detail window
11, *And all the
trees shall sing*

The Torah (the Five Books of Moses) is considered in the Jewish religion to be the earthly equivalent to the original Tree of Life. The central window which carries this title (window 6, FIG. 11) faces the *bimah* (platform in front of the ark which contains the Scrolls of the Law) and has special significance as an embodiment of the wisdom, understanding and knowledge housed therein. The apparent simplicity of its design belies a subtle dialogue in amber, grey/blue and turquoise, its harmonies modulated to form a minor key, encouraging the viewer towards reflection.

FIG. 10:
Detail window 4,
And it Took
Deep Root

Materials and Techniques

The panels were made at Goddard & Gibbs Studios and were completed in June 2002. Lamberts flashed antique glass was used, with every piece either heavily etched (SEE PLATE 3, p. 119) or sandblasted. The antique glass was bonded to 4mm toughened float. There was a layer of 8mm laminated glass to the outside and a layer of 6mm toughened float to the inside. The text and painted lines were screen printed to the back of the 6mm inside toughened float. Each light was 6.30m high and 0.45m wide and was made up of three triple-glazed sealed units. There were thirty-three sealed units in total, each unit approximately two metres high. Both the Head Teacher and architect expressed a preference for bonding the glass which would allow for multiple layers and colour to flow unfettered by lead lines. As an adherent of leading I was conscious of the absence of the dialogue that should exist between glass and lead. For this reason I introduced painted lines to provide linear accents to the structure.

The rough etched surfaces reminiscent of ancient bark or eroded stone are a reminder of the past whilst the coloured areas floating in their own space are a statement of hope for the future.

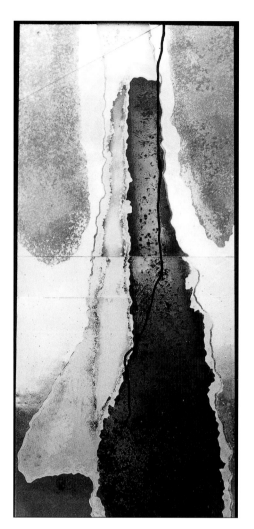

FIG. 11:
Detail of etched
surface of window
6, *It is a Tree
of Life*

*There's so much hate in the world: you have
to counteract it with loveliness.*

Stan Getz

Our youth is confronted with tragedy and
uncertainty on a daily basis and must somehow
make sense of this world. I wanted to create a place
which would be at once tranquil and uplifting, a
room for the soul. These windows have been
compared to layers of gauze – which takes me full
circle back to the essence and spontaneity of my
original collages and watercolours. I only hope I
have managed to achieve something of my original
aspiration: the transformation of heavily surface
worked glass into an atmosphere of weightlessness
and spirituality.

*Visits to the school synagogue are by
appointment only Monday to Friday. Please apply
in writing to: David Lerner, JFS School, The Mall,
Kenton, Harrow HA3 9TE.*

ACKNOWLEDGEMENTS
The success of this project was due entirely to my
having an outstanding team at Goddard and Gibbs.
Here I would like to acknowledge their huge input.
My thanks are due to Sharon McMullin, Chris
Madlin, Sophie Lister and Annie Ross for their
contribution to the acid etching and their superb
interpretative skills; to Ryan Roberts and Paul
Bradbury for the bonding process; to Brian Goddard
for screen-printing; to Zoe Angle for staining and
enamelling; to Laura Pes for her contribution to window 6; to Mick Welch in his
capacity as head of surface decoration and finally to Bernard Becker who co-ordinated
the project between Goddard & Gibbs, Jarvis and JFS. Calligraphy was by Ruth
Bruckner. The interior co-ordinator for JFS was Clemy Lazarus. All photographs with
the exception of FIGS. 1, 2 and 3 are by Michael Greisman.

Prizes and awards from the Worshipful Company of Glaziers and Painters of Glass: 2003

The excitement of designing a feature window for the foyer of a new Drama Centre at Chigwell School attracted forty-four entries to the 2003 Stevens Competition. Addressing the Prize-Giving Ceremony in the Garry Weston Library of Southwark Cathedral, Susie Bridges from the Arts Team, architects for the new building, described her conviction that a glass feature will give great life and focus to the foyer. The school intends that a commission will follow from the competition.

Ms Bridges served on the judging committee along with glass artists Harry Cardross, Amber Hiscott, Douglas Hogg, and John Patsalides. Speaking on behalf of the judges at the Prize-Giving, Douglas Hogg emphasised that there had been no preconceived ideas in the judges' minds of how the area should be treated. They had enjoyed looking at all the work very much and observed that the entries showed great engagement with the site and the project, as well as being of an overall high standard which had made their final selections quite difficult.

As always the work was required to be submitted under a pseudonym and judged anonymously. Each entrant had to submit a scale drawing of the design for the space, a statement of purpose and costing and a sample panel executed at full scale to show how they would take their design into glass.

Joint First Prize, the Brian Thomas Memorial Prize, was awarded to Denise Mt. Basso (FIG. 1), studying at Chelsea College of Art and Design, and Sun Ju Park (FIG. 2), a student at Central Saint Martins College of Art and Design. Lucy Batt, also studying at Chelsea College of Art and Design won Third Prize (FIG. 3). The entries from Helen Chick (FIG. 4), trainee at Holy Well Glass, and Robert Pratt McMachan (FIG. 5), studying at the Royal College of Art received Commendations. McMachan was also the first to be awarded the newly-established John Corkill Memorial Prize for Best Presentation.

The diversity of glass treatments evident in these winning submissions is representative of the range of imaginative approaches across the whole field of entries. Mt. Basso conceived a well-composed feature incorporating three layers suspended with a broad enough spacing between that the effect varied interestingly as one moved around it, while Park's multiply-etched flat mirror panel incorporated depth and movement through the reflectivity of the myriad tiny areas of unetched mirror. Batt's entry again utilised suspended layers, including metals and fabrics with a light-hearted reference to the theatre curtain as a theme. Chick's commended offering was created in traditionally assembled etched, painted and leaded glass with a suitably humorous treatment of figures forming a wheel. Pratt McMachan prepared a sandwich with calligraphy overlying reflective areas and a stacked series of media based images which was visually rich as well as apt to the drama centre setting.

The imaginative site, the strong responses to it from the entrants and the energy and dedication of the judges in considering each entry deeply, combined to make the Stevens Competition 2003 a particularly positive event.

Further awards were announced at the Prize-Giving Ceremony. Mike Lees, studying at North East Wales Institute, Wrexham, has won the Arthur and Helen Davis Travelling Scholarship, which will enable him to travel in Iceland, where he intends to meet contemporary artists and sketch and draw the dramatic landscape, a favoured influence in his own art work.

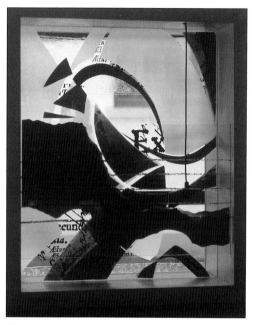

The Award for Excellence which enables the Awardee to undertake forty weeks of supported work placements in studios in the UK and abroad was awarded to Sigrid Blekastad who is just completing her BA (Hons) at Swansea Institute of Higher Education. This year, for the first time, it was possible to award three Ashton Hill Awards, each for ten week supported work placements in studios specialising in conservation. These will be undertaken by Helen Coyle, studying at Dudley College, Ruth Fisher, completing her BA (Hons) at Swansea Institute of Higher Education and Luke Wilkinson, completing his BA (Hons) at North East Wales Institute.

Adelle Corrin
Glass Information Officer
July 2003

FIG. 1

FIG. 2

FIG. 3

FIG. 4

FIG. 5

Portfolio of new work by Fellows and Associates 2002

FIG. 1

FIG. 2

Susan Ashworth AMGP

St Olave's Grammar School, Orpington, Kent
South Cloister, 20 panels, each 840 mm H x 420 mm W

The Millennium frieze stretches over the twenty upper panels of the glazed cloister. The theme is 'a young person's journey, confronting the ups and downs of the passage through school.' This is expressed in glass as progressing changeable weather through which cuts and dances a golden line, that streak of special stuff that carries one along. The weather, from dark obscure beginnings, reaches lightness in the rare prism of colour in the central panels. It contains the marks made on paper, some immature, some sophisticated and of differing legibility within the layers of paint.

1, 2.   Beginning: A, alpha and a simple tune from Leopold Mozart. Number sequences, i.e. prime, square, Fibonacci. Calculation of Pi.

3, 4.   'Tyger, tyger burning bright'... Why. OK (most used word world-wide).

5.   Spirit. Extracts from teachings of Sikh, Buddhist and Hindu religions. The Law given to Moses.

6, 7.   Algebra and co-ordinates.

8, 9.   Language. Without each other – nothing; with communication – everything.

10, 11.   Yes. Simple affirmation of a high day.

12, 13.   Science. Energy, nitrogen cycle, molecular structures, the double helix. (FIGS. 1, 2)

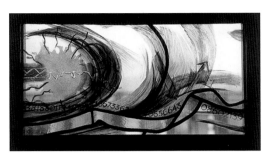

FIG. 3

FIG. 4

FIG. 5

14, 15.   Humanities. London transport
          implications. Global warming.
          Twentieth-century protest. (FIGS. 3, 4)

16.   Spirit. Essential tenets of Taoism,
          Islam, Christianity and Jainism.

17, 18.   Literature. Prologue from Chaucer's
          Canterbury Tales: the Pilgrims set
          out for Southwark 'the holy blissful
          martyr for to seek' (St Olave's was
          an ancient grammar school
          foundation in Southwark until
          1966). Shakespeare's *Sonnet no. 116*.
          (SEE DETAIL OF PANEL 17, FIG. 5)

19, 20.   Old and new technology. Hands and
          the internet with a nod to the earliest
          artist's hand in a cave painting at
          Pech Merle. Aristophanes's *Clouds*
          and a light-hearted spelling rhyme on
          weather. Winning and losing and
          onwards. One nil, one nil! Nil points.
          Eric Clapton's *Layla*. A winged arrow
          reaching for the stars. No closing
          with Z or Omega as this is the start
          not the end. Pi marches on, currently
          to fifty-seven billion places…

FIG. 6

Glenn Carter AMGP

St Mary and St John, Cambridgeshire (FIG. 6)
West-facing single quatrefoil
Painted and stained panel
depicting elements of local
topography.

St Mary, Horncastle, Lincolnshire
2-light window with typographical
inscription to Lord Tennyson.

St Matthew, Sutton Bridge, Lincolnshire
3-light west-facing window on the
theme of 'Repent and be Baptised'.

St Nicholas, Skirbeck, Lincolnshire
2-light west-facing window,
dedicated to the Barkham family
and depicting elements of the life
of St Leonard, to whom the oldest
hospital in Boston is dedicated.

All Saints, Eagle, Lincolnshire
Single east-facing light depicting a
Lily with the word 'Resurgam' at
the base of the panel.

Andrew Taylor AMGP

St George's Church, Altrincham, Manchester
For a window on the theme of Word and Sacrament, the start of St John's Gospel
was taken. The left-hand light illustrates John 1:1, 'In the beginning was the Word,
and the Word was God', while the right-hand light illustrates John 1:14 'The Word
was made flesh, and dwelt among us.'

For 'Sacrament', a Chalice and Host is shown on the right, in balance, a Bible
is set in the left. The colours are darker on the left, as in the 'Beginning', but more
light flows through on the right, indicating our enlightened awareness in the passing
of time. The blue background and shading marks suggest the Waters of Baptism.
Lightning comes from above, piercing the dark colours and striking the *Bible*, this
then penetrates the next panel, where the shaft of light comes to rest on the word 'Us'.

Employing streaky glass and flashed glass, the techniques of paint, silver stain
and acid etching were used to create the letters to bring out a somewhat ambiguous
effect – the words may not be immediately obvious but will become clearer as one
contemplates the window.

Mel Howse AMGP

St Wilfred's Hospice, Chichester
(DETAIL, FIG. 7)
The windows are located in the newly-built chapel, which is designed to be multi-faith. The windows face north and have a total of 6 square metres. The theme of the design draws on the Hospice's desire to create a 'Haven of Peace' and conveys the message of life moving forward.

Painter's Hall, City of London
(FIG. 8)
The window was installed in celebration of the Quincentenary of the Worshipful Company of Painter-Stainers and is located in the principal window in the Livery Hall. It displays the dynamic symbol of the phoenix rising from the flames. This represents the survival of the Company and its hall through fires and wars over the centuries. A phoenix also features on the Company's own Coat of Arms.

FIG. 7

FIG. 8

FIG. 9

Gareth Morgan AMGP

West windows, Christchurch, Quinton
In memory of Mr Lawson Darby and
Mrs Shirley Darby
Central lancet 2730 mm x 717 mm
Roundels 1103 mm in diameter

FIG. 10

The theme given for the central lancet was Charity
or Love. I was asked to make the Cross the central
feature of the window as a symbol of love and to use
certain colours and flowers in memory of Mrs Darby.
    Looking for a visual context which would allow me
to combine these requirements, I found my inspiration in the
Song of Solomon, Chapter 4, verses 12-15. This book of the
Bible speaks of gardens and flowers; it is also a poetic expression of
the joy of human love and, on a spiritual level, has been interpreted as a
picture of Christ's love for the Church. Thus I have grouped patterns from flowers

FIG. 11

taken from the *Song of Solomon*
around a stylised cross (DETAIL, FIG.
9). Linked to various flowers are
vignettes containing representations
of incidents from the life of Christ
which are indicative of love.
    I have related the roundels to
the central lancet by designs which
also use flowers and figure groups.
As a symbol of Faith, in the left-hand
roundel (FIG. 10), I have chosen to
portray the testing of Abraham's
faith in the call to sacrifice Isaac
(*Genesis*, Chapter 22, verses 1-13
and *Hebrews*, Chapter 11, verse 17).
In the small circle I have placed a
stylised mustard seed, and expanding
from this, mustard pods and flowers,
recalling Christ's words on faith in
Matthew, Chapter 13, verses 31-32.
The strong tree shape which
overshadows the scene of sacrifice is
derived from the same source.
    In the right-hand roundel, to
symbolise Hope, I have chosen to
represent the Annunciation (DETAIL,
FIG. 11), thinking of Christ as 'the
hope of nations'. I have surrounded
the scene with lilies – traditionally
associated with Mary and in a
smaller circle, top right, I have placed
a 'window', looking forward to the
Nativity with Christ's 'natal star'.

FIG. 12

Jude Tarrant
AMGP

Holy Cross Church, Chiseldon, Wiltshire
(FIG. 12)
3-light Millennium window with tracery, on south side nearest west end
1550 x 1550 mm
Acided, painted, stained antique glass

The left-hand light describes Christ's life from the Annunciation (illustrated by the lily), to the calling of the Disciples (the netted fish, 'fishers of men'), and the Last Supper (bread and wine), to the Crucifixion (Calvary's three crosses). His thirty-three years are measured by circles and marks in red on the left-hand border. The bottom edge of the three panels alludes to a timeline.

The central panel begins with the spread of Christian teachings by St Paul's conversion on the road to Damascus. Constantine Christianised the Roman Empire and his vision of the cross and the Christ sign are shown. Teachings are brought to England by St Augustine. The lower section shows the familiar landscape of Chiseldon's Ridgeway and Liddington Castle, with the quill and crown of Wessex king and scholar Alfred the Great, and the founding of Holy Cross church in 903.

The right-hand panel continues with the first mechanical printing of the Bible, the Reformation and *The Book of Common Prayer*, and concludes with the Ordination of Women Priests in our own time. Installed December 2000 and dedicated by the Bishop of Ramsbury.

Blake Lapthorn Solicitors, Southampton
Five contemporary windows for the firm's new headquarters in Southampton.

Chandler's Ford Infant School, Hampshire County Council
A six-panel window incorporating children's paintings about their school.

Goldsmith Infant School, Portsmouth
A memorial window to a pupil.

Alan Younger FMGP

St Mary the Virgin, Enville, Staffordshire
2-light and tracery window on the north wall of the nave. Theme: 'The Sower'

Emma Butler Cole Aiken AMGP

Nativity Window, Longforgan Parish Church, Perthshire
(FIG. 13)
The window was the gift of Dr and Mrs Prain in
appreciation of their family's historical connections and
long involvement with this church. Longforgan is a small
town near Dundee, historically associated with farming
(represented here by the patchwork of fields) and weaving
(the strip of partially woven cloth).

   This is a simple Nativity scene with a shepherd peering
curiously at the Christ Child. At the top is the Natal star
with the wise men's gifts at the base. Touches of red
symbolise the Crucifixion. The larger faces can represent
several things. One interpretation is Joseph looking in from
the left, with the lower face a second look at Mary as she
'ponders these things in her heart'. Another is different
peoples' reactions to Christ both at the time of his birth and
today. One embraces Christ – his glory is reflected in their
face; the other turns away mystified or unbelieving. The
window unashamedly asks the congregation or casual
observer alike: 'what do you think? What is Jesus to you?'

Caroline Benyon FMGP

Our Lady and St Peter, Leatherhead, Surrey
2-light window, south transept.
36 in x 15 in

The subject is the Baptism of Christ. Three years ago
I added a 2-light north window to the nave glazing scheme
established by Paul Woodroffe in the 1920s. This new
window now completes the glazing in the body of the
church and balances the light. Both windows are rich with Catholic symbolism and
are the result of hours of 'discussion', the main topic being what to leave out rather
than what to include.

FIG. 13

Christ Church, Shooters Hill, London
Single light, north side
10 ft 6 in x 30 in
The subject is St Francis, based on the Canticle of St Francis.

St Simon Zelotes, Chelsea, London
3-light east window with tracery in Lady Chapel
Outer lights 9 ft x 12 in, centre light 9 ft 6 in x 5 in

3 lancet lights on north side of chapel, each 8 ft x10 ins
(SEE BACK COVER)

The subject of the Lady Chapel East window is the Nativity, with an emphasis on
Mother and Child. Each of the lancet lights has one of the three kings positioned
centrally and facing eastwards. All the figures are set against quarry backgrounds
cut from antique sheets and slabs, providing much-needed light to a gloomy interior.

BSMGP Fellows and Associates in 2002

Fellows

Keith Barley
Rodney Bender
Caroline Benyon
Susan Bradbury
Roy Coomber
Mike Davis
Alfred Fisher
Jane Gray
Rosalind Grimshaw
John Hayward
Douglas Hogg

Kuni Kajiwara
John Lawson
Lawrence Lee
Paul Lucky
Shona McInnes
Keith New
Joseph Nuttgens
Paul Quail
Geoffrey Robinson
Paul San Casciani
Beverley Shore Bennett

Sebastian Strobl
Caroline Swash
Christopher Wallis
Sep Waugh
Alan Younger
Klaus Zimmer

Honorary Fellows

Margaret Bell
Nicola Gordon Bowe
Sarah Brown

Peter Cormack
Martin Harrison

BSMGP Associates

Emma Butler Cole Aiken
Peter Archer
Susan Ashworth
Jean Bailey
Alan Baker
Jennifer Bayliss
Peter Berry
Pippa Blackall
Christine Boyce
Philip Broome
Jane Campbell
Linda Cannon
Harry Cardross
Glenn Carter
Gerald Coles
Adelle Corrin
David Cowan
Alan Davis

David Esler
Eric Fellows
Ginger Ferrell
Laura Gilroy
Judy Hill
Robert Holloway
Mel Howse
Derek Hunt
Andrew Johnson
Nicola Kantorowicz
Samuel Kelly
Ruth Kersley
Michael Lassen
Meg Lawrence
Deborah Lowe
Deanne Mangold
Lydia Marouf
Patrick Martin

Gerald Miller
Roland Mitton
Gareth Morgan
Arthur Pearce
Simon Ratcliffe
Kathy Shaw
Ann Smyth
Ann Sotheran
Lou Spencer
Colin Stokes
Jude Tarrant
Andrew Taylor
Ruth Taylor Jacobson
Helen Whittaker
Trevor Wiffen
Sachiko Yamamoto

Craft Associates

Mark Bambrough
Patrick Costeloe
Tracy Smith

Technical Inquiry

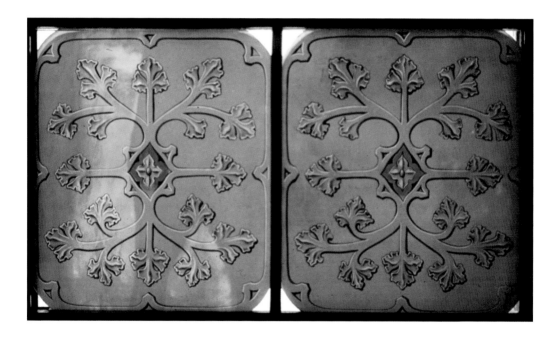

Sebastian Strobl and Leonie Seliger

Learning by doing: the restoration of the Indian Kiosk glazing at Shuttleworth, Bedfordshire

The Task
Sebastian Strobl

It may be the privilege of the head of a studio to accept challenges on behalf of colleagues who will have to bear the brunt of the consequences. It may even be that such acceptance is one of the more painful ways to progress and to further our knowledge. Be that as it may, now that we have gone through such a challenge, neither my colleague in charge of the project nor I might have agreed to go into it in the first place, but I am glad that we did, more for our profession's sake than for our studio's. But let me start from the beginning...

The Shuttleworth Estate at Old Warden in Bedfordshire looks back on almost 200 years of creative but little recorded history. Bought toward the end of the seventeenth century by the Ongley family, the estate appears to have accommodated a garden of some note by at least the end of the eighteenth century. The Swiss Garden – as this particular part of the estate is now known – was probably the work of the third Lord Ongley, who inherited the property in 1814.

The garden has an intricate network of paths that wind their way along avenues, through shrubbery and trees, over decorative iron bridges, across ponds and beneath rose arbours. Dotted about are exotic follies – picturesque buildings, urns, statues, a grotto with a fernery, a tiny thatched Swiss cottage and, located at the top of a mount, the so-called Indian Kiosk, the glazing of which is the subject of this article (FIG. 1).

In 1872, the property was sold to a Lincolnshire man, Joseph Shuttleworth, who pulled the old estate house down and had the gothic-style Shuttleworth mansion built in its place. The garden received some remodelling at the same time. Two of the four surviving main panels of the Kiosk glazing (panels L18 and L20, FIG. 2), which are so evidently of a later Victorian period than the original panels (L19 and L21), may be part of a restoration campaign contemporary with this remodelling.

When the last heir of the family, Richard Shuttleworth, was killed in a plane crash in 1939, his mother formed a trust to administer the entire estate, which by that time already included a notable collection of items relating to historic transport. Unfortunately, the trust failed to fulfil its obligations towards the upkeep of the garden and it was left to deteriorate for almost forty years. Bedfordshire County Council agreed in 1976 to take over the management of the garden and to restore it, and it was finally opened to the public in 1981.

Before the opening, however, the Kiosk was to be thoroughly restored, a project which also included its glazing. In early 1980, the late Francis Skeat received instructions to restore the stained glass. Skeat opted for a complete replacement of all damaged or missing glass, a method which was common practice at the time, although it would inevitably lead to substantial loss of historic material. It is therefore regrettable that no written records have survived, in particular since no pre-restoration photographs have so far come to light which would help to explain why Skeat was forced to replace seventeen out of twenty-one main panels with new glass.

Thus far, only two of Skeat's letters have been discovered, with only one reference to the original glass. In a letter dated 30 May 1980,[1] he mentions his drawings and 'the bits of the original glass', now disappeared. The letters also reveal the problems encountered in manufacturing the replacement glass and provide a hint as to why Skeat's efforts to restore the Kiosk to its former glory had been obliterated by the elements within a short period of time. In an earlier letter, dated 14 March 1980,[2] he identifies the glass as being etched, a conclusion we now consider unlikely. More importantly, in the second letter he admits to difficulties with staining the glass. These problems clearly proved insurmountable, and a decision was made to abandon the correct procedure of staining glass in favour of using cold paint – a non-fired and short-lived substitute.

Whether this happened with the blessing of Bedfordshire County Council, as the client ultimately responsible for the project, is unclear. Skeat was under tremendous pressure to have the glass installed by mid-1980 and he may have sought permission to resort to this rather unconventional method. He must have been aware, however, of the high risk of failure in using unfired material. Indeed, there are reports that most of the golden-orange pigments, shining bright on the day of installation, had disappeared within months of the garden's reopening.[3] A few years later, little remained of the cold paint – most pronounced in Panel L12 – rendering the glazing a mere shadow of its former glory.

Looking at the Kiosk as it appeared in December 2001, it was not surprising that the Friends of the Swiss Garden wished to restore the glazing. I was asked to prepare a survey of the glass, to provide an opinion on possible ways forward and to submit a quote for the restoration of the glazing. The survey underpinned the conclusion drawn by the Friends from the scarce amount of information available. It was obvious that the majority of the glass (panels L1 to L17) had been replaced in 1980 by Francis Skeat, with only four major panels (L18 to L21) and all smaller inserts (S1 to S32) left *in situ* (FIGS. 1, 2). Since that time, hardly any further damage had occurred. All glass except S5 was undamaged and surrounded by a border of dark-blue glass. The panels were set with putty into the rebate of what I originally thought was a cast iron frame, which although suffering some deterioration, did not pose danger to the panels themselves.

In fact, in terms of material survival, I was able to describe the glazing and its framework as being in a satisfactory condition. However, the stained glass itself indubitably failed to function in visual terms, and a revisit of the 1980 restoration was imperative if the Kiosk was to regain its rightful place within the ensemble of the garden. Thus it was agreed to remove and replace the glass inserted by Skeat,

FIG. 1:
The Indian Kiosk, Shuttleworth, before restoration.

providing that appropriate techniques could be found to recreate or at least to approximate the original manufacturing process, to guarantee a long-lasting satisfactory solution. My colleague in the studio, Léonie Seliger, carried out some research and trials to find the right base glass and mix of silver stain and flux. When, perhaps naïvely, we were confident that our studio could indeed create a good match, we were given the go-ahead for the project.

The agreed terms were to replace only the Skeat glass. The 1872 restorations (L18 and L20), even though inconsistent with the original glass, are of excellent craftsmanship and in contrast to the later restoration, represented a valuable part of the history of the Kiosk. Admittedly, such a differentiation between levels of quality in former restoration campaigns could be considered unacceptably subjective and is normally to be avoided, but in this case we considered our position to be fully justifiable.

The actual removal of the glass, however, revealed further questions – the framework holding the panels was not of delicately constructed cast iron, as I had previously assumed. Instead it consisted of a tinned metal strip, slotted into the groove of a triangular-shaped lead came and soldered firmly to the latter to provide a rebate for the glass (FIG. 3). Wherever such a strip met another to form the intricate framework, the metal and lead were accurately tapered in elongated mitres and soldered neatly together, retaining its fine profile (FIG. 4). The framework thus produced would take the panels like any glazing frame, with putty used to hold the panels in place rather than sealing the window (FIG. 5).

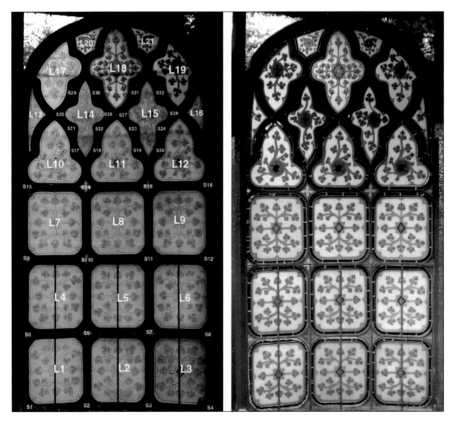

FIG. 2:
Glazing of the Indian Kiosk, left numbering, immediately following restoration.

The frame was still moderately stable after the removal of the panels and therefore remained untouched during the project. The question nevertheless remained why a lead frame was used when an iron frame could have delivered greater stability. One possible answer may be the fact that the base frame, made of timber and holding the lead frame, is set on hinges and was clearly intended to open. During my initial survey, I had not fully considered this fact, assuming it was for ease of removal should it ever prove necessary.

When pointing out the arrangements to those who look after the Swiss Garden, they mentioned the former existence of a secret walkway on a 'higher level' in the grounds of the park. And indeed, there is a revealing paragraph in Mrs Shuttleworth's short monograph on the garden, where she writes: 'Lord Ongley had platforms in the trees... and he used to walk about, it is said, to hear what people said about him walking below... . He entered by the stained glass door in the little summer-house...' There are no obvious remains of this secret walkway, but it is clear from this account that Lord Ongley embarked on his intelligence gathering from the Indian Kiosk, and that 'our' window had in fact once been a door, and had therefore to be as lightweight as possible.

FIG. 3:
Cross-section of metal strip/lead came.

Be that as it may, the use of this particular framing technique may have brought us closer to solving the riddle of the maker of the stained glass. It is by no means a rare technique, as many Georgian fanlights have been glazed in this way. However, so far I had come across such frames only twice in church windows, and more specifically, only once in stained glass. The first example was a window with quarry glazing from a church in Northern Ireland, which had been extensively damaged during a storm. I retained a sample of the strip (SEE FIG. 3), but never discovered its origin. This was a disappointing dead end, but a second window, which I saw two years later, provided more information. The East window of the former church of the Holy Trinity in Tunbridge Wells displays the same technique, this time in a figurative depiction of the Four Evangelists. The church is now an arts centre and the window is covered up, however an image in Martin Harrison's *Victorian Stained Glass* shows the glass in all its splendour. In his book, Harrison dated the window to 1839 and attributed it to Joseph Hale Miller (1777-1842), one of the few outstanding pre-Victorian pioneers of the revival of medieval stained glass techniques. However, in a later addendum, he re-attributed the window to William Miller, son (?) of Joseph Hale Miller, or to a possible collaboration between the two.

Not only is the framing technique the same as the one applied in the Indian Kiosk, but the painting technique is similar too. I have yet to revisit the Trinity Arts Centre, but if my memory serves me correctly, the background quarries were produced using the same process of matting and staining, albeit in much smaller dimensions. The date and technique would thus fit, so perhaps in the Swiss Garden we are looking at another window which could be attributed to one or both of the Millers. I am now convinced more than ever that we are. Without final proof, however, I am still on the hunt for further examples of his work. Is there anybody out there who can help?

The Solution
Léonie Seliger

In 2002 I was shown a photograph of the surviving original glazing in the Indian Kiosk at Old Warden (SEE FIG. 1). The prospective client wanted to ascertain whether it would be possible to produce an acceptable match to the original glazing. Even from the photograph it was obvious that this was high quality Regency glass painting, with several pigment layers on the front and silver stain on the reverse.

The client's particular concern was whether it would be possible to reproduce the depth of the silver stain in the originals. This concern was born from the experience of the last attempt at restoration in 1980, when the cold paints had virtually disappeared within months of the installation. Furthermore, an earlier restoration in the 1870s had clearly encountered a similar problem; two large pieces in the tracery (L18 and L20) dating from this campaign, although executed in fired stain and thus permanent, are far lighter in colour.[4]

Initially, using only the photograph as reference, I reproduced one of the smaller pieces (L21), using *Johnson and Matthey's 42 H 1005* amber stain – the strongest stain I had available.[5] The result was encouraging. However, things always look easy on a photograph and the problems only started when all the panels were removed to the studio, first by choosing the right glass.

The original glass was very thin, only about 1.5mm, but this in itself is quite usual for Regency glass. It may, however, explain why so little of it survives today. Whilst such thin glass is still available, its use was rejected; firstly, the modern glass does not take silver stain well enough to reproduce the original tone and secondly it would be very vulnerable in such a public place. Furthermore, the original glass showed very faint concentric curved lines in its surface, indicating crown glass, a glass-type no longer made to the quality required. Although the use of a mouth-blown glass would have been preferable, none of the glasses I tested (amongst them *St. Just Cordelé* and *Lamberts Goethe Glas*) accepted stain well enough or evenly enough.

In response to this problem, I employed instead modern 3mm thick float glass, which has excellent staining qualities. It is produced by floating molten glass on a bath of molten tin. The surface of the glass that was in contact with the tin takes silver stain extremely well and evenly. The difference between the two sides can only faintly be seen in ultraviolet light, so keeping the individual pieces the right way up while cutting them is very important.

Painting could now begin. A close examination of the original showed that it had been painted in several stages:

FIG. 4:
Detail of
framework.

1. An initial dark brown trace-line defining the edges of the floral ornament was applied and fired.

2. A thin but dense layer of opaque white enamel was applied all over.

3. The shading of the leaves was added, employing brown glass paint bound in oil.

4. Highlights on the leaves and alongside the edges were picked out using quills and scrubs.

5. The glass was fired for a second time.

6. The silver stain was applied to the reverse side and fired for the final time.

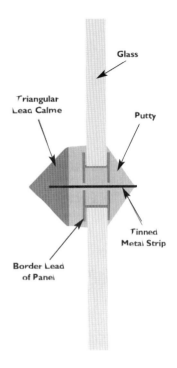

FIG. 5:
Diagram of
cross-section.

I was able to match the tracing and shading colours from commercially available paints (*Reusche Bistre Brown* and *Deancraft 3988* respectively). *Johnson and Matthey's 42 H 1005* amber stain mixed with 25% copper sulphate gave a good colour for the stain.

However, the white enamel, used extensively in the Regency period, proved difficult to match. A recipe from 1827 for 'white in imitation of ground glass' suggests mixing three parts of flux with one part of white tin oxide and then sprinkling it through a sieve from a great height onto the oiled glass surface. This does indeed work, but results in an even coverage of not just the glass, but also the painter and half the workshop, with a very fine toxic dust, unacceptable for health and safety reasons. Moreover, since the shading of the leaves had to be done in oil onto the unfired white enamel, the enamel had to be bound in a different medium to prevent mixing of the two layers. Thus the enamel was mixed with water and matted onto the surface using a badger brush.

Reproducing the white enamel was complicated. The original was surprisingly dull in transmitted as well as in reflected light. At the same time it was extremely dense, a very important quality to copy, as the wire guard on the exterior of the window would otherwise shine through. Starting with the 1827 recipe of a mixture of tin oxide and flux, I progressed through numerous tests with commercially available enamels, as well as a plethora of flux and tin oxide and/or titanium oxide combinations. Some enamels approached the colour, but proved much too transparent. Increasing the thickness of application or adding metal oxide to increase density resulted in far too white an appearance.

Finally, a mixture of 4 parts of *Johnson and Matthey's flux 44C2* combined with 4 parts of aluminium oxide and 1 part white titanium oxide produced an acceptable result. Moreover, this mixture proved easy to apply evenly, with no need even for the addition of gum arabic to provide sufficient resistance to the application of the oil shading.

After covering each piece with the white enamel and allowing it to dry thoroughly, the entire surface was covered with oil to allow for the shading to be added without tidemarks appearing. The shading technique is one more commonly associated with porcelain decoration, in which only one side of a flat brush is dipped into the paint. The brush strokes are thus already shaded from dark to light, and a light softening with a squirrel brush smoothes the appearance even further (FIG. 6). A variety of oils was tried. The best results were achieved with clove oil, initially purchased from the local aromatherapy shop. However, after working on the first tests for four hours and nearly fainting from its therapeutic effects, I wisely switched to rectified oil of clove from *Kremer Pigmente*.

While this was easy to work with, it had the unfortunate tendency to produce large circular crystallisations on drying, which remained very visible even after firing. In order to prevent this, the highlights were picked out of the still moist surface and the glass fired immediately.

The original method of application of the silver stain remains a mystery to me. No brush marks were visible, indicating it was painted only onto the floral ornament. However, close examination revealed that the stain may have been applied over a masking medium, which had then been removed, either before or after firing. I tried masking off the white areas with masking fluid and with thin *Fablon* and then badgering stain over the whole piece. Both masks had to be removed before firing, producing static electricity. This resulted in extensive coverage of the white areas with tiny flakes of dry stain dislodged from the masking material. Despite careful cleaning, there were always pale yellow smudges in the white areas after firing. Sometimes the ability of glass to take stain well can become a curse! Finally, I used this method only on the interior surface, where the centre of the design was stained both on the outside and on the inside. I also experimented painting the white areas with ground chalk mixed with water and gum. The stain, this time mixed with oil, was again badgered over the whole glass surface. The glass was then fired, and the chalk removed after firing. Although this technique works very well with paint, the stain penetrated the chalk layer and stained the white areas as well. All methods had another major drawback: along the edges of all the different masking media the stain either accumulated or in the case of the chalk was absorbed, leading to a visible edge to the stained area, a characteristic not evident in the original. I now think that the stain may have originally been printed onto the glass.[6]

A possible workable alternative was to cover the whole surface evenly with stain, and after firing, to etch away those areas intended to be white. In order to shield the interior decoration from the effects of the acid, it was covered with *Fablon*, and the edges painted with molten beeswax to prevent seepage.

However, a new problem was to emerge: all my stain tests employed unpainted and unfired glass. Firing had an unsuspected effect on the tin surface of the float glass: any air that came in contact with the surface during firing changed its ability to take stain. As the tin surface was placed onto the kiln bed during the

first two firings, only small portions of it hovered above the very slightly uneven kiln bed. This was enough to oxidise the surface, resulting in streaks of lighter yellow cutting through the otherwise perfectly even orange (SEE PLATE 4, p. 141). Fingerprints, invisible before firing, changed the surface in a similar way.

The remedy was to start again, and clean each piece of glass with something bordering on compulsive obsession before each firing. In addition, the individual pieces were placed in the kiln on thick beds of soft whiting and then pressed down firmly to prevent air getting underneath.

You may ask, why not fire the stain first, and then add the internal decoration? The answer is simply that the stain had to be fired at 520° C, while the internal decoration was fired at 640°C. Refiring the stain at a higher temperature bleached it from rich orange to yellow.

The size of the individual pieces (310 x 360mm) meant that only two or three fitted into our kiln each firing, a very slow cooling process essential to avoid stress forming in the glass, allowed only one firing per day.

It was all worth it, though. With the colour scheme of its secret door restored, the Indian Kiosk has regained its oriental splendour. What was previously a disappointing white expanse is once again a pleasure to behold. And interestingly, since the door faces north, the best place to see it from would have been the raised walkway, now disappeared, of the third Lord Ongley!

FURTHER READING
Mark Bambrough, 'On white enamels: "The Alternative Veil"', *Stained Glass, Newsletter of the BSMGP* 1 (1996): 13-15.

ACKNOWLEDGEMENTS
With thanks to Keith Barley, who made available to me *The Decorative Painter's And Glazier's Guide*, Nathaniel Whittock (1827).

NOTES

[1]   Letter to Alan [no surname], now held in Bedford Public Record Office.

[2]   Letter to Alan [no surname], now held in Bedford Public Record Office.

[3]   Information received from the Rev. Gabriela Thau.

[4]   Reproducing the flat orange and ruby stain found on Regency glass is difficult today mainly because Kelp glass is no longer manufactured. Basically, with Kelp glass you could fire the stain several times until it became a deep ruby colour. See 'A Glossary of 19th and 20th Century Glass Terms for Stained Glass' published in the BSMGP's *Stained Glass Magazine* (1995): p. 7, which states: '...the use of wood ash was prohibited in this country towards the end of the 16th century, and 'Kelp' ash was introduced as an alternative source of alkali. This was made by burning various species of seaweed... . Kelp glass had extraordinarily good staining power. It absorbed silver stain readily on firing and the compound which first forms deposits the silver gradually on further heating, a rich orange stain being developed, which repeated firing can deepen to a red approximating to that of a ruby pot metal...'. The stain on glass became lighter because the glass was made using wood ash instead of kelp ash. Information by courtesy of Caroline and Tony Benyon.

[5]   Johnson and Matthey have now discontinued 42 H 1005 and have replaced it with 42 H 1006. I am told the two are identical.

[6]   Patents were also taken out at the beginning of the nineteenth century on various methods of 'printing' silver stain onto Kelp glass in ways that did not require the use of a brush. Information by courtesy of Caroline and Tony Benyon.

Reports,
Reviews
and
Obituaries

Helen Dunstan

Highlights from the auction rooms

PLATE 5: *(overleaf)*

October 9th, 2002, Sotheby's, Bond Street, saw the start of the most important and successful sale in any fine or decorative arts field over the last twelve months. The statistic 91.54% sold by value is without doubt a rarity, especially in the unstable market that we have all witnessed during the past year. 'The Beck Collection of German Expressionist and Modern Art' was the legacy of two and a half generations of a family's passionate and inspired relationship with the artistic and social fabric of their country. Founded by Paul Beck (1887-1949), his dedicated and often dangerous acquisitions of 'degenerate art' as an enemy of the state under Nazi Germany formed the basis of one of the most highly regarded private collections of early twentieth-century German art in the world.

World record prices for artists lay in tatters as US and European private buyers snapped up works entirely fresh to the market, the majority having been purchased directly from the artists or their estates. In the first session Lot 2 was a rare oil painting on glass by Wassily Kandinsky (1866-1944), entitled *Reiter und Apfelpfluckerin* (*Rider and Woman Picking Apples,* 1911). Acquired by Dr Helmut Beck, son of Paul, in 1949 from Fraziska Dengler (the artist's housekeeper) via the Galerie Gunther Franke, Munich, this work was one of the last of a series of 'primitive art' paintings on glass that Kandinsky executed in March 1911, which had remained in private hands. The majority are now held in major museum collections in Germany such as the Stadtische Galerie in the Lenbachhaus, Munich. The work reflects the artist's keen interest in the ancient folk tradition of *Hinterglasmalerei* (behind glass painting) that he discovered in 1908 on a trip to Murnau in Southern Bavaria. This was a medium he was to exploit time and again, returning to it as late as 1936 in *Formes en Tension*, now in the collection of the Musée National d'Art Moderne, Centre Georges Pompidou, Paris. The glass painting considerably exceeded its estimate at €468,650 (£293,870) against €180,000-€250,000.

Session three of the sale included two *glasfenster* (stained glass windows). The catalogue illustrates Paul and Margaret Beck in their Stuttgart home seated in front of the central section of Adolf Holzel's stained glass window for the Stuttgart Rathaus, which they acquired and had built into their own house. Purchased in 1937 from the estate of Holzel (1853-1934), Lot 363 sold at the top end of the estimate €40,000-€50,000 for €50,190 (£31,368.75). This was one example of many works by the Stuttgart artist included in the sale, which had never been publicly viewed before: some were originally acquired as offerings to Paul Beck in exchange for the installation of a central heating system in the artist's home! (the Beck family ran a central heating firm in interwar Stuttgart). Lot 362 was the other example of stained glass included in this sale. By the artist Ida Kerkovius (1879-1970), her work was fittingly sold alongside that of her mentor Holzel, whose colour concepts she strove to develop and advance. Her panel sold at the reserve for €16,730 (£10,456) against an estimate of €20,000-€30,000.

At the end of October, this time at Bonhams, Bond Street, a sale was held entitled 'The 19th Century and Decorative Sale, including a Private Collection of Art Bronze'. Lot 141 was a decorative but uninspiring panel of late nineteenth-century glass portraying St Raphael the Archangel that sold below an estimate of £1,200 - £1,500 for £1,205. The following day, the 30th, an interesting little panel of seemingly German nineteenth-century stained glass, depicting a scholar engrossed in his books (FIG. 1), sold in an auction of scientific instruments for

£529, double its estimate of £100 - £200. Earlier that day at the same location, Sotheby's Olympia, in 'Masterpieces from the Time Museum', Lot 17, a rare example of a seventeenth-century European painted glass sundial was sold. Iconography of time, the zodiacs and the seasons was accompanied by Jesuit symbolism and two mottoes: the first from Virgil, Georgics III, 284-5: FVGIT IRREPARABILE TEMPVS (time passes never to be retrieved), and the second: DICO LVCIDAS TACEO NVBILAS (in the light I speak, in cloud I keep silence). A charming little panel, it is a rather miraculous survivor from a tradition of stained and painted glass sundials which first evolved in Germany in the sixteenth century. This lot sold under an estimate of £3,000-£4,000 for £2,115.

FIG. 1

Sotheby's Olympia 'Decorative Arts and Design from 1870', held on 7 November, contained two lots of rather uninspiring stained glass. Lot 303 was a late nineteenth-century Arts and Crafts panel of an angel, after designs by Sir Edward Coley Burne-Jones for his *Nativity* window in Birmingham Cathedral, completed in 1887. This sold for £940 against an estimate of £800 - £1200. The second lot, 306, consisted of twelve late nineteenth-century panels bearing the civic arms and mottoes of various British cities, towns and boroughs including Leeds, Chelsea and Newcastle Upon Tyne. They sold against the bottom of their estimate of £2,000-£3,000 for £2,350.

At Christie's South Kensington on 13 November, in the 'Oak, Country Furniture, Folk Art, Works of Art and Sculpture Sale', Lot 75, a pair of attractive panels (late 19th-/early 20th- century?), depicting scenes of chivalry (SEE FIG. 4) sold at double their estimate of £300-£500, for £1058. Lot 76, a Continental panel dated 1539, decorated with landscape scenes above a central armorial set into later glass, sold for £1528 against £500-£800. On the 27th in the same sale room, the 'English and Continental Furniture, Tapestries and Works of Art' sale included Lot 269, a somewhat over-estimated group of four Victorian Biblical figures reputedly from Hockwold Hall, a Tudor Manor House on the Cambridgeshire/Suffolk border, which went unsold against a fairly ambitious estimate of £7,000-£10,000.

The best examples of stained glass to be found at Bonhams, Bond Street, this year were in the 'European Works of Art' sale on 10 December. Lot 185, a set of three stained glass composition panels generated considerable interest: formerly belonging to a deceased collector who had pieced together at the beginning of the last century numerous early fragments of armorials, Romayne heads, flowers and fauna, they reached £4,099 against an estimate of £600-£800. Lot 186, catalogued as a sixteenth-century Flemish leaded glass panel of the Madonna and Child was unsold against an estimate of £600-£800 but sold after the sale for £602.

The Priory sale held by Dreweatt Neate on 14 January 2003 at Donnington Priory included an Aesthetic Movement panel of glass depicting a riverside scene; a heron catching fish amongst the pebbles and reeds, an attractive subject in a

FIG. 2

rather unfortunate dull palette. This lot had previously been unsold in a Decorative Arts sale on 27 November but did find a buyer in this sale, selling against the reserve at £626.

The year 2003 however really began with François De La Vaissière, who held his specialist stained glass sale with Rieunier & Associés in Paris on February 5th. Over the last fourteen years De La Vaissière has become one of the world's few specialists to mount regular stained glass auctions, with a dedicated and loyal following. Since his first sale with Francis Briest in 1989 and subsequent sales with Libert-Castor in Paris and occasionally in the provinces, he now collaborates in the main with Rieunier and Associates. This was an eclectic sale of some 222 lots which ranged from medieval fragments to substantial Art Deco panels; the main focus appeared to be sixteenth- and seventeenth-century Continental works and numerous examples from the nineteenth century.

Only 123 lots found buyers, but this 55% sold statistic reflects closely the average performance figures from the majority of auction rooms across the arts over the last twelve months, in such an uncertain economic climate. The best result came from a large five-part Art Deco tropical rainforest screen, Lot 146, which sold above the estimate at €9,199 (£6,012). Other results appeared sporadic and somewhat hit and miss, with no apparent reason for one lot selling and the next not reaching its mark. This is perhaps best exemplified in the failure of a beautiful five-fold Art Nouveau-style stained glass fire screen, Lot 172, designed by the contemporary artist Eric Bonte, to reach its reserve. This was a stunning piece with floral and bird decoration set within an engraved wrought iron frame. Failing to sell against a reserve of €20,000-€25,000, De La Vaissière himself had sold a very similar piece for 120,000 Francs in 2000. Consistently strong and steady prices could be found amongst the fifteenth- and sixteenth-century works. De La Vaissière concludes that prices for such pieces are: 'rising steadily as works become fewer and fewer, and more and more people become interested'. Grisaille medallions proved particularly popular providing that damages were minimal. A seventeenth-century Flemish work once in the ownership of one of my esteemed predecessors, the late Dr William Cole, had the unusual subject of a man in an open carriage drawn by two grey horses, shaking hands with a passer-by, with the monogram CENSRD in the bottom right hand corner, this sold for €1,350 (£880). English nineteenth century glass was strong, De La Vaissière preferring English glass from this period to French, as it is 'much closer to the medieval spirit' with its 'softer faces and greater warmth'. Two restored French glass cupolas c.1880, Lots 116 and 117, made by the Lobin glass works in Tours for the Café du Commerce in Saumur, disappointingly failed to sell during the auction and indeed after the event despite the receipt of numerous offers. None of these was high enough to accept, the vendors having invested a considerable sum in removing and restoring the pieces in preparation for the sale. The majority of works that did sell sold to German, Belgian, Swiss and Italian private buyers and the trade from the UK. De La Vaissière feels the latter have a more dynamic approach to dealing than the French, being far readier to buy and sell than their Continental counterparts.

February also saw glass in London and Amsterdam. The first in Sotheby's Amsterdam from the 'Princely Collection of the Princes of Liechtenstein', was a magnificent

FIG. 3

comprehensive treasure chest of old master paintings, drawings, works of art, palace furniture, books, weapons and the decorative arts: the history of which goes back to the Medieval period. The complete reorganisation and redisplay of the works in select palaces has meant the 'thinning out' of various pieces. Consequently Sotheby's 'Of Nobel Descent' sale included Lot 199, two South German leaded stained glass windows, mostly nineteenth-century but incorporating fourteenth-century elements. With a provenance of Johan II, Palais Rossau, Vienna, despite significant condition problems the panels sold for €8,294 (£5,420) against an estimate of €2,500-€5,500. Also from this provenance was Lot 308, a mixed collection of panels in varying condition which sold for €5,688 (£3,717) against

FIG. 4

an estimate €2,500-€5,500. On the 26th at Christie's South Kensington, Lot 88 of the 'Oak, Country Furniture, Folk Art, Works of Art and Sculpture' sale, was a rather over-estimated nineteenth-century stained glass cresting, modelled as a crown. This failed to sell against an estimate of £2,000-£3,000.

On April 9th at Sotheby's Bond Street, in the 'European Sculpture and Works of Art' sale, three lots of stained glass all sold fairly comfortably, either within or above estimate. Lot 8 comprised four nineteenth-century English gothic revival armorial panels, the first inscribed EDWARD I AND QUEEN MARGARET, the second WILLIAM AND MATILDA, the third KINGDOM OF BRITAIN and the fourth quartered with a profile of demi-rampant lions: a good lot which sold well above an estimate of £1,000-£1,500 for £3,600. Lot 7 was French; the *Dormition of the Virgin* (SEE PLATE 5, p. 151) a very attractive example of fifteenth-century glass with later additions portraying the sleeping Virgin with five apostles around her. This sold for £6,600 against £3,000-£5,000. Finally Lot 9, a stained glass panel from the Upper Rhine dated 1646: to the right a female figure, to the left a coat of arms, a cartouche with inscription above and inscribed below: ROHT ZU KAMULI UND HANS FURST, ANNO 1646. This sold for £1,440 against £1200-£1,800.

In May, Sotheby's Sussex auctions held a garden statuary sale which included four lots of decorative twentieth-century glass; 540, 543, 544 and 545 all sold within their estimates for between £400 and £1000. June and July saw the regular appearance of a series of specialist sporting sales in London. It was in Sotheby's Olympia on the 8th July that four rather special panels of stained glass could be found (FIGS. 2, 3). Special not for any outstanding quality (and the workshop is unknown), but the provenance in this case was quite spectacular. K. S. Ranjitsinhji was the first Indian to win a cricketing Cambridge Blue in 1893, this predates India's Test status, a period when racism in the sport was still rife. In 1897 he was voted Wisden 'Cricketer of the Year' and in 1899 he became the first cricketer ever to score 3000 runs in an English season. His passion for sports resulted in the commissioning of four stained glass windows c.1915, each depicting a classic English sporting scene: Polo, Rugby, Cricket and Tennis. The panels were entered into the sale by a private vendor who had purchased them directly from the estate of Ranjitsinhji after they were removed from his Middlesex riverside home, Jamnagar House, following his death in 1933. It was this provenance and the never-ending international enthusiasm for British sports that led to substantial results for all four panels; the tennis match sold to an American tennis collector for £12,000, a UK dealer purchased the rugby and cricket panels for £7,200 each, and the polo panel went for £6,600 to the US trade.

In New York at the Rockefeller Plaza in the 'Twentieth Century Decorative Arts' sale on June 13th a highly decorative American stained glass panel c.1904, portraying a dancing woman accompanied by her musicians, went unsold against an estimate of $15,000-$20,000. On the 25th at Donnington Priory, Dreweatt Neate sold eleven stained glass doors, each with a star-shaped arch and leaded panels in red, green, blue and turquoise, reputedly originating from the Palais Royal, Paris, totalling over £2,500. On the 26th, McTear's in Glasgow held an auction of Decorative Arts: Lot 53 was a pair of Art Nouveau stained glass doors in the style of stained glass artist Stephen Adam, who was initially apprenticed with the Edinburgh firm of Ballantine & Allan, before setting up his own studio in Glasgow in 1870. Dated 1886, the panels sold for £2,411.

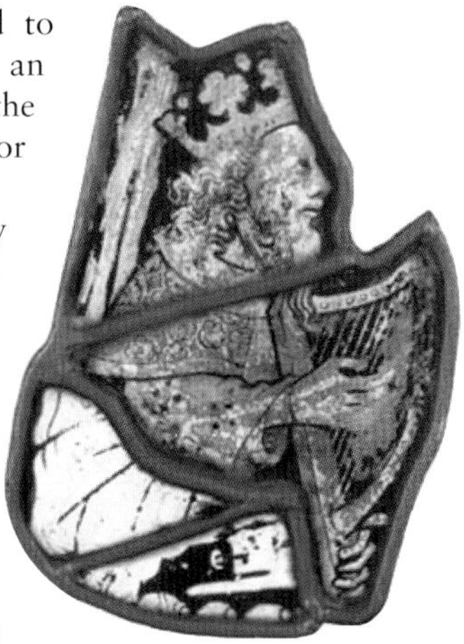

FIG. 5

Above is just a small selection of the stained glass that has sold over the last twelve months. Many more examples could be found in the UK alone; rooms included Bonhams in Leeds and Chester, Bracketts in Tunbridge Wells and Thomson Roddick and Medcalf in Dumfries. This year I *have* included the buyers' premium in the results – some premiums have been raised and some reduced – so to do otherwise would only have lead to confusion. In the major rooms, additional minor pieces sold, including a delightful sixteenth-century leaded fragment in Christie's, South Kensington (FIG. 5) which realised £529 against an estimate of £200-£300. In Bonhams, Bond Street, on 1st July three armorial fragments were sold: these were rescued by the vendor as a boy in the 1930s from the smouldering ruins of a country house. The owner kept them in his greenhouse for many years propped up against the glass to 'cheer him up in the mornings when he was watering'! How very appropriate.

Anna Eavis

Gothic: Art for England 1400-1547
Victoria & Albert Museum, London,
9 October 2003 – 18 January 2004

Gothic: Art for England 1400-1547 sets out to show that, far from being a cultural backwater in the fifteenth and early sixteenth centuries, England was commissioning, producing and importing works of art in vast quantities. Anyone who was anyone, either nationally or locally, spent money on art. The exhibition curators have assembled over 300 objects, produced for patrons as far afield as Cornwall and Cumbria, and made by artists and craftsmen all over Europe. They are arranged according to who paid for them and why. Patrons appear according to social status and role, while the objects themselves are clearly presented in terms of their purpose and use. This is not art for art's sake. All the exhibits, from the Dunstable Swan Jewel to William Waynflete's capacious ankle boots have a function, whether it be liturgical, devotional, chivalric, combative, ceremonial or domestic. Although determinedly not a social history, the exhibition vividly evokes the look and feel of late medieval life in England.

Inevitably, this approach has some disadvantages. With plate, sculpture, paintings and glass scattered throughout the exhibition, rather than grouped according to medium, the technical and stylistic development of particular forms is not immediately apparent, particularly as relatively little prominence is given to the craftsman. And the lack of a chronological survey can be confusing; for an exhibition entitled *Gothic*, it certainly seems to begin with a lot of Tudors. This is, of course, a deliberate challenge to the viewer. The placing of Torrigiano's head of Henry VII not far from an exquisite collar of 'SS', or Henry VIII's jousting armour near the delicate Reliquary of the Order of St Esprit, reminds us that the Tudors were rooted in a medieval world. Henry VIII was born in the Middle Ages. This realisation adds poignancy to his swaggering portrait at the very end of the exhibition.

Such illuminating juxtapositions are one of the exhibition's strengths. The placing of Sir John Donne's triptych alongside his book of hours and above an altar frontal from Cothele House reveals more about the triptych's importance as an object for private devotion than is apparent at the National Gallery, where it usually hangs. The contrast between Donne's smart continental commissions and the Edgecumbes' broadly contemporary, but decidedly old-fashioned English altar frontal, is also instructive, cautioning those who believe that changes in taste and style may be easily mapped onto a timeline.

The exhibition rightly recognises the importance of the patron in shaping taste, and shows how fashions embraced at the top of the social scale could filter down through the lower classes. High status patrons encouraged technical innovation, as well as insisting on high quality materials. The richly coloured Beauchamp Chapel glass, with its jewelled inserts and beautiful streaky rubies, is exceptional for two reasons. One is that its maker – John Prudde – was a consummate technician and artist. The other is that Richard Beauchamp paid him to produce work of the very highest calibre. We can see its enduring influence in the Stockerston figure of St Clement made around twenty years later for another patron with good taste, if less cash.

For glass enthusiasts there is much to enjoy, ranging from the early fifteenth to the early sixteenth centuries and emanating from all the major stained glass centres of the period. The panels were created for a variety of locations and purposes, from the image of Princess Cecily (FIG. 1), made for the exceptionally high profile 'Royal Window' at Canterbury Cathedral, to a devotional image of the Annunciation, possibly made for the Chapel at Hampton Court, Herefordshire. The inclusion of a newly conserved panel from the St William window in York Minster provides a unique opportunity to get close to a piece that will soon be far out of reach.

FIG. 1:
Princess Cecily
(1469-1507),
c.1482-7 ©
Glasgow
Museums: The
Burrell Collection.

For those who did not see the *Wonder* show at the Henry Moore Institute last winter (and possibly for those who did), the sculpture will be a revelation. It includes remarkably expressive heads, both from Westminster Abbey and the Great Screen of Winchester Cathedral, as well as a serene Virgin and Child, also from Winchester. The extraordinary statue of St Peter, until 1986 still adorning the front of 187 High Street, Exeter, and the figure of Temperance, made for the porch of London Guildhall, show that ecclesiastical patrons did not have a monopoly on quality.

The logistical challenge of securing such a high number of loans from so many different institutions is not to be under-estimated and the curators are to be congratulated for meeting it. It has to be said, however, that the unevenness of the overall installation does not always do justice to the exhibits. In design terms, the exhibition begins very well, with the magnificent Dacre beasts heralding one's approach to the fairytale crown of Margaret of York. It ends well too, the final sections dominated by a nicely judged evocation of a parish church bringing together sculpture, woodwork, alabasters, vestments and stained glass. The glass is beautifully lit – especially the Transfiguration window from the church of St Mary the Virgin, Fairford. But the middle section of the show, which includes exhibits relating to the patronage of noble families, churchmen and guilds, suffers by comparison, with poor visibility blighting some of the manuscripts and plate. Bishop Fox's crozier too is only partially visible, while the statue of Henry Chichele is so unsympathetically top-lit that the subtlety of the facial modelling is almost lost. Supporters of the controversial loan of Richard Beauchamp's effigy will be disappointed by its presentation here, while critics are unlikely to be appeased. As it is impossible to walk round, it is very difficult to see, while the awkward placing of the Beauchamp Chapel stained glass and sculpture in relation to the effigy creates a dislocated effect. In short, it looks far better *in situ*.

Architecture, although well represented in the superb catalogue, does not really have enough of a presence in the exhibition. It is an essential part of the story. Many of the exhibits, including movable objects like plate, were expressly designed for particular buildings. The statues of Henry Chichele and Henry VI, here seen apart, were conceived as a pair fronting the archbishop's major foundation, All Souls' College, in Oxford. And at a time when the most influential patrons were increasingly turning towards the continent for their art, English architecture remained confident and innovative enough to please them. This contrast is perhaps most vividly expressed in the chapel of King's College, Cambridge, whose architecture – a flowering of English Gothic – houses glass designed by foreigners. The stone-coloured display cases, generally unrelieved by texture or line, do not successfully evoke an architectural context, and with one or two exceptions the large scale photographs are simply not good or numerous enough to do the job either.

Evoking architecture in an exhibition space is not easy, the only good recent example in this country being the Royal Academy's *Sir John Soane* exhibition which used drawings, models, full-scale reconstructions, photographs and virtual reality to impressive effect. This is hardly a fair comparison, however, since the subject of the Soane exhibition was explicitly architectural and, as so many of his buildings have disappeared, their recreation was an essential part of the show. Happily for us, a large number of our magnificent late Gothic buildings survive. Once you have visited this exhibition and feasted your eyes on the sculpture, metalwork and glass, I urge you to visit the buildings for which they were made.

The BSMGP Library

The steady stream of requests for articles and information stemming from the Society's *Journal* continues, and responding to them constitutes the principal activity in the Library.

While the Library is not suitable for holding extensive archival material, information available on disc is a very useful resource when responding to enquiries and in this connection many thanks are due to Mrs Wendy Woods for her spreadsheet of information on windows she has visited as a church recorder for NADFAS. Also Donald Green has kindly made available his extensive catalogue of works by William Glasby. Both these compilations are held on disc and any enquiries should be addressed to the Hon Librarian.

Michael Peover
Hon Librarian

Catalogue of Additions to the Library since Summer 2002

ALBUTT, Roy *Stained Glass Windows of Bromsgrove and Redditch, Worcestershire*, Published by the author 2002

AYRE, Kerry *Medieval Figurative Roundels*, CVMA Great Britain Summary Catalogue 6, Oxford University Press for the British Academy 2002 *[Review copy, donated by the Hon Librarian]*

FOSTER, Paul (Ed.) *Chagall Glass at Chichester and Tudeley*, Otter Memorial Paper 14, University College Chichester 2002 *[Kindly donated by the editor, Paul Foster]*

HONEY, Thomas *The Stained Glass of Gordon Webster*, copy of recent compilation containing biographical notes, appreciations and an extensive list of the artists' works with illustrations in colour. *[Generously donated to the Library by the author]*

Leonard Evetts – Master Designer. Privately printed, 2001

MacDONALD, Juliette *Visions Through Glass. The Work of Douglas Strachan (1875-1950)*, Crawford Arts Centre 2001

PURCHLA, Jacek (Ed.) *Vernacular Art in Central Europe*. Proceedings of the International Conference 1-5 October 1997, Crakow 2001 *[Exchange copy given by the Research Institute for European Heritage at the International Cultural Centre, Cracow, Poland, donated by the Hon Editor]*

ROGERS, Frank '*Innocence in the Fields of Paradise': A Study of Tower-of-Glass Stained Glass Windows in County Fermanagh*, Published by the author 2001

RUSSELL, A. C. *Stained Glass Windows of Douglas Strachan*, 3rd edition, Pinkfoot Press 2002

Michael, Michael, *Images in Light: Stained Glass 1200-1550,* Catalogue 26.

London, Sam Fogg, 2002. Softcover, 124 pp., profusely illustrated with colour photographs. ISBN 0-9539422-3-6, £25 (available from Sam Fogg, 15D Clifford Street, London, w1S 4JZ, or by e-mail at info@samfogg.com).

Sam Fogg is well known as a dealer in illuminated manuscripts, but he has now proved himself equally formidable in the medium of stained glass. Over a ten year period, he put together a collection of Medieval and Renaissance stained glass of remarkable quality, the cream of which was recently exhibited in his London gallery between 21 November 2002 and 10 January 2003. Since the works were also up for sale, this book functions principally as a sales catalogue, yet it has the look of an exhibition catalogue. It is a sumptuously produced book. The colour photographs are stunning, and on top of that, the analysis of the stained glass is more informed and authoritative than might be expected of a sales catalogue.

The photography is remarkable and highlights many of the distinctive aesthetic qualities of stained glass. The cover photograph is an excellent example: a detail of the Christ Child from a splendid early 16th-century St Christopher image, probably from eastern France (no. 28), it has been taken with a strong light source behind the panel, creating an ethereal effect very different from the photographs of the same item in the catalogue, the general shot of the whole light on p. 68 and the detail on p. 71, which were illuminated more neutrally. These photographs provide three distinctive experiences of the same image, each highlighting different creative aspects of the work in particular and of the medium in general. And throughout the book, many enlarged details of works sensuously reveal their exquisite artistic quality. Such sensitivity is characteristic of the photography in this book, which must be considered one of its most appealing features.

Each of the fifty works catalogued here receives, as well, a brief but informative entry, which is supplemented at the back of the book, pp. 112-24, with technical descriptions, a bibliography and, where necessary, a restoration chart which identifies original pieces, stopgaps and 19th-century and modern repairs and modifications. It is not just in this respect that *Images in Light* calls to mind the publications and research methods developed by the CVMA. As well, both the author and many of the impressive list of scholars acknowledged for their research belong to various national committees of the CVMA. This participation and structure bring an impressive authority to the treatment of each work. In this respect, it is remarkable how thoroughly the activities of the CVMA have engineered a new awareness of connoisseurship in pre-modern stained glass.

Stained glass sales catalogues have certainly not always exhibited such scholarly authority. The art market has long realised the financial benefits of prestigious identifications. An artist's name or provenance from a well-known monument, no matter how flimsy the attribution, can substantially increase the market value of a work. But stained glass is a peculiar medium, and studies of authorship for this period ideally take into account the highly collaborative nature of stained glass design and workshop practice. Thus, the attribution of a magnificent, early 14th-century half-length figure of the Virgin and Child (no. 6), which appears to have come from the cloister of the Cistercian abbey of Klosterneuburg in Austria, to 'the Master of Klosterneuburg' seems curiously anachronistic from the perspective of recent stained glass scholarship. Such attributions, however, are common within the tradition of sales catalogues, and betray the synthetic character of this book, which has one foot in the world of contemporary scholarship and the other planted firmly in the art market. It should be said that this is the only such attribution in the book, and the entries usually content themselves with a more judicious – and less categorical – appraisal of compositional models and style. Even here, some of the connections made with the works are open to debate – the association of an Italian roundel of the Virgin Annunciate (no. 27) with Ghirlandaio, for example – but nowhere does one find analysis that is completely inappropriate. Not only does this book provide potential buyers with a fairly reliable assessment of works that they might be interested in purchasing, but it does so in a manner which – while it may fall short of CVMA standards – can satisfy specialists in the medium as much as collectors of stained glass, who are much more knowledgeable today than they were generally in the past.

Besides acting as a sales catalogue, this book can also be usefully treated as an exhibition catalogue. Not only is this significant collection of works documented at a particular place and time – no small advantage, seeing that all but one of the works have now been sold and are thus dispersed – but many of the works are previously unpublished and are thus available to the general public now for the first time. Moreover, the exhibition provides valuable evidence of the current nature of the market for stained glass. Although there are some larger pieces – such as two early 16th-century lights from eastern France depicting a Crucifixion and a St Christopher and donor (no. 28), each 2.25 x 0.64 m. – most of the works are quite small, including many roundels and heraldic panels, as well as a substantial number of single pieces and fragments. As well, the bulk of the collection is fairly evenly divided between works of the fifteenth and of the early sixteenth centuries; there are only two small 13th-century pieces and five mostly fragmentary 14th-century pieces. The geographical range of the works spans most of western Europe. England, France and the Low Countries are particularly well represented, and the collection is also strong in German works. There are also four Swiss panels, and both Austria and Italy are represented by a single work. Altogether, it makes an excellent study collection, and highlights many useful aspects of the stained glass medium.

These works were apparently selected from a larger collection, which Sam Fogg is continuing to supplement, with the intention of mounting another exhibition/sale of stained glass. Presumably, then, this catalogue will be followed by others, and we can look forward to a continuation of this new level of supply-side connoisseurship.

James Bugslag

Sprakes, Brian, *The Medieval Stained Glass of South Yorkshire*. Corpus Vitrearum Medii Aevi, Great Britain, Summary Catalogue 7.

Oxford: Oxford University Press for the British Academy, 2003.
Hardcover, 206 pp., 12 pp. col. plates and numerous b/w ills.
ISBN 0 19 726265 1, £55.

The purpose of the CVMA summary catalogue series is to describe and illustrate all the medieval glass remaining in a given location. The latest volume in the series, which covers the county of South Yorkshire, began life as a summary of ancient stained glass in the Deanery of Doncaster and was produced for the now defunct

South Yorkshire County Archaeology Committee. First of all therefore, one must commend the patience and effort which Brian Sprakes has put into rewriting his original text to produce a volume which fits the CVMA format.

As Sprakes concedes, South Yorkshire is not rich in medieval glass, which remains at only twenty-eight sites in the county, all of them parish churches apart from one private residence. The most extensive remains are to be found in the churches of Ecclesfield, High Melton, Thrybergh, Tickhill and Kirk Sandal, where one north window contains substantial remnants of the 1520s glazing from Archbishop William Rokeby's mortuary chapel. The inclusion of both pre- and post-restoration photographs of this window is most welcome. They demonstrate how dramatically a skilled conservator can improve the legibility of jumbled panels of medieval glazing by a combination of judicious rearrangement and restrained restoration of missing pieces. It is fortunate that this important glazing was entrusted to Keith Barley's studio, which is the best in the business when it comes to this type of work. Comparison of the window at Kirk Sandal with the over-restored lancet at Hooton Roberts, in which a few medieval fragments have been incorporated into a spurious figure of Archbishop Melton of York, shows how far the approach to conserving medieval glass has progressed over the course of a century, although it must be said that many conservators fall far short of the standards set by the Barley Studio and some do not even make a proper photographic record of panels before rearranging them.

Other noteworthy pieces are to be found at several other sites, including Kirk Bramwith, where two figures originating from a Cologne workshop constitute the only early foreign glass in the county, and Todwick, where fourteenth-century roundels depicting kings' heads parallel examples to be found elsewhere, for example at Radcliffe in Greater Manchester. Such comparisons can be made much more easily since the recent launch of the CVMA website (www.cvma.ac.uk), which offers free access to thousands of photographs of English stained glass. Many of the sites represented only by black and white photographs in this book are illustrated more fully in colour on the website, which thus provides a valuable supplement to the printed publication.

This volume is strong on the manuscript sources and provides comprehensive details of extant and lost heraldry both in the general introduction and in the individual introductions to each site. Occasionally one wishes for more detail in the catalogue entries: for example, some (admittedly intruded) blackletter inscriptions in panels sIV 1a and 1c at Thrybergh, which one hoped would have been transcribed, are not mentioned at all, and nothing is said concerning the technique of the Talbot shield at Ecclesfield which appears to be executed in flashed glass with charges and fields abraded, although this type of information is provided for other shields such as that of Gascoigne at Sprotbrough.

Each of the previous CVMA county catalogues (*Oxfordshire* 1979, *Lincolnshire* 1996 and *Northamptonshire* 1998) has improved on its predecessor in some small but useful points of organisation and detail. This one is no exception, particularly in the distribution map, which shows and differentiates between the locations of extant, lost and excavated glass, and in the appendices. The two preceding county volumes each contained only one appendix, devoted to excavated glass, and that was limited to simple bibliographical references and a very brief summary of the material for each site. Sprakes's appendix on excavated glass is much fuller, including descriptions of the material and large clear drawings of many of the fragments (far more useful than photographs of these often heavily corroded pieces). There are two further appendices. One reproduces a description of Hatfield Church recorded by a monk just before the Reformation. Although no medieval glass remains at Hatfield, detailed descriptions from this period (as opposed to the accounts of seventeenth-century antiquarians), are so rare as to justify quoting this in full. The other is a pedigree of the Fitzwilliam family, useful for reference given the number of South Yorkshire churches where their arms appeared in windows. It is to be hoped that future authors will follow the pattern established by Sprakes. The one glaring omission, in this volume as in its predecessors, is the absence of an appendix listing sites where medieval glass is known to have existed but none now remains. This is something which must be rectified in future volumes.

In this type of book the photographic record is as important as the text. Remnants of medieval glazing, with corroded and opaque fragments set on expanses of plain glass, pose a real challenge to the photographer, so it is good to report that with a very few exceptions, such as a blurred panel from Ecclesfield on p. 37, the images are of a high standard. Only insignificant fragments are not illustrated, with the exception of two shields at Mexborough, one depicting Passion emblems. Their omission is a pity, although possibly their poor condition rendered the photographs illegible. In this volume, as in that covering Lincolnshire, the CVMA has been lucky to have the assistance of the Reverend Gordon Plumb. Experienced photographers who are prepared to devote their expertise to the project on an expenses-only basis are a great rarity and one wishes that more like him could be found.

The copy-editing is careful, apart from a few insignificant errors. These include the mention on p. xliv of a shield at Sprotbrough in window nVIII which is actually in sV; the reference on p. 72 to an eagle and sunburst at Royston in window sIII panel A3, whereas the accompanying photograph shows them in panel A2; and on p. 78 the direction of the reader's attention to figure 2 in the introduction, which is a portrait of the antiquarian Joseph Hunter instead of the expected page from Henry Johnston's notes. However there is nothing as jarring as the opening sentence of the introduction to the Northamptonshire volume, where the phrase 'Elizabeth I's accession in 1559' somehow made it past the copy-editor.

This volume has two major drawbacks. The first is the cut-off date of 1540, which in fairness to Sprakes was imposed against his wishes. Although this date coincides with the dissolution of the last of the monasteries, it makes little sense in the context of parochial glazing in northern England, where both surviving glass and documentary evidence show that the production of overtly Catholic imagery in the medieval tradition continued throughout the 1540s and 1550s, if not even later (a point already tacitly conceded by the inclusion in the Northamptonshire volume of the 1550s glazing at Stanford-on-Avon). Since the current CVMA guidelines allow the inclusion of glass produced up to the beginning of the Gothic Revival in volumes published under its aegis, it would be sensible to allow authors more discretion in the choice of end-date, particularly in an area such as South Yorkshire, where the medieval material is rather sparse. Several sites in the county contain post-Reformation glass, notably Aston, where there are several armorials by Baernard Dininckhoff, and Wentworth, where Henry Gyles worked. A case could even be made for the inclusion of all glazing by William Peckitt, since some of his work is covered anyway by virtue of his arranging and supplementing Thomas of Oxford's glass at High Melton. It is on such post-medieval glazing that Sprakes's expertise and interest centres and little extra work would have been required to include it. The result would have been a fuller, more satisfying volume demonstrating the contraction of subject matter, the ascendancy of heraldry, and the technical progression from the mid-sixteenth-century armorials such as that of Brandon at Silkstone, which relied on the laborious and often unsightly abrasion and staining of the flashed coating of the coloured glass to depict the correct tinctures, to the introduction of enamel paints, which allowed the glass painter to display his artistic skills, using plain glass as his canvas. As it is, readers must consult a variety of other sources, such as Sprakes's articles on Dininckhoff in previous editions of the *Journal of Stained Glass*, for this later material.

Secondly, the geographical area covered poses a problem. Apart from Northamptonshire, other volumes in the series have used (or will use) the pre-1974 county boundaries, so the use of a wholly modern county in this one will cause difficulties for subsequent authors and readers. The local historian in Derbyshire or Nottinghamshire who five years hence buys the CVMA catalogue covering these two counties will not be amused to find that he has to track down Sprakes's volume for the entries on Beighton and Finningley, both of which became part of South Yorkshire in 1974. Moreover, a future volume will have to cover either the West Riding of Yorkshire while omitting a large chunk of its former territory, leaving readers feeling short-changed, or the modern county of West Yorkshire, in which case a swathe of old West Riding sites now in Lancashire which are not included in the pre-1974 Lancashire volume currently in preparation will fall into a black hole. One wishes that the CVMA had been more flexible regarding the temporal limits of Sprakes's volume but more stringent regarding the geographical ones.

Finally, although it is cheaper than most of its predecessors in the series due to the smaller number of sites it contains, this volume is still too expensive. It must be said that this is the fault of the British Academy, who have as usual set an unreasonably high price and who will consequently in a few years' time end up remaindering copies which would otherwise have been sold to the Yorkshire historians and genealogists who will form the majority of the readership. Brian Sprakes deserves their gratitude as well as that of devotees of stained glass for making a valuable contribution to the artistic and social history of pre-Reformation Yorkshire.

Penny Hebgin-Barnes

French, Thomas, *York Minster: The Saint William Window.* Corpus Vitrearum Medii Aevi, Great Britain, Summary Catalogue 5.

Oxford: Oxford: Oxford University Press for the British Academy, 1999. Hardcover, 168 pp., 25 col. plates and 115 b/w ills. ISBN 0 19 726202 3, £50.

Mention St William of York to today's citizens or to the thousands of tourists who visit York Minster every year and there will be very few for whom his name has any significance. None of the city's pubs, tea-rooms, schools or churches is named after him and, the St William window apart, the only major monument that helps to keep his name alive is St William's College at the east end of the Minster, an institution founded in 1461 in an attempt to impose some discipline on the lives of the Cathedral's chantry priests. In the early 21st century William appears a sadly neglected figure, in urgent need of rehabilitation, but for the Cathedral clergy and citizens of late medieval York he was the focus of considerable devotion and local pride.

Prior to the Reformation the impact of his cult on the visual appearance of the Cathedral was of huge significance. The beginnings of the construction of the Minster into the imposing Gothic building we know today, virtually coincides with

Archbishop William Fitzherbert's canonisation in 1227, seventy-three years after his death in 1154. The removal in 1541 of the lavishly decorated tomb in the nave, a 14th-century structure which may have supported William's head reliquary, and of the principal shrine in the choir, made for the rededication of the newly completed Cathedral in 1472 and positioned immediately behind the high altar, brought to an end the Minster's role as a pilgrimage centre and dealt a huge blow to its artistic heritage.

Battered fragments of the nave and choir shrine bases, usually stored in the Yorkshire Museum, have been displayed in London at the *Age of Chivalry* exhibition in 1987-8 and at the current *Gothic* show at the Victoria & Albert Museum. They were structures which were not only exceptionally large in scale, but were also of exceptional artistic quality. Also belonging to the Yorkshire Museum are pieces from a 15th-century alabaster altarpiece dedicated to St William, which was dug up in York in 1957. Yet another work of unusual size and quality, it must have been commissioned for a major altar, possibly the one dedicated to the saint in the south transept of the Cathedral, where a roughly contemporary image of the archbishop, dating from c.1434, can still be seen in one of the windows.

Despite these spectacular commissions, the canons of York were not as obsessive about their saint as the monks of Durham were about their patron. Documentary evidence shows that in late medieval Durham the windows of the Cathedral and the cloisters were used to bombard the viewer with images of St Cuthbert. While William's appearances in the Minster windows were more restricted, they were often associated with key areas of the building such as the main east, south and west gable windows, the high altar, the afore-mentioned St William altar and the Chapter House.

Tom French's Corpus volume is dedicated to what is by far and away the largest and the most historically significant of the windows associated with the saint, the huge St William window in the mini-transept on the north side of the choir. Paired with the St Cuthbert window opposite, the windows honouring the two great northern saints originally flanked the high altar and marked out its position on the exterior of the building. Proximity to William's shrine allowed the window to function as a spectacular piece of saintly propaganda for the pilgrims, just like the series of 13th-century Becket windows which enclosed the rival shrine at Canterbury.

Unlike Becket, however, William remains a shadowy and even dubious figure, attacked by his enemies as a loathsome character, not worthy to hold sacred office, let alone the archbishopric. Opposition to his election was organised by the great reforming party of the 12th-century church, the Cistercian order, led by another future saint, Bernard of Clairvaux, who described William in a splendidly vituperative letter to Pope Innocent II as 'rotten from the soles of his feet to the crown of his head.'

The dispute over William's election, his deposition, reinstatement and eventual death by poisoning are key events in the lower section of the window where forty-five panels illustrate William's life. Based on a Latin *vita* written in the early thirteenth century, this section of the window presents William as a great hero whose opponents are confounded. Any doubts about the validity of his election are countered in a panel depicting the Holy Spirit, as a dove, hovering beside William as he prays devoutly at an altar.

In a spectacular series of sixty panels, further up the window, William becomes the great thaumaturge, healing the blind, the lame and the infirm, freeing prisoners and, in a scene borrowed from St Nicholas imagery, rescuing sailors from the North Sea. In deference to his high birth, William rescues King Edward I from a nasty fall, but for the most part he is shown as a popular figure, interceding, often at his tomb and shrine, on behalf of the common men, women and children of York. According to French 'the St William window certainly ranks among the greatest masterpieces of fifteenth-century stained glass.' It is the largest surviving medieval window to narrate the life and miracles of a saint, as well as a fascinating compendium of medieval life and misfortune. This book makes all this invaluable material easily accessible for the very first time.

Considering the fate of the other major works of art associated with William, it is miraculous that this potentially fragile window managed to escape destruction, especially as its principal messages about the cult of saints, the importance of pilgrimage, the power of relics, the roles of the monasteries and the papacy, were rooted in the very beliefs and structures that the reformers set out to destroy.

The appearance of this second volume in the Corpus Vitrearum's Summary Catalogue of York Minster glass, following on from the same author's catalogue of the East window, published in 1995, is a cause for real celebration. There may initially have been doubts about the wisdom of publishing a St William window volume while the window itself was undergoing major conservation and restoration at the York Glaziers' Trust, work which has involved quite radical alterations to some individual panels, as well as an attempt to reorder the window, as far as possible, back to its original sequence. Tom French's work completely vindicates the CVMA's decision. A future volume, in full Corpus format, could present the latest research on the design, format, historiography and restoration history of the window, much of which has been written-up recently by Janice Smith for an M Phil. Thesis at the University of York. Such a volume could also include exciting new research by Christopher Norton on the textual sources which inspired the window, and on the cult and iconography of St William of York. A larger volume could include more detail on the antiquarian sources for the window, such as James Torr's description, written in the late seventeenth century, when even the identity of the saint represented in the window had been lost. More could no doubt be done in a future volume on earlier restorations, like J. W. Knowles's in 1895, and on the current conservation programme. The great strength of Tom French's book though, and what will ensure its lasting significance, is that it will remain as a permanent record of the window as it existed in the late twentieth century, before current restoration commenced. Its scholarly text and superb illustrations have already proved invaluable to those currently engaged in further art historical research and on conserving the window.

The success of individual Corpus volumes rests in part on the detail in the panel-by-panel catalogue entries and in the scope and quality of the accompanying illustrations. Even allowing for the summary format, the reader will not be disappointed with either element here. Of particular value, especially to the general reader, are the opening essays which provide a concise, lucid and interesting introduction to many different aspects of the window: the historical and architectural contexts for the glazing, William's life, cult and role within the Minster and the style of this brilliantly designed and superbly executed window, associated with John Thornton of Coventry, the master glazier of the Minster's East window.

In a cautious and sensible account of the iconography, French mentions the literary sources which influenced the design and outlines the general principles underpinning the structure of the narrative. More could have been made of the visual sources available in the Minster, especially the St William window in the Chapter House, glazed around 1280-90, at about the time that the saint's body was translated from the nave to the choir. Representations of the saint in windows outside the Minster are only alluded to in footnotes. While it is true that such representations are rare, or at least difficult to identify, William does appear on occasions as a patron's name-saint, as in the East window of St Peter Mancroft in Norwich or at Edington Priory in Wiltshire. Doubtless because of his high birth there is evidence for some devotion to William in royal circles. William's image, along with the Fitzherbert arms, appeared in the series of royal saints commissioned for the windows of the Greyfriars church in Greenwich by Henry VII around 1490.

In a previously published article on the donors that fill the bottom row of the Minster window, the Ros family of Helmsley in Yorkshire, French was able to push its date back from the early 1420s to around 1414. This depends, like much of the research in this book, not only on the author's detailed knowledge of the glass and of the building as a whole, but on his awareness of the immense value of heraldic and antiquarian sources.

The volume on the St William window proved to be Tom French's final contribution to the CVMA project on York, as he died not long after its publication. There can be no more fitting memorial to its author than this splendid book in honour of York's most prestigious saint. It is appropriate to conclude with the opening words of yet another great work of art inspired by the saint, the antiphon to St William commissioned by a later archbishop of York, Cardinal Wolsey, from the Tudor composer, John Taverner, in about 1525:

O Wilhelme pastor bone,	William, good shepherd,
Cleri pater et patrone,	Father and patron of the clergy,
Mundi nobis in agone	To us in the trials of the world
Confer opem, et depone	Grant help, and remove
Vitae sordes, et coronae	Life's baseness, and give us
Coelestis da gaudia.	The joy of a heavenly crown.

David O' Connor

Ayre, Kerry, *Medieval English Figurative Roundels.* Corpus Vitrearum Medii Aevi, Great Britain, Summary Catalogue 6.

Oxford: Oxford University Press for The British Academy, 2002.
Hardcover, 192 pp., 156 b/w ills., numerous b/w photographs and 8 col. plates.
ISBN 0-19-726251-1, £65.

For many, the term roundel is associated primarily with the painted glass produced in the Netherlands, and to a lesser extent Germany and Switzerland, in the late fifteenth to seventeenth centuries. So the fascinating article by Kerry Ayre on English roundels in the 1989-90 *Journal of Stained Glass* was both an eye-opener and provided an intriguing taster for the present compilation by her for the CVMA Great Britain. It covers around 600 roundels in English churches, museums (including the Burrell collection, Glasgow) and private houses yet is only a preliminary catalogue, relying as it does on drawing together material primarily from county-based published work, which was then subjected to additional scrutiny before incorporation in this volume. Even so, what impresses is the range of surviving roundels, from the early fourteenth century to the sixteenth, and the varied and lively treatment of their subject matter. Strange hybrid animals and *drôleries* provide links with designs on misericords. There are heraldic beasts, series representing the labours of the months, signs of the zodiac, donors or local types and Evangelists and their symbols, although there are relatively few surviving narrative religious scenes. A study of facial types and of the decoration of borders and background diapers has given some information on regional styles and there are detailed drawings of over ninety border designs and over sixty of diaper and ground designs. About fifty of the later designs have some Netherlandish characteristics which may simply be the result of the prevailing influence on the English glass painter and they lack the detailed backgrounds so typical of Netherlandish work of the period. As the author comments, this is a fruitful area for further research.

The presentation of the material will be familiar from previous Summary Catalogues in the CVMA Great Britain series. Over 100 roundels are described but not illustrated, no doubt due to cost constraints. Most of the illustrations are in black and white, and their size on the page is limited by column width, about 80mm or roughly just under half the actual dimensions of the roundels in most cases. This is a considerable and welcome improvement over some earlier CVMA publications, William Cole's *Netherlandish and North European Roundels* for example, in which the illustrations are only half this size although containing more detail than the English roundels. However, in those cases where there is significant corrosion and pitting of the glass, the grey tones in the photographs make the main image difficult to discern. It is in just these instances where a colour reproduction would allow the subject to emerge more clearly, as the few excellent colour plates demonstrate. The usefulness of this volume would be much enhanced if the CVMA website under development contained a comprehensive group of colour images of all these roundels which could be related directly to the numbering system employed in this catalogue, rather than being listed on a location by location basis.

So this volume is in the nature of an interim report on a fascinating and little researched branch of English glass painting, and it is good to see existing knowledge brought together in such an authoritative way. Each of us will have our own personal favourite, mine is the lovely Virgin and Child in Nowton of 1460-80, incidentally surrounded by later Netherlandish roundels. No doubt we can look forward to further examples which will be forthcoming from those areas yet to be tackled in detail.

Michael Peover

Raguin, Virginia Chieffo and Zakin, Helen Jackson,
with contributions from Elizabeth Carson Pastan,
Stained Glass before 1700 in the Collections of the Midwest States,
Corpus Vitrearum United States of America, Part VIII, 2 vols.

London and Turnhout: Harvey Miller Publishers for Corpus Vitrearum Inc., 2001. Hardcover, 600 pp., 46 col. and 570 b/w ills. ISBN 1 872501 00 1, £181 or $270 US (orders: info.publishers@brepols.com; UK orders: direct.orders@marston.co.uk; North American orders: david.brown.bk.co@snet.net).

The end papers of these two hefty volumes are formed of maps. At the front is the United States of America, with a compact grouping of four midwestern states highlighted: Illinois, Indiana, Michigan and Ohio. At the back is the whole of Europe, showing a wide diversity of locations, from Concarneau, France, in the west to Toruń, Poland, in the east, from Gresford, England, in the north, to Cortona, Italy, in the south. The sites on these two maps form a 'homology' relating to 182 individual works of pre-modern stained glass. The works are now located in collections in these midwestern states but originated in a bewildering variety of European contexts. Many are in major collections, such as those of the Detroit Institute of Art and the Cleveland Museum of Art, while others are in much smaller collections. None, obviously, is *in situ*. This situation has made access to these works particularly difficult for those interested in European stained glass, and this publication by the American Committee of the CVMA can be said to fill an important gap in stained glass scholarship.

The various European committees of the CVMA have long been producing publications on their invaluable artistic legacies. This work, however, is the first monographic CVMA treatment of pre-modern stained glass outside of Europe. It is, thus, a milestone in the CVMA project, as well as a pioneering effort that pertinently reflects the distinctive nature of the study of all displaced glass. In this respect, it will undoubtedly form a touchstone, not only for further volumes from the non-European committees, but also for the substantial displaced collections within Europe – such as those of the Victoria and Albert Museum in London, the Musée national du Moyen Age / Thermes de Cluny in Paris, and the Germanisches Nationalmuseum in Nuremberg, *inter alia* – none of which have received a monographic CVMA publication to date. The authors, and the American CVMA Committee, are thus to be congratulated on an important and splendidly produced publication.

Anyone who has ever looked closely at pre-modern stained glass knows what a challenge its study poses, in the best of circumstances. The previously published European CVMA volumes typically represent an enormous effort, combining scrupulous observation and penetrating research. But in a sense, the European committees have 'had it easy', since, for the most part, their glass is still *in situ*. If, added to all of the other problems they have faced, the glass they were dealing with had been removed from its original locations a couple of hundred years ago, if it had changed hands several times, often being shuffled together with completely unrelated material, and if most, or all, of this bewildering activity had been largely undocumented, then their problems would have been compounded exponentially.

This was exactly the situation faced by the American CVMA Committee. Some works can be traced quite precisely back to their original source; for example, the splendid early 16th-century Martyrdom of St Eustace in the Detroit Institute of Art originated as the lower part of Window 13 in the Church of St Patrice in Rouen. Difficult problems arise with many other pieces, however, just to propose a general region from which they may have originated. The art market, through which these pieces invariably filtered, was not primarily interested in questions of provenance unless, of course, that could influence the prices they might charge, and dealers were not above manufacturing provenances for this purpose. Even more worrisome is the often extreme 'restoration' or modification that many of these works underwent to prepare them for the market. At its most unscrupulous, clever 'fakes' were circulated, but the sheer variety of changes that many of these works have undergone is staggering, and most were intended to be undetectable. Virtually every piece in these volumes, thus, poses distinctive individual problems.

The first task that the American Committee faced was simply to locate all of the pre-modern stained glass that had made its way into their country. This required considerable effort, since many pieces were hidden away in private collections, often installed in the windows of private houses, or gathering dust deep in museum reserves. In order to facilitate this collation of material, a series of 'Checklist' volumes was compiled, providing a brief catalogue of all known pieces. Two of these pertain to this publication: Madeline H. Caviness et al., *Stained Glass before 1700 in American Collections: Midwestern and Western States* (Corpus Vitrearum Checklist III), Studies in the History of Art, Monograph Series I, vol. 28 (Washington, D.C.: National Gallery of Art, 1989); and Timothy B. Husband, with assistance from Marilyn Beaven, *Stained Glass before 1700 in American Collections: Silver-Stained Roundels and Unipartite Panels* (Corpus Vitrearum Checklist IV), Studies in the History of Art, Monograph Series I, vol. 39 (Washington, D.C.: National Gallery of Art, 1991). The Checklist project must have been of considerable value as a foundation for the regional monograph volumes that, with this publication, have now begun to appear. For example, the Checklists mention seven pieces in the Art Institute of Chicago, but this publication lists no fewer than fifteen works. Further research undertaken since the Checklists were published has also resulted in some changes in attribution, date and even subject.

The first volume of this monograph opens with an Introduction, and follows with the collections of stained glass in Illinois and Indiana; Michigan is begun as well, with the extensive collection of the Detroit Institute of Art, which, in fact, constitutes about half of the book (pp. 144-304). Volume II completes Michigan and inventories Ohio; it ends with a Glossary, a Bibliography, an Index and a list of all CVMA publications to date. The lengthy introduction (vol. I, pp. 11-68), is entitled 'The Collections of Stained Glass before 1700 in the Midwest States'. Its most instructive areas are the later sections on the collecting of stained glass. This is a subject that has benefited enormously from the activities of the American Committee. It is, after all, the reason that any of these European works have crossed the Atlantic, and research on collections, collectors and dealers has been necessary in establishing provenances, both on an individual basis and in terms of more general trends. The Introduction begins, however, with a heterogeneous selection of themes, including 'Form and Meaning' and 'Chronological Development' and also discusses narrativity, workshop structure and methods, prints and the dissemination of designs, and heraldic display. Although an attempt is made to focus on works of stained glass in the collections included here, these sections are less satisfying, since accidents of geography and collection interests have not resulted in a thorough enough representation to sustain a homogeneous treatment of many of these themes.

The inventory is organized by state, then by city, and then by collection, all in alphabetical order. Each collection is introduced with a history of the collection and its stained glass, followed by the holdings in approximate chronological order. The entry for each work is very complete, including, where appropriate, most of the following sections: History of the Glass, Related Material, Original Location, Reconstruction, Composition, Bibliography, Description, Colour, Inscriptions, Condition, Composition, Iconography, Heraldry, Costume, Technique, Style, Date, and Photographic References. There is also a black and white photograph, a Restoration Chart where necessary, and often photographs of comparanda. Colour views of some works are also included. The quality of the photographs is generally good (with occasional exceptions, e.g. vol. I, p. 98; vol. II, pp. 106, 213), and they are printed on high quality paper stock. It should be mentioned, however, that colour plate 12 seems to have been printed in reverse.

The entries are comprehensive and provide a solid foundation for further research. One may occasionally quibble with a proposed date, region of origin, or attribution, but it should be made very clear that any such quibble falls into the realm of continuing scholarly debate and in no way compromises the high level of scholarship maintained throughout the book. The authors of record, in fact, might be likened to 'conductors' who have directed a large orchestra into a harmonious symphonic performance. The participation of other members of the American CVMA Committee is constantly apparent, and the debt owed to a wider community of scholars and experts in specialised fields is generously acknowledged. The biannual International CVMA Colloquia have regularly created opportunities for slides and photographs to be shown to colleagues from other national committees, for lively discussion, and for valuable contacts with a wide-ranging diversity of expertise. The many links that have been forged in the pursuit of this project have helped to form a closely-knit international community of stained glass scholars. As such, this book represents the distillation of considerable valuable scholarly exchange, the results of which are now available to a much broader audience.

Although, understandably, the content of these midwestern collections is varied and disparate, there are some notable strengths. There are a handful of early pieces – the early 13th-century panel of *Two Clerics* from Soissons Cathedral, now in the Detroit Institute of Art; the half-length *Seraph*, possibly from the west rose of Rheims Cathedral, in the University of Michigan Museum of Art; a couple of decorative fragments from Canterbury Cathedral – but the focus of these collections lies in the fifteenth and sixteenth centuries, including, for example, a splendid *Nativity* by Guillaume de Marcillat from Cortona Cathedral, now in the Detroit Institute of Art. For those interested in the 'problem' of the early 16th-century glazing of the Louvain Charterhouse, there are several relevant panels represented here: a *St. Catherine Seized for Martyrdom* in the Indiana University Art Museum; a *Horse and Rider* in the Cranbrook Educational Community, Bloomfield Hills, Michigan; and four Old Testament scenes, *Jacob Returning to Canaan, Elias and the Widow of Sarepta*, the *Judgement of Solomon*, and *Esther Interceding before Assuerus*, in the Cleveland Museum of Art. With many other displaced panels on both sides of the Atlantic attributed to the Louvain Charterhouse (too many, perhaps!), the publication of these pieces is timely in aiding on-going research on this important site. Equally rich are works related to the St Cecilia Workshop, emanating from around Cologne in the late fifteenth century: the Detroit Institute of Art has twelve half-length figures of Prophets and Psalmists from a *Biblia Pauperum* series, and Trinity Cathedral in Cleveland, Ohio, has two panels from a Passion series, the *Nailing of Christ to the Cross* and an *Entombment*, that relate to other displaced panels attributed to the same workshop now in Cologne Cathedral and the English parish churches of St Mary's at Stoke d'Abernon and St Nicholas at Great Bookham, both in Surrey.

Since much pre-modern stained glass now in the United States was initially intended for installation in the homes of paragons of American industry who aspired to 'aristocratic' pretensions, these collections are rich in smaller pieces – roundels, *Kabinettscheibe* and heraldic panels. The US Committee, and Timothy Husband in particular, have been at the forefront of recent scholarship on stained glass roundels, and several important works are included here, including examples attributed to, or after, Dirick Vellert, Pieter Cornelisz. Kunst, Jacob Cornelisz. van Oostsanen and the circle of Jan Gossaert. Although not by such generally well-known artists, a high percentage of the Swiss domestic panels have also received attributions, and here, as well as in the considerable wealth of English armorial panels, an impressive amount of heraldic scholarship is evident, with properly described blazons and many specific identifications.

As should be evident from this all too brief overview of the stained glass included in this book, there is a rich diversity of material here, capable of accommodating a wide variety of interests. Although the assiduous researcher is provided with extensive information about all of this material, however, I can't help thinking that it might have been made a little more 'user-friendly'. The colour plates, for example, have very incomplete captions which do not give original locations, whether known or attributed. Moreover, in order to find the entry for each item, and in general throughout the two volumes, identification codes have been devised, consisting of an abbreviation for the collection, followed by a number which seems to represent a more or less chronological ordering of the pieces, e.g. CCSP 9 is the ninth work inventoried in the collection of the Cathedral Church of St. Paul in Detroit, Michigan. However, the system is not explained in full, and the abbreviations are listed in a 'Note to the Reader' which in the first volume is found as late as pp. 70-72 – a problem for anyone who might begin with the Introduction preceding this explanation. The Reader's Note is repeated, more conveniently, at the opening of volume II, where it is easy to find, since it must be consulted by anyone not intimately familiar with the identification codes. It might have been preferable to use a numerically sequential system of identification codes, or to include page numbers with this system. Once familiar with its peculiarities, the system makes sense and can be negotiated, but the book's undisputed usefulness as a reference work is compromised by this awkwardness. One might also have wished for a tabulated finding aid, so that one could locate at a glance all of the, say, 14th-century French pieces, or all of the roundels.

I reserve my greatest criticism for the price: $270 U.S. or £181. Ouch! Although sumptuously produced and undoubtedly worth the outlay, even university libraries balk at such prices in these straitened times. To use a metaphor not inappropriate for the midwestern states, the American CVMA Committee has provided a 'Cadillac', while many potential buyers can only afford a '*deux chevaux*'. Undoubtedly, the cost of quality illustrated books has rapidly escalated, but some economising measures might have been considered. In the interest of providing exhaustively authoritative entries for each work, there is much repetition, particularly for provenances; the History of the Glass given for DIA 50-53 (vol. I, p. 271) is repeated exactly for DIA 54-62 (vol. I, p. 278). Likewise, the history of Canterbury Cathedral given in the entry for the border piece in the Martin d'Arcy Gallery of Art at Loyola University in Chicago (vol. I, pp. 120-21) is repeated verbatim for one on an ornamental boss from Canterbury Cathedral now in the Detroit Institute of Art (vol. I. pp. 159-60). Arguably, anyone interested in the Cathedral's border elements and ornamental bosses might already be expected to know something of the building's history, but surely a cross-reference might have been used. Extensive hagiographical details are often provided, for which reference to standard iconographic sources could easily have been made. The 12-point type used for sections of text might also be judged an unnecessary luxury, although it certainly adds to the overall excellence of production.

If one can afford it, or obtain access to it, this magnificent book is a valuable resource. As the first of eleven regional catalogues planned by the American Committee, it will be interesting to see how subsequent volumes compare. Inevitably, since it is the first of the series – and as pointed out earlier, pioneering in many respects – this has become more than just a review. Many of the criticisms mentioned here are (unfairly, perhaps) prescriptive and aimed more at future publications than the present one. The authors have provided a rich and stimulating work which must be considered an important milestone in the history of stained glass scholarship. This book joins a distinguished series of CVMA publications which have set a benchmark for contemporary scholarship on pre-modern stained glass.

James Bugslag

Scherrer, Jacques, ed., *La Rose de la cathédrale de Lausanne.*

Lausanne: Editions Payot Lausanne, 1999. Hardcover, 215 pp., 39 col. and 126 b/w ills. ISBN 2 601 03239 1, €53 (available from Centre Suisse de recherche et d'information sur le vitrail de Romont, CP 225, CH-1680 Romont, Switzerland, fax +41 (0)26 652 49 17, email: centre.recherche.vitrail@bluewin.ch).

In 1989, Alice Mary Hilton published an article in the *Revue Suisse d'art et d'archéologie*, in which she described the condition of the Rose window at Lausanne Cathedral as alarming. To understand the huge efforts which were initiated by the article and which eventually led to the publication of this book, one has to remember that this Rose is a national treasure, unique not only as the sole survivor of the medieval glazing of the Cathedral, but also as a monument which, despite its prominence within the circle of 13th-century French Rose windows, had stylistically never found followers.

According to the latest research, the Rose is earlier than previously thought, predating a devastating fire in 1235 by several decades and thus not created by maître Pierre d'Arras after all. Werner Stöckli, in the course of his studies on the sequence in which the building was erected, believes the masonry to be of the year 1205, a date supported for the glazing by Claudine Lautier.

Having miraculously survived the fire, the Rose then endured centuries of exposure to the elements and to a string of restorations. Not all of these interventions are recorded but still, a fair amount is known about the Rose's restoration history, both from documents and the scars left behind by the restorers. In 1520, the glass painter Etienne Capyenz was paid for the repair of the 'fenestre rotonde', which was followed by numerous repairs in the eighteenth century. Characteristically, the nineteenth century was prone to intervention, beginning with Monnet's campaign of 1817 and ending with Hosch's restoration carried out between 1891 and 1899. It was the latter which by and large gave the Rose its present appearance.

When the Department responsible for the buildings of the Canton Waadt, alarmed by Hilton's article, embarked on the latest conservation project, it was not surprising that this time the authorities wanted to 'get it right'. The Centre Suisse de recherche et d'information sur le vitrail de Romont was asked to prepare a report which was subsequently presented to an international team of experts in 1992. Three fundamental decisions were taken in the wake of this meeting, which determined the conservation procedure: the glass was not to leave the Cathedral but to be restored on the premises; the panels were to be protected by isothermal glazing and Romont, under the guidance of Stefan Trümpler, was to establish a multidisciplinary team of conservators for the actual work.

The preparations were thorough and took some time. It was not before in-depth analysis of the glass had determined the parameters of the conservation that work on the panels could begin in 1996. The main problem with the glazing was the deterioration of the pigments and their loss of adhesion, the cause of which baffled the experts and which necessitated the assistance of a painting conservator. Cleaning was easy by comparison and could be reduced to a minimum, which proves how much can be achieved with minimal intervention. The lead could be preserved, due to the protection the isothermal glazing provided. Last but not least, a new documentation system was developed, on computer of course, containing 6079 documents. Together with three small panels which have been left unrestored, these records make future studies on the effect of this most recent intervention possible, following the return of the glazing to its rightful place in 1998.

An exemplary conservation project has been followed up by an equally exemplary account, published quite rightly so in French, but unfortunately without English and German summaries. Edited by Scherrer, the list of contributors to this book is impressive: Kurmann-Schwarz, Lautier, Schweizer and Trümpler, to name but a few. Hence the book not only reports on the conservation, with charts and excellent colour images of each panel. It covers the history of the masonry, investigates the meaning of Rose windows in general and of Lausanne ('*imago mundi*') in particular and even touches on the influence the Rose has on modern Swiss stained glass. It is sometimes controversial, when for example Stefan Trümpler, quite correctly in my view, emphasises the influence the masters of the glass had on the concept of the Rose, an issue disputed by Brigitte Kurmann-Schwarz, if not in the same publication.

And one other hotly discussed issue, controversial at least in England. Whoever advocates isothermal glazing, puts her/himself into a no-win situation, and the Rose of Lausanne is no exception. There is hardly another issue in conservation where experts point in so many different directions. It makes interesting reading that for Lausanne, a thermoformed layer was rejected on the basis of deontology, while in a recent article by Peter van Treeck, the doyen of German stained glass conservation, this method is hailed as the only acceptable way.

The book makes extremely good reading, and is written for the expert and lay-person alike. It is an ideal starting point for research into all subjects surrounding this window and conservation in general, and hence should have a firm place on the bookshelf of anyone who is interested in stained glass and its preservation.

Sebastian Strobl

Kulturstiftung DessauWörlitz, *Die Glasmalereien im Gotischen Haus Wörlitz, Sicherung und Schutz. Abschlussbericht zum Projekt der Deutschen Bundesstiftung Umwelt.*

Leipzig: Kulturstiftung Dessau-Wörlitz, 2000. Large format softcover, 64 pp., 7 full-page and 24 smaller col. plates, and 11 b&w ills. and diagrams. ISBN 3 361 00519 1, £10 (plus £3 P&P in UK from Morris & Juliet Venables, 270 Henbury Road, Bristol Bs10 7QR, tel. 0117 950 7362, fax 0117 959 2361); or €13 (in Europe from Centre Suisse de recherche et d'information sur le vitrail de Romont, CP 225, CH-1680 Romont, Switzerland, fax +41 (0)26 652 49 17, email: Centre.recherche.vitrail@bluewin.ch).

This slim but important work is the final report on the project to restore the stained and painted windows in the Gothic House at Wörlitz, near Dessau, Sachsen-Anhalt in the former German Democratic Republic. It is also the most recent of a series of books published by Edition Leipzig which bear witness to the surge of interest in stained glass as an important feature of the heritage of the former East German *Länder*. The text is in German, although several of the later diagrams have (very tiny) captions in English.

Wörlitz is unique in Germany. The estate was the ancestral home of the Princes of Anhalt-Dessau, and consists of magnificently landscaped 'English' gardens, a large stately home, believed to be the first Neo-Classical country house built in Germany, a church, and, most significantly for stained glass enthusiasts, the Gothic

House (Germany's equivalent of Walpole's Strawberry Hill House). Built partly as an occasional residence for Prince Leopold III, Friedrich Franz von Anhalt-Dessau, it was primarily intended to house his large collection of objets d'art and stained and painted glass. With over two hundred mainly late fifteenth- to seventeenth-century Swiss panels and fragments acquired by the Prince between 1783 and 1814 at the instigation of Johann Caspar Lavater, it has long been regarded as one of the most important and complete collections in Germany, and is of primary significance for the history of Swiss glass painting. It contains works by many of Switzerland's best known glass painters including the Murers, the Blunschlis, the Nüschelis, Ulrich von Bergarten, Carl Egeri, Jakob Sprüngli and Lukas Zainer. There are few, if any, single collections in Switzerland which offer such a comprehensive view of what must be one of the country's foremost contributions to late- and post-medieval European culture. The status of the Wörlitz collection was recognised as early as 1797 when Carl August Boettiger in his *Journey to Wörlitz* described it as 'a treasure-house for the history of glass painting'.

The panels were removed for safety during World War II and survived the bombing and subsequent invasion of Sachsen-Anhalt relatively intact. However, attempts at restoration in 1944 proved inadequate, and thirty years of exposure to high levels of atmospheric pollution from nearby chemical industries and from the ubiquitous burning of lignite, caused serious corrosion to glass, ferramenta, stonework, woodwork and even to the unsightly chicken wire which had been used as external protection, with the result that many items in the collection were left in a dangerous state of disrepair. The initial decision to restore the windows was taken in 1978 and a preliminary survey was carried out followed by limited restoration of windows in three of the rooms. Inevitably in the former GDR, funding for the project ran out (in view of later findings this was probably a stroke of good fortune), and nothing further was done until 1992 when, under the aegis of the Kulturstiftung Dessau-Wörlitz, a number of respected artists, scientists and craftsmen were commissioned to restore the Gothic House, including the windows, as part of an overall plan to reinstate important cultural landmarks in Sachsen-Anhalt and protect them from the threat of pollution and vandalism. The experts and agencies involved in the project included Drs Karin Adam, Wolfgang Müller and Manfred Torge of the Bundesinstitut für Materialforschung und-prüfung, Dr Lutz Gärlich of Domglas, Naumburg, Dr Erhard Drachenberg of the German CVMA, Dr Arno Weinmann of the Deutsche Bundesstiftung Umwelt, Dr Stefan Trümpler of the Centre Suisse de recherche et d'information sur le vitrail, Dr Reinhard Alex of the Kulturstiftung Dessau-Wörlitz, Dr Stefan Oidtmann of the well known Linnich glass studios and Dr Helmut Steltzer of the Büro Architektur und Denkmalpflege, Halle.

Planning for the task was meticulous, possibly more so than would have been the case two decades earlier under the former East German regime, when it was difficult to obtain the high quality materials necessary to complete the task to the required standard. Funding was for a period of four years and consisted of a grant of DM 881,936 from the Deutsche Bundesanstalt Umwelt, supplemented by DM 220,454 raised locally, for a grand total of well over DM 1,000,000, excluding the cost of locally employed bricklayers, stone masons and carpenters. One precondition for the grant was that research into the Wörlitz windows should provide a methodology that could be applied to future similar restoration projects elsewhere in Germany. The conservators and restorers were also required to consider the potential value of external protection and to investigate the viability of isothermal glazing.

The report sets out clearly the condition of the windows following attempts at restoration in 1888, 1944 and 1978 and lists the many problems facing the restorers in 1992. Iron frames, saddlebars, other metal fixings and leads were damaged. In some cases missing pieces of coloured glass had been replaced with thicker domestic window glass, the leads having been broken open and realigned in order to accommodate it. The bowing resulting from decayed leadwork and saddlebars had become a serious hazard in the face of strong winds. Some elements had already fallen out and were handed loose to the conservators.

Although the painted panels had survived in reasonable condition, there were problems with the thinner surrounding ornamental glazing – the yellow glass in particular, but also the violet had crazed and was threatening to crumble away. Laminated heat-resistant glass tried elsewhere in Switzerland had proved to be inadequate as external protection against solar heat and, if anything, had increased temperatures on the painted surfaces (+56° C at one point, which over a period of time would have been hot enough to render the enamels unstable). Any attempt at external protective glazing had to take into account the temperature and humidity within the house and their possible effect on the interior fittings and other artefacts.

The major chapters in the report give an account of the conservation work undertaken. Of particular interest are those dealing with the use of thermal imaging to record the heat absorbed and emitted by the south façade of the Gothic House, and the use of newly-developed glass sensors to determine the potential rate of future corrosion of the windows, measured at various points on the exterior surface of the protective glazing and the exterior and interior surfaces of the original glass. Surprisingly, it was discovered that sunblinds, which had been used in the nineteenth century, and for which fixings were already present, offered the best means of reducing surface temperatures, although external protective glazing would still be required to counter possible effects of atmospheric pollution or vandalism. Results of the chemical analysis of a range of enamels and coloured glass and of the composition of the glass itself are given in tabular form and the photogrammetric method used to survey the windows is described in detail.

The colour illustrations are excellent and the report is economically constructed, clearly written and of considerable significance for the future conservation of collections comparable to Wörlitz. It is clear that this work is sufficiently important to warrant a full translation.

Paul Sharpling

Marks, Richard and Williamson, Paul, eds. (assisted by Eleanor Townsend), *Gothic: Art for England 1400-1547*.

London: V&A Publications, 2003. Hardcover and softcover, 496 pp., 410 col. and 65 b/w ills. ISBN 1 85177 401 7, hc, £45; ISBN 1 85177 402 5, sc, £29.95

This magnificently produced book – good value in hardback and a real bargain in paper – brings together coloured photographs and detailed descriptions of over 350 late-medieval objects, placed in their historical context by eleven introductory essays and twenty-one brief overviews. The latter are thematically organised to complement the various modules of the exhibition to which the book forms the catalogue.

The introductory essays and overviews provide a comprehensive *tour d'horizon* of the period that takes full account of modern scholarship – the enormously useful bibliography alone runs to twenty pages of close print – and are all stimulating, accessible and jargon-free. The strange title of the book makes it sound like the strapline to a sporting event but it expresses its purpose succinctly enough. The subject matter is art commissioned by English men and women of all classes, irrespective of provenance. And increasingly through the period, markedly so in some fields, the art came from mainland Europe or was made by foreign craftsmen living in England. The dominance by the early sixteenth century of Low Countries glass makers such as Galyon Hone is well known, but modest objects for the mass market were imported, too, such as pipe clay devotional images or the moulds for tin pilgrims' badges.

Inevitably in a book that is primarily an exhibition catalogue, the pattern of survival of displayable artefacts means that coverage is skewed towards the rich. But even from the wealthiest echelons of society – not least the royal family – one is struck by the extent of what has been lost. In some cases this represents the late-medieval imperative to be up-to-date, not only the vicissitudes of time. The scale of deliberate destruction in the sixteenth and seventeenth centuries is constantly apparent. This dearth is something of a *leitmotiv* of the book, the purpose of which is to reinstate the period in England as one of significant artistic achievement within the European mainstream. As such, it follows self-consciously in the vein of other recent blockbuster exhibitions (and splendid catalogues) – on the art of the Anglo-Saxons (1984, 1991), the Romanesque (1984), and the Age of Chivalry (1987). But Alexandrina Buchanan's interesting essay on perceptions of late Gothic in England suggests these might lie within an even older tradition of exhibitions dating back to the 1890s when a number attempted to counter the prevailing view that art in England 'was of no interest before the eighteenth century'.

Refined by John Harvey and Nikolaus Pevsner, one wonders now whether this apologetic approach to late-medieval English art is still really necessary. It can lead to hyperbole: can the period really be characterised as one of 'mass politics and media management'? Our knowledge of the period has been transformed over the last fifty years. Perhaps *Gothic: Art for England* will finally put this defensive tradition to bed.

The constraints of what can be exhibited exacerbate this aspect of the book. Given the emphasis on the visual arts, late-medieval literature inevitably receives little attention, although illuminated manuscripts, particularly the exquisite small-scale products designed to enhance personal devotion, feature well. One of the great achievements of the period, the huge flowering of government and legal records, remains unsung although the remarkable private letters of families such as the Pastons and the Celys are mined for illustrative material. But one of the criticisms made of the exhibition itself can hardly be levelled at the book: that it misses out architecture, the one area where the visual record is rich. Christopher Wilson and others tackle the subject squarely in a number of important essays although most insights attach to the upper end of the market and relatively little use is made of new thinking in the fields of vernacular building.

Among the most vulnerable targets of the iconoclasts, of course, was stained and painted glass although, as Wilson points out, its utility and the cost of replacing it with plain glass might have slowed the rate of destruction. Also the fact that some was set so high that it can only now be seen clearly with the aid of binoculars, may mean that the iconography could not then be easily 'read'. Precisely when most of our medieval glass disappeared is a moot question that deserves further research. Many insights and some clarifications of attribution are contained throughout the text and in the sixteen detailed entries on glass (or *vidimuses*) contributed by Marks, Sarah Brown and David King.

One of the great virtues of this book is its determination to place what remains of the art of late-medieval England in an historical, economic and social context. This broad approach is underpinned by detailed analysis of individual artefacts and full scholarly apparatus. As such, especially when set beside the catalogues supporting the earlier English medieval art exhibitions, it will remain of lasting value.

Martin Cherry

Neri, Antonio / Merrett, Christopher, *The Art of Glass (L'Arte Vetraria).* 3rd ed. with minor corrections.

Sheffield: Society of Glass Technology, 2001. Softcover, 436 pp., 4 b/w ills. ISBN 0 900682 37 X, £17.50 (incl. P&P, available from the Society of Glass Technology, Don Valley House, Savile Street East, Sheffield S4 7UQ or see www.sgt.org).

In October of 1662 the gentlemen of a certain learned Society received, with thanks, the translation of a famous Italian treatise, undertaken by one of their number and at their instigation. This was not the first or last occasion on which the gentlemen of the newly incorporated Royal Society of London, dedicated to the 'further promoting by the authority of experiments the sciences of natural things and of useful arts', were to render inspirational service to British manufactures, but their actions in this instance were to have far-reaching and long-lasting consequences for the British glass industry overall. The translator? One Christopher Merrett (1614-1695), a Fellow and Librarian of the Royal College of Physicians. And the treatise? Only 'The World's Most Famous Book on Glassmaking', published in Florence in 1612 by the well-travelled Antonio Neri. Indeed, Merrett's was the very first translation anywhere of Neri's *L'Arte Vetraria* from the original Italian, and was itself to be the subject of further translations throughout Europe over the following century.

As a severely practical manual of glass-making methods and practice, Neri's text is of course an invaluable historical document, but Merrett's is no mere translation. If it may seem odd that a physician should undertake such a labour, this merely reflects the multi-facetted *virtuoso* interests of the members of the Royal Society. It is however quite apparent that Merrett was well acquainted with the London glasshouses, especially as suppliers of medical and experimental glassware, no doubt to order – he must have discussed technical matters with them on numerous occasions, and in the course of preparing his translation. Merrett therefore not only edits Neri's text (removing for instance, a large number of repetitious elements), but also appends his own critical and scholarly commentary and practical observations, amounting to nearly half the text. Thus the speculative empiricism of Neri, just this side of alchemy (and the constant references to cleanliness, purity of materials and diligent labour must be read as more than merely practical instructions) is overshadowed by a newly sceptical and experimental cast of mind, with fascinating results.

Neri's text is divided into Seven Books, and it is perhaps at first surprising that there is so little mention of window glass, as opposed to vessel glass. Nevertheless, the recipes will give the reader a fair summary of the underlying chemistry of various glass colours and enamels (and the fourth book has some valuable discourse on the difficulties to be had in the manufacture of lead glasses). That these colours are almost always compared to gemstones betrays the chief ambitions of the 16th-century glassworker's art, a hangover from medieval speculation on the properties of gems as inhering in their colour and brilliancy, not in the stones themselves.

Neri addresses himself exclusively to his fellow glassworkers, and a considerable degree of practical knowledge is assumed – as he says in his foreword (and notwithstanding the address to his Medici patron) 'to please and delight… men understanding in this profession'. Virtually no reference is made to the construction and operation of the predominantly wood-fired furnaces of his day, whereas Merrett, addressing the businessman and entrepreneur wishing to set up in glass-making, gives us a fascinating description of the coal-fired reverberatory furnaces seen in the glasshouses of 17th-century London. Reader beware – the quantities recommended are therefore on a semi-industrial scale – 'do not try this at home'!

Merrett is not without a certain wry humour, and faced with the impossible task of defining this marvellous material – glass – he notes, 'Glass is one of the fruits of the fire, which is most true, for it is a thing wholly of Art, not of Nature, and not to be produced without strong fires. I have heard, a singular Artist merrily to this purpose say, that their profession would be the last in the world: for when God should consume with fire the Universe, that then all things therein would vitrifie and turn to glass. Which would be true upon supposition of a proportionable mixture of fit Salts, and Sand or Stones'.

The present edition under review, published by The Society of Glass Technology, and reproducing the original layout of Merrett's text in an A5 format, is prefaced by Professor W. E. S. Turner's fascinating historical paper, originally published in 1962 as a 300th – and indeed a 350th anniversary tribute to Merrett's and Neri's 'Most Famous Book'.

Neil Moat

Fawcett, Richard, ed., *Glasgow's Great Glass Experiment.*

Edinburgh: Historic Scotland, 2003. Softcover, 92 pp, 59 col. and b/w ills. ISBN 1 903570 78 6, £16.50 (available from www.historic-scotland.gov.uk/shop or tel. 0131-668-8638, fax. 0131-668-8669).

The debate surrounding the controversial scheme to reglaze St Mungo's Cathedral, Glasgow would be a perfectly feasible event on which to hinge the analysis of the aesthetics of nineteenth-century stained glass in the whole of Britain. The Glasgow programme was begun in 1859 and largely completed by 1864. Fierce reaction to the appointment of the Königliche Glasmalereianstalt (Royal Bavarian Stained Glass Manufactory) to make all of the more than fifty principal windows in the 'upper' Cathedral only subsided after the last of them was taken down in the 1950s: *Glasgow's Great Glass Experiment* re-opens the debate. The six essays in this timely and scholarly reassessment explore the impact of the German glass on its contemporaries and its subsequent vicissitudes, and are also revealing about present-day attitudes to historic stained glass.

The contributions of James Macaulay on the contemporary liturgy of Presbyterian Scotland, George Rawson on the background to the ambitious campaign and George Fairfull-Smith on its patronage are invaluable in placing the glazing in its social and historical contexts. Rawson's chapter extends his essay in

Missionary of Art (2000), an informative study of Charles Heath Wilson, Headmaster of Glasgow School of Art and prime mover in the glazing scheme. A pioneer in art and design education in both Scotland and England, Wilson intended the scheme to be didactic on two levels – as a display of biblical iconography (in a country with almost no surviving figurative stained glass), and as an exposition of academic glass painting designed by artists working in the Italian Renaissance tradition he favoured.

Wilson's tastes automatically precluded, therefore, all of the English Gothic Revival glass painters; Rawson details the determined lobbying of the one Scottish contender, James Ballantine, which, to his chagrin, was equally unsuccessful. For in 1856 Wilson decided to consult his friend Charles Winston, whose advice (thirty-three of his letters to Wilson were included in the posthumously published *Art of Glass Painting*, 1867), was liable to generate more heat than light; moreover, he had come to the conclusion that no British artists were up to the task of securing the future of stained glass.

Sally Rush takes up the story of what she almost describes as the Winston-Wilson 'conspiracy'. Winston advocated that the only viable modern style was a synthesis of medieval technique and Raphaelesque drawing. Rush is right, therefore, to draw attention to the claims of the window at St Paul's, Alnwick, designed by William Dyce and made (under Max Ainmiller) at the Königliche Glasmalereianstalt in 1856. Arguably the most triumphant vindication of Winston's theories, certain passages within it are scarcely surpassed in the history of stained glass. Why Dyce (an Aberdonian) was passed over for the Glasgow commission perhaps only Winston could explain; he admitted that what was placed in St Mungo's was not 'true' glass painting (although he influenced Ainmiller to use more pot-metal and less enamels), nor did he get more than competent academic drawing. In 1955 Douglas Percy Bliss (a successor of Wilson's at Glasgow School of Art) called the figures 'drearily correct' and the ornament 'rigid and mechanical'. Rush informs us that consideration of Dyce was linked to his joint pitch for the commission with the glass painter Frank Oliphant (another Scot); but Oliphant had engaged in two very public rows with Winston, which must have militated against their chances.

Elgin Vaassen, whose exemplary *Bilder Auf Glas* (1997) deserves to be familiar to all of our members, appears to be slightly defensive about the work of the Glasmalereianstalt, as though forced onto the back foot by its predominantly unenthusiastic reception. While the outcry against this huge job being assigned to foreign artists may have been motivated partly by envy or nationalism, there were legitimate grounds for criticism of the results. This is a debate that could fill a complete issue of the *Journal*: an initial proposition *contra* might be that none of the designers – Von Schwind, Hess, Strahuber, Friesz *et al* – was as imaginative or fluent a draughtsman as Dyce. But Dr Vaassen provides a thorough survey of these and other Munich 'Stained Glass Windows for the United Kingdom' and includes an illuminating discussion of the adaptation of porcelain painting techniques in pictorial stained glass.

Dr Rush essayed her highly original perceptions concerning the influence the Glasgow scheme exercised on Daniel Cottier, Stephen Adam and the 'new' Scottish stained glass in *Missionary of Art*. Here she concentrates on a broad and balanced discussion of the relative merits of the German glass in the context of such disparate British figures as James Ballantine, William Morris and Christopher Whall. Local pressure had some effect on the authorities, for several British glass painters were offered the sop of windows in the 'lower' church and the crypt. Henry Hughes's disappointing *Acts of Mercy* remain *in situ*, as does a better effort by Ballantine & Allan, but those by William Wailes and Thomas Willement, for example, are lost (the latter's angels, to judge by the designs in the British Library, were among his finest late work).

Plans to remove the German glass gathered pace in the 1930s and twenty years later it was nearly all banished. It was not destroyed but placed in storage; while its future remains uncertain, the volume concludes with Mark Bambrough's discussion of the conservation techniques he employed on the panels that were brought out for the Charles Heath Wilson exhibition in 2000. Rush astutely notes that paint loss, which was the principal reason given for the removal of the Glasgow glass, was a fairly widespread problem in the nineteenth century, and remains a crucial factor in important windows being condemned (she cites the Daniel Cottier window displaced from St Giles's Cathedral, Edinburgh, in 1985 and the Pugin window removed from Sherborne Abbey in 1996). It might be noted that as early as 1869 the *Building News* reported fading in both the Glasgow glass and the four Munich windows in St Paul's Cathedral. Bambrough's essay will be of particular interest to members, and provides a welcome airing for the question of whether to repaint and refire fugitive pigment on historic glass – still a contentious issue. The book is well produced (although some of the colour plates are slightly fuzzy): indeed it is essential reading and can be very warmly recommended.

Martin Harrison

Albutt, Roy, *Stained Glass Windows of Bromsgrove and Redditch, Worcestershire.*

Pershore: Roy Albutt, 2002. Softcover, 128 pp., 25 col. and 1 b/w ills. ISBN 0 9543566 0 8, £12.95 (available from the author, 11 Great Calcroft, Pershore, Worcestershire WR10 1QS).

The author of this very useful book has carried out a survey of stained glass in forty-two churches and chapels in and around the towns of Bromsgrove and Redditch, listing all the buildings with their windows in a Gazetteer section. Preceding this are essays on the history of the craft and on the procedures entailed in the commissioning of a window from design to installation (although it is not made clear that these differ for non-Anglican denominations), with a series of extended entries highlighting some of the most significant windows and their designers and makers. It is a pity that no map is included, as such a book seems tailor-made for the vitreous-minded church-crawler who finds the opportunity to focus on this particular area of the English Midlands.

Roy Albutt has clearly undertaken a considerable amount of research into parish and diocesan records. Especially illuminating are the occasional quotations from the contemporary correspondence of dissatisfied or contented clients, as are the details given of prices charged for particular windows. It is, for example, remarkable to read that J. E. Nuttgens was charging only £200 for a window (at Holy Trinity church, Lickey) as recently as 1979! In general, the author's style of writing is appealingly direct and personal, although sometimes a little baldly interjectory: why single out the Camm windows at St Cassian's, Chaddesley Corbett, simply because, with no other explanation, they 'are not to my taste'?

There are a few fragmentary examples of medieval glazing featured – among them a charming fifteenth-century *Virgin and Child* at Hewell Grange, Tardebigge – but the majority of the windows listed and described are by nineteenth- and twentieth-century designers and makers. Not surprisingly, there are many individual and multiple commissions by the Birmingham-based firm of Hardman, but also a good selection by less prolific makers such as Frederick Preedy, Chance Bros. and the various members of the Camm family of Smethwick. The Arts & Crafts Movement is well represented, notably by the work of the local Bromsgrove Guild (whose output in several media brought international renown to the town in the 1900-1950 period) and by the lesser known but equally interesting Alfred Pike, whose 'rediscovery' was chronicled by Albutt in the last volume of this *Journal*. One curious oversight in the Gazetteer, therefore, is Pike's impressive *Ruth, Boaz and Naomi* window (1918) at Alvechurch, here listed as 'maker unknown'. Any future, revised edition should also give the full dates (1870-1964) of Baron Arild Rosenkrantz, the Danish-Scottish designer of an important Arts & Crafts window at Hewell Grange, and George Parlby should be credited with cartooning the Henry Hughes memorial window (made by Ward & Hughes, 1885) at St John's, Bromsgrove, which is illustrated.

The colour plates are generally good and have wisely been chosen to show the more interesting glass and not simply representative examples. An appendix listing all the artists/makers alphabetically with their respective windows provides a handy means of tracing work by particular individuals or schools, and there is a good bibliography with details of obscure sources as well as more standard works. In this book, Albutt has made a valuable contribution to the inevitably gradual – but increasingly more systematic – process (pioneered by the late Birkin Haward) of recording our national heritage of stained glass. In so doing, he has also highlighted the distinguished achievements of regionally-based craftworkers, such as A. J. Davies and A. E. Lemmon of Bromsgrove and Alfred Pike of Hewell, whose work has hitherto been unjustly neglected or forgotten.

Peter Cormack

Waters, William, *Stained Glass from Shrigley & Hunt of Lancaster and London.*

Lancaster: Centre for North-West Regional Studies, 128 pp., 58 col. and 40 b/w ills. ISBN 1 86220 140 4 , £26.95 (plus £3 P&P, cheques payable to Lancaster University, orders to CNWRS, Fylde College, Lancaster University, LA1 4YF or see www.lancs.ac.uk/users/cnwrs)

The publication of Paul Thompson's monograph on William Butterfield in 1971 signalled British architectural history entering welcome new territory. But it proved to be something of a false dawn, and thirty-two years later many of Butterfield's peers – Street, Bodley and Sedding, for example – still await serious critical attention. In the context of such an apparently arbitrary scholarly programme it is not surprising that nineteenth-century stained glass, which has attracted minimal interest as an academic discipline, is being published in a more haphazard way. Charles Sewter's catalogue raisonné of Morris & Company (1974-75) was followed by my own general survey (1980); thus Margaret Stavridi's study of C. E. Kempe (1988) was, notwithstanding its flaws, the first substantial monograph of its kind. No doubt a thin primary bibliography and the consequently huge research burden have discouraged others from tackling individual artists or workshops; to a meagre list – Peter Cormack's scholarly catalogues and essays on Arts and Crafts stained glass workers and Michael Kerney's narrower but exemplary *Stained Glass of Frederick Preedy* (2001) – can now be added William Waters's pioneering reassessment of the Lancaster workshop of Shrigley & Hunt.

Although Shrigley & Hunt's stained glass is mainly concentrated in North-West England, Arthur William Hunt opened a London office in 1879 and actively sought to promote their work across the whole of Britain; his diligence helped the company to achieve national prominence. Hunt was, first and foremost, an entrepreneur, and one of the many good things about this book is that it opens with what is basically a business history of the firm he founded. This is an apposite perspective from which to frame an artistic retrieval: reconciling art and commerce was, after all, a core dilemma of the Victorian stained glass industry.

The first Shrigley & Hunt stained glass was made in 1875. Initially their designs coincided closely with the aestheticism of the London *avant-garde*, but during the 1880s this style itself became outmoded. Rather than forge an innovative idiom of their own, Shrigley & Hunt reorientated, like many other firms, towards the highly-wrought (and commercially viable) late-Gothic of Burlison & Grylls and C. E. Kempe. The broader national context that one misses at times in this volume would have allowed this shift to be examined in greater depth. It might have been argued, for example, that originality is not a *sine qua non*, and that the skilful and attractive stained glass produced by Shrigley & Hunt provides paradigmatic support for such a view: Waters, however, suggests that their principal designers in the nineteenth century, Edward Holmes Jewitt and Carl Almquist, were artists of 'genius'. While his obvious enthusiasm for Shrigley & Hunt is preferable to earnestly detached art history, this claim is somewhat excessive. Although Jewitt and Almquist were accomplished figure cartoonists, their designs were invariably indebted to Henry Holiday's Neo-Classicism and Burne-Jones's Neo-Renaissance. Moreover, as many of the illustrations demonstrate, after 1885 Shrigley & Hunt increasingly set these late-Pre-Raphaelite echoes within complex fifteenth-century style micro-architecture; this was precisely the kind of historicist stylistic incongruity absent in the work of, say, William Morris, and the gulf between them requires explication if the author is to substantiate his contention that Shrigley & Hunt were 'equal to any of their national compatriots'.

The text is well arranged and includes informative appendices with a chronology, list of artists and craftsmen and a select gazetteer (the author, we are told, is preparing a catalogue raisonné). Shrigley & Hunt had a long, if latterly chequered, history and Waters is to be commended for following the story through until the firm's demise, on the death of Joseph Fisher, in 1982. The post-war contributions of John Blyth, Harry Harvey and Keith New will be of special interest to many members, as will the designs of Henry Wilson and J. C. N. Bewsey around 1910. We learn that in 1909 George J. Hunt quarrelled with his father and left to set up his own firm in London; among other former employees who, like Hunt Jnr, established independent workshops exploring late-Gothic idioms were Edward J. Prest and Gilbert Gamon. The book is generously illustrated but the editing is occasionally slipshod, with several mis-spellings and excessively repetitive language. Nevertheless there is much to admire in this balanced and engagingly presented survey, which elucidates many aspects of nineteenth- and twentieth-century workshop practice. Let us hope for many more productions of this kind.

Martin Harrison

Warrener, Rodney and Yelton, Michael, *Martin Travers 1886-1948. An Appreciation.*

London: Unicorn Press, 2003. Hardcover, 352 pp., 32 col. and 162 b/w ills. ISBN 0 906290 70 8, price £35 (incl. P&P, UK only; plus £4 for Europe or £8 for rest of world, available from Unicorn Press, 76 Great Suffolk Street, London SE1 0BL).

If Christopher Whall was the most influential British stained glass artist of the first quarter of the twentieth century, Martin Travers arguably had a similar status for the following generation working in the craft, so this fine new monograph – the first full-length study of its subject – is a major addition to the literature. It combines a well-researched biography with detailed studies of his work as an architect, designer of church furnishings, stained glass artist and graphic artist. A comprehensive gazetteer lists architectural work in various media, including unexecuted projects.

Before their careful analysis of the stylistic phases which Travers's career underwent, the authors introduce the man himself, a complex personality with a challenging personal life and a paradoxical attitude to the work for which he is best known. For although he is now indelibly associated with the more ultra-montane movement in High Anglicanism between the world wars, Travers himself was apparently an agnostic detached from the lavish piety his designs expressed and promoted, and with an antipathy to the Roman Church (which most of his Anglo-Catholic clients believed they were emulating). The story of Travers's home life is sufficiently 'dysfunctional' to be the stuff of television dramas. The cast of characters includes his glamorous but erratic first wife Christine, her brother, the self-Gaelicised actor Michael Mac Liammoir, the necromancer Aleister Crowley and Christine's female companion 'Poker' Hartley. Their exploits, recounted with tact and sympathy by the authors, are in marked contrast to the disciplined beauty (and sometimes austerity) of Travers's designs, as if the designer was intent on retaining in his artistic work the control which eluded him in the domestic sphere.

Martin Travers's training was almost schizophrenic: four years imbibing Arts & Crafts philosophy under Lethaby at the Royal College of Art, followed by the rather drier atmosphere of Comper's office. He not unnaturally took some elements of his style from both experiences whilst repudiating others. His personal manner did in fact emerge very early, characterised by an unerring sense of spatial organisation in his designs, excellent lettering and a creative use of sometimes disparate historical sources. Travers's 'Baroque' is far from being a pastiche of any particular period or national school. Instead, it blends late-Gothic, Wren-inspired, Hispanic and other seemingly historicist components to create a peculiarly clean-cut idiom which is, above all, modern. One of the most perceptive remarks made by Warrener and Yelton in their discussion of Travers's church furnishings draws attention to the similarity with contemporary cinema design. Indeed, perhaps it is in the context of Art Deco that his work can best be understood.

The fact that neither of the authors is an art historian does not seem to have been a significant handicap. There are a few errors of terminology – archive photographs of windows being wrongly captioned as 'designs', for example – but most of the detailed descriptions of stained glass, woodwork, statuary and graphic art are both concise and helpful. If there is a missing dimension, it is most conspicuously in the absence of contextual discussion. Although undeniably original, Travers's prodigious multi-media output was influenced by and competing against work by many talented contemporaries. It would, for instance, have been interesting to relate his distinctive use of source material to that of F. C. Eden, who (though not as prolific) was almost as versatile as an ecclesiastical designer.

Readers of the *Journal* may be aware of Travers primarily for his stained glass, which is fully illustrated (though mainly in monochrome) in this book. Perhaps fewer people know his considerable *oeuvre* as a graphic artist, which is very closely related in style and equally distinguished, so it is good to have the two areas of work featured at some length. The graphic quality is very evident in Travers's glass-painting style – linear and well-defined, with a very structured use of leading (and, sometimes, false leadlines) to reinforce the painted line. One regrets that the illustrations, although plentiful, do not adequately show the evolution of his increasingly self-limited colour sense, from the Arts & Crafts richness of the East window at St Andrew's, Catford (1920) to the more delicate hues of the Annunciation window (1943) at St Edward's, Corfe Castle.

There may be room for further detailed publications on aspects of Martin Travers and his influence, but there can be little doubt that this is the definitive monograph. It is elegantly written as a seamless collaboration by its two authors and, in chronicling Travers's achievements, it also presents a compelling study of that cultural phenomenon – 'Baroque' High Anglicanism – which, in his curiously ambivalent way, he articulated with such panache.

Peter Cormack

Greensted, Mary and Wilson, Sophia, eds., *Originality and Initiative: The Arts and Crafts Archives at Cheltenham.*

Cheltenham Art Gallery and Museum, in association with Lund Humphries, 2003. Softcover, 160 pp., 53 col. and 142 b/w ills. ISBN 0 85331 873 5, £25.

In view of the close association between the Cotswolds and the Arts and Crafts Movement, it is entirely appropriate that the Cheltenham Art Gallery and Museum should have made a special effort to collect in this field, and it has been triumphantly successful. Since 1981 credit for this has been due largely to George Breeze, who was until recently the Head of the Gallery, and this book, which is the third and last of a series publicising the collection, is suitably dedicated to him.

The first two volumes dealt with 'objects' and with furniture, while this one covers 'the archive of drawings, designs and photographic records, together with the Emery Walker Library'. In his foreword Breeze refers to the book as a 'catalogue', and that is how the second part (compiled by Sophia Wilson) is titled, but the various parts of the collection are only summarily described, with the exception of Emery Walker's library, acquired by the Gallery in 1990. Even this, however, is not a complete catalogue of the over '1,000 books', but of only 214 personalised books and manuscripts (including three which did not belong to Walker). It would, however, be unfair to complain about this, as a complete catalogue would scarcely have been an economical publishing project.

The first part of the book consists of five fascinating and beautifully illustrated essays. Three are by Mary Greensted – on Emery Walker, on 'William and May Morris: images of Kelmscott', and on Ernest Gimson. Mike McGrath writes on Sidney Barnsley.

The fifth essay will be of most interest to readers of this journal: Peter Cormack gives an elegantly succinct account of the work of Paul Woodroffe, whose output of stained glass is documented in six 'design albums' bought by the Art Gallery in 1988. Compiled by Woodroffe himself, they contain 122 watercolour designs and 273 photographs and printed reproductions of his glass, covering the years between 1900 and 1945. The essay supplements Cormack's catalogue for the exhibition at the William Morris Gallery in 1982-3, which dealt mostly with Woodroffe's work as an illustrator and book designer. It gives a good idea of what the albums contain, and the twenty illustrations (seven in colour) make possible an assessment of Woodroffe's achievement – not so personal as that of his master Christopher Whall, or Karl Parsons, but always displaying fine drawing and craftsmanship, and skilful adaptation to the architectural context. Three of the illustrations relate to his largest and most important commission, the fifteen large windows for the Lady Chapel of St Patrick's Cathedral, New York. Woodroffe's own assistants included Gabriel and Michael Pippet and Joseph Nuttgens.

For all those interested in the Arts and Crafts Movement, this book will provide both a visual treat and a treasure house of information and enlightenment.

Peter Howell

The Stained Glass of Liverpool Cathedral. Pitkin Guide by Canon Noel Vincent.

Liverpool: Jarrolds, 2002. Softcover, 21 pp., 50 col. and b/w ills.
ISBN 0 7117 2589 6, £2.99 (available from SPCK, Liverpool Cathedral, St James Mount, Liverpool L1 7AZ, Tel: 0151 702 7255, Email: liverpool@spck.org.uk)

The Liverpool Cathedral in question is the Anglican Cathedral designed by Giles Gilbert Scott and begun in 1904. The last Gothic Cathedral to be built in Europe, it also contains the last glazing scheme to be executed by three consecutive generations of stained glass masters and their apprentices.

John W. Brown of Whitefriars, a pupil of Edward Burne-Jones and William Morris, designed the East window, while the work of his pupil James Hogan features in the great central space, and in turn his pupil Carl Edwards completed the glazing in 1978 with the West window, a monumental *Benedicite*. Each designer was also responsible for other windows but, historically and stylistically, the scheme developed from East to West. Unfortunately, the numbering of the windows in the booklet begins at the west entrance, but if you wish to enjoy the chronological development of the glazing it is essential to start at the east end.

The firms of Morris & Co, Kempe and Burlison & Grylls were well past their inventive best when they contributed glazing to the Cathedral. But the Scottish designers William Wilson and Herbert Hendrie were still creative forces and competently adapted their styles to complement the work of James Hogan already *in situ*, although Hendrie did go astray by applying matts to the glass, a technique which the linear school of Hogan had eliminated.

The glass in the Anglican Cathedral is the antithesis of that found in the Catholic Cathedral. It was created within constraints established by a powerful and opinionated stained glass committee which originally included Giles Gilbert Scott, who preferred visitors to look at his architecture and not be distracted by the glass. The committee determined that the nave windows must include men of both local and national acclaim: hymnologists, parsons, musicians and even stained glass craftsmen stare down from between the giant mullions. Choice of subject or freedoms of expression were not available to the glaziers; these are windows that had to be designed to a well-defined and detailed brief. It is to the credit of James Hogan that he developed a style of glazing, influenced by Christopher Whall and by his experiences in North America, that took a different direction to those of his contemporaries.

The handbook is an essential guide to the stained glass for any visitor. It consists of twenty pages in full colour, heavily illustrated and with two fold-out features displaying the East and West windows in their entirety. Colour reproduction is not precise as the glass occasionally appears too blue, but this may partly be due to details of the windows being shown out of their architectural setting. The later windows were generally designed in cooler tones to balance the hot red sandstone.

Quibbles about an iconographic overload and a scarcity of technical information would be unfair, because many readers will have experienced the sheer frustration of entering cathedral gift shops lumbered with everything from key-ring angels to medieval fudge – everything except a decent guide to the stained glass. The booklet is a gem and Canon Noel Vincent should be congratulated.

Tony Benyon

Foster, Paul, ed., *Chagall Glass at Chichester and Tudeley.*

University College Chichester, 2002. Reprinted with additions 2002. Softcover, 102 pp., 3 b/w and 47 col. ills. ISBN 0 948765 78 X, £7 (plus 75p P&P, cheques to University College Chichester, Bishop Otter Campus, Chichester, West Sussex PO19 6PE).

The Otter Memorial Papers (this is Number 14), launched in 1987, were established to provide an opportunity to consider a religious or associated secular subject from several perspectives: contributions are primarily expository, but others offer a meditative or an original artistic response to the chosen subject. Policy and control rests with an editorial panel drawn from the staff of University College Chichester, where the editor, Paul Foster, is Emeritus Professor of English.

The subject of this volume is Marc Chagall (1887-1985) and his stained glass in the North Quire aisle of Chichester Cathedral, a predominantly ruby-coloured window, and the twelve windows filling All Saints, Tudeley, in Kent, where blue is the enveloping colour. Together they comprise the entirety of Chagall glass in Britain.

The twelve contributors to this study describe the background to the commissioning of these windows, the themes expressed, the interpretations from maquette to stained glass by Charles Marq, details of the Services of the Dedication and various responses to the glass, including some in verse as well as photographs of an embroidery inspired by it, which seems out of place in this publication. In a long essay Patrick Reyntiens sets the cultural scene that greeted Chagall, an exile from Vitebsk, on his arrival in Paris in 1910, where fellow artists soon referred to him as the 'poet', and the political and religious climate between the two World Wars and after 1945, the years when the French state and the Catholic Church encouraged and financed a number of astonishingly good ecclesiastical buildings and sacred art. Architects and artists of the stature of Le Corbusier, Perret, Braque, Manessier, Leger and others accepted commissions and in 1957 Chagall, at the age of seventy, designed his first stained glass work for the chapel at Assy, Savoy. His three lights in Metz Cathedral, perhaps the most architecturally satisfying of all his windows, were installed the following year and, in 1961, glass for the synagogue in the medical centre of the Hadassah Hebrew University in Jerusalem was put on show in the Louvre.

Among visitors to this exhibition was the remarkable Walter Hussey, then Dean of Chichester, who earlier had commissioned work from Sutherland and Moore for his church, St Matthew's in Northampton. In Paris, Hussey conceived the idea of a window by Chagall for Chichester and approaches were made in the early 1960s. However, a series of events delayed progress and the window was not installed until 1978, the year after the Dean's retirement. Another visitor to the Louvre exhibition was Sarah d'Avigdor-Goldsmid who was enraptured by the Jerusalem windows. Tragically, two years later, she drowned in a sailing accident off the Sussex coast. Her parents invited Chagall to design an East window in Tudeley Church as her memorial. At the unveiling in 1967, Chagall exclaimed: 'C'est magnifique. Je ferai les tous!' The remaining eleven windows were glazed, the whole scheme being completed in 1985, but only after lengthy negotiations to obtain a Faculty to remove existing stained glass in the chancel.

The chronology charting the progress of each commission is set out and good colour plates show complete windows, details and exterior shots. Dates and the location of other windows by Chagall are listed. This is an attractive and informative publication.

Alan Younger

Cowen, Painton, *Six Days: The Story of the Making of the Chester Cathedral Creation Window Created by Artist Rosalind Grimshaw.*

Softcover, 112 pp., full colour throughout. ISBN 01275 464 891, £12.99 (available direct from Alastair Sawday Publishing, Home Farm Stables, Barrow Court Lane, Barrow Gurney, Bristol BS48 4RW, tel. (0)1275-464-891 or visit www.fragile-earth.com/sixdays).

This is the story of a window told in a most unusual way. The writer Painton Cowen is well known for his thoughtful book *Rose Windows* (Thames and Hudson, 1979). Rosalind Grimshaw is also known to the stained glass fraternity. She is a Fellow of the BSMGP and a warm-hearted and observant creator of lively stained glass panels and windows. That she has Parkinson's disease is also somewhat known, but not taken much notice of, because what matters about Ros is her glass.

This book reveals the complex development of the *Creation* window made for Chester Cathedral from the first letter commissioning the work in May 2000. Painton, with gentle skill, guides the reader through the processes needed to complete the substantial six-light window. These include the intellectual effort required for the reinterpretation of the Biblical texts, followed by an exciting period spent designing, cartooning, cutting and glazing the glass. Finally there is the shared joy of achievement in the completion of a very important work of art. For this is no ordinary task, it is nothing less than a keynote statement of Faith in one of the country's finest ecclesiastical buildings.

Six Days is an intensely moving book. It is about struggle and triumph against tremendous odds. Hardly surprising, therefore, that people burst into tears in the text. Indeed one is tempted to do the same when reading that Rosalind must arise at dawn to take her medication in order to be able to get going on her work during the day. Later, we find out that the early stages of the cartoon were sorted out in the ward where she was undergoing a readjustment of her treatment. I can well imagine the delight and enjoyment of the staff. Here was a patient determined to take full advantage of their care and do something utterly splendid with their aid!

The inclusion of a chapter by Patrick Costeloe (Rosalind's partner in every sense of the word) was especially moving. He writes: 'The more I use the metaphor of travelling in a strange land to try to illuminate the predicament posed by Parkinson's disease, the more apt it seems. One's landscape, one's environment, is so much part of one it is like breathing: miraculous, but taken for granted'.

Painton's method of tracing the passage of the commission from enthusiastic design acceptance to the flat aftermath of the triumphant dedication in Chester Cathedral is unusual. His description of the progress of the project is a bold departure from the restrained and edited version of events usually produced in written form for general consumption, while the glowing photographs on every page greatly enrich the text, enabling the reader to respond to the charm and humanity of the artist.

I particularly enjoyed the inclusion of tiny sketches and diary notes by Ros and the poems that suddenly seemed apposite, and the comments by neighbours and friends. One of these, Lavinia Ferguson, wrote with engaging clarity about the dedication, 'I looked at it up there in all its glory and felt very proud of Ros and so glad that I had been involved in a small way in this massive, vibrant and thoroughly idiosyncratic work of art'.

Caroline Swash

Farnsworth, Jean M., Croce, Carmen R., and Chorpenning, Joseph R., eds., *Stained Glass in Catholic Philadelphia.*

Philadelphia: St. Joseph's University Press, 2003. Hardcover, 528 pp., 880 ills. ISBN 0-916101-43-6, $70 (US, plus $8 shipping in US or $38 airmail, available from Saint Joseph's University Press, Attn: Book Orders, 5600 City Ave., Philadelphia, PA 19131; tel. 610-660-3400, fax 610-660-3410, email sjupress@sju.edu)

Whatever may be said about this publication, it is, quite simply, an extremely beautiful book. Whether or not one is interested in the history of the Roman Catholic Archdiocese of Philadelphia, it is a joy to leaf through – almost every page has a gloriously coloured image, including the index and front matter, where delightful details of windows have been silhouetted like the marginalia of medieval manuscripts. Extraordinary care has been taken in the illustrations, with digital cutting and pasting to provide even exposures. Although the studios represented may not top the lists of the world's most popular (Munich glass figures large here), their presentation allows the reader to judge them equitably, in accurate colour and sharp detail.

Unfortunately, beauty alone does not a great book make. It is hard to know how to critique this work: as art history, as social history, as church history, as gazetteer, as picture book? In trying to be all of these, the editors have set themselves too high a goal.

The text is oddly unsatisfying. Individual chapters seem truncated, eliminating the meat and leaving only the bones. Overall, there is less about stained glass than the title leads one to expect: while we may find that a particular church has windows by this or that firm, we learn little about the firm, about the congregation that purchased the windows, about the role of the windows in their building, or their place in the history of the church, the congregation, or the medium. Perhaps in the end the book is about Catholic Philadelphia, but the reader comes away without a notion of what the rest of the city is like, in order to ground the information in history and context.

Called a 'labour of love' in the foreword (a phrase often used to excuse a lack of excellence, as though good intentions were enough), the preface explains that the book evolved as a means to use a 50,000 image photographic archive, compiled since 1997 by the Archdiocese of Philadelphia. It includes the windows of 450 sites. These are very impressive statistics. No other organisation in the United States can boast such an organised and effective record in a similar time frame, and their desire to make part of this archive available to the public is highly commendable. Although no credit is given to any individual, the publisher, St Joseph's University, appears to have spearheaded the effort to bring together this group of essays by local scholars and church officials to explain and contextualise the 880 color illustrations drawn from the archive.

The idea of 'Catholic Philadelphia' is a concept that requires explanation. When one thinks of Catholic cities in the US, Boston or Chicago are the first to come to mind, with their notable Irish and Italian immigrant populations. Philadelphia, the 'City of Brotherly Love', is viewed as a Quaker city. David R. Contosta's chapter on the social history of Catholics in Philadelphia begins with the story of its Quaker founder, William Penn, and traces the growth of Catholicism, from 378 Catholics in a city of 10,000 in 1750, to about one-third of the population by 1850. Violent anti-Catholic riots in 1844 seem to have been a pivotal event and are referred to in several chapters. But they receive short shrift here; there seems to be an assumption by the author that readers already know about these events. This tendency is pervasive throughout the volume, leaving one feeling that only the most devout Catholic readers raised in Philadelphia will be able to understand most of the book's content. The rest of Contosta's chapter (one of the more interesting), deals with the development of individual parishes based on their ethnicity. The only non-stained-glass chapter to do so, he integrates the windows of these parishes into his story, showing how the Polish parish windows depicted St Stanilaus Kostka; the Irish, St Patrick; the Italian, St Anthony of Padua; and the Native Americans, Blessed Kateri Tekakwitha. Compelling as this is, the reader is left wanting more contextualisation: did Polish communities in other archdioceses venerate Stanislaus Kostka, or is he a peculiarly Philadelphian saint? What was the role of Native Americans, African Americans, and Chinese immigrants, mentioned only briefly here, in the Catholic church in Philadelphia, and elsewhere?

Of the eight chapters that deal directly with stained glass (including the Introduction), only one presents new historical information: Jean Farnsworth's chapter on the stained glass in Philadelphia's Catholic churches. Since this is really what the book purports to cover it is a shame that she was not given more space to devote to her subject (or even a whole book). An independent stained glass historian, her research is fascinating and important, and one craves more. Subtitled 'Reflections of Faith and Culture', she traces the history of the medium from the

1820s through the present day. Although few pre-1880 windows survive, she has located references to domestically-produced stained glass as early as 1827. This fact is a stunner: previously published information on American stained glass history dates its domestic production no earlier than the 1840s. Yet she devotes only two sentences to it. She also mentions windows made of glazed paper or linen, stained glass substitutes, a topic which has received no attention in the literature, despite its apparent prevalence around the country (at least a dozen patents exist from the late nineteenth century, and various homemakers' texts discuss them). But she provides no context for them: why were they used, who produced them?

Farnsworth's most important discovery is the dominance of the Munich school in Catholic churches in Philadelphia, whose windows became 'the definitive Catholic style' in the last decades of the nineteenth century. Promoted by the Church, which preferred their academic, neo-classical realism to the Gothic Revival styles developed in England (and closely associated with the Anglican and Episcopal Church), at least seven different German and Austrian firms exported glass to Philadelphia, led by Mayer of Munich and F. X. Zettler. Germanic stained glass was so popular in the Archdiocese that many churches replaced their earlier American-made windows with it. The Munich studios were adept at translating famous religious paintings from the Renaissance and by the Nazarenes into stained glass, a process decried by English and American stained glass pundits seeking to make new art in the medium. Farnsworth deals with this heretofore almost taboo subject in stained glass with professionalism and care, but again, one wishes for more detail, especially on the dissemination of the images used by the studios. She passes no judgement on the artistic quality of the windows, but presents them as their patrons saw them: as emotive, communicative religious education, rather than as religious decoration, as windows were often treated in churches of other denominations.

Farnsworth also contributes a brief history of the revival of the craft in the United States and an essay on patronage. Perhaps the most important aspect of the book, at least from the perspective of a stained glass historian, is her appendix of biographical information on the studios illustrated. Representing a tremendous amount of research, her chapters and appendix are the meat of this book, and constitute a significant contribution to the history of the medium in the United States. Much more than the other writers, Farnsworth makes us understand the difference in purpose between stained glass in Catholic and Protestant churches – that it is part of the liturgy – without making us feel like outsiders bereft of the secret handshake that will illumine this arcane medium.

The same cannot be said of essays by Joseph F. Chorpenning, OSFS (the publisher's editorial director) and Stephen Happel (Dean of the School of Religious Studies at Catholic University). Their role is to explain Catholic art. Chorpenning discusses iconography, and in general, although there is little new in his explanations of scenes from the life of Christ or the Virgin Mary, his text may be helpful for those unfamiliar with the importance of these scenes to Catholics. He does better with more specialised or rare saints, like St Margaret Mary Alacoque and St Catherine Labouré, figures of particular significance in the Philadelphia area. Happel's afterword, 'Lights and Mirrors: Stained Glass as Metaphor for the Catholic Soul', may appeal to the devout, but has little to do with stained glass *per se*.

Likewise the two chapters on Catholic architecture in Philadelphia, by Professor Sandra L. Tatman and Victoria Donohoe, senior art critic for *The Philadelphia Inquirer*: each would be fascinating if fleshed out more and published on its own. Critically, they fail to relate the architecture to the stained glass in any way. Tatman deals primarily with the work of Philadelphia's most important architects of Catholic churches, Napoleon LeBrun (1821-1901), Edwin F. Durang (1829-1911), and Henry D. Dagit (1865-1929). As architectural history, this is a fine piece of writing, but once again, it seems incomplete. The reader is left wanting to know how these buildings compare with other religious architecture. The most salient point presented is that Gothic Revival was not a favoured style; other authors mention this as well, but none succeeds in explaining why. Pugin is mentioned frequently, as are Ruskin and the Ecclesiological Society, but their connection (or rather, the lack thereof) with Catholic architecture is not adequately analysed. The impression is that these writers know the history of the Gothic Revival, but not of Catholic architecture, and are struggling to place the latter within a framework in which it was never meant to fit.

Donohoe's chapter deals more with the decoration of Catholic churches and how it reflects to the liturgy. But she, too, barely mentions stained glass. More problematic is that although her text is ostensibly about the 'evolution of taste and aesthetics in liturgical art from the mid-nineteenth century to the post-World War II era' (the subtitle), she does almost nothing to explain the vast changes wrought by the Second Vatican Council's *Constitution on the Sacred Liturgy* (1963), a monumental shift in liturgical design that is single-handedly responsible for the decorative ruination of more Catholic church interiors than one wishes to count. Curiously, none of the authors deals with this at all, leaving the reader with the very distinct impression that the book is by the faithful for the faithful, and underwritten by the Church.

Chapters on the technical aspects of the subject, by Joseph Beyer, a stained glass restorer, and Virginia Raguin, Chair of the Census of Stained Glass in America (although this august body is not mentioned), are at best arguable. Beyer relates how the Archdiocese removes windows from redundant churches and resells them to other Catholic churches around the country. This is not widely done in this country, but the Archdiocese of Philadelphia appears to have a mechanism in place (meaning funding, storage, and publicity) to accomplish it. Commendable as the practice may be, the illustrations suggest that little effort has been made on the receiving end to appropriately display the glass: although some installations are quite striking, the majority have far too much ambient or surface lighting to show the windows to their best advantage. Also regrettable is that neither Beyer nor Raguin appears to have current information on state-of-the-art conservation and restoration of architectural stained glass. Beyer claims that tracery cannot be reused because aluminum framing cannot be fabricated in its complicated shapes, as though wood and stone are no longer used for frames. Raguin trots out the old chestnut that windows do not have to be releaded every century because there are 800-year-old windows in Europe with their original leads, completely ignoring the fact that all lead is not fabricated the same way or of the same alloy. Similarly, she implies that nineteenth-century glass is subject to the same 'glass disease' or corrosion that affects the softer potash glasses of the Middle Ages. Beyer and Raguin patently contradict one another on at least one point: Beyer states that the conditions of lead cannot be determined without removing the window, while Raguin states that lead deterioration is a 'readily visible issue'. Most shocking is their lack of any mention of standards and guidelines for restoration by the Corpus Vitrearum, the American and International Institutes for Conservation, or even the Stained Glass Association of America or the Census of Stained Glass in America. Raguin, an art historian by profession, also surprisingly omits footnotes and bibliographic references.

Other chapters deal with the development of medieval stained glass; one by Michael Cothren is a well-written, engaging essay that presents nothing new and fails to connect well to the subject. There is also a single case history of one church. Interesting, but one wonders why it was included.

A gazetteer follows the text, comprising almost a quarter of the volume. Not all windows of any given building are illustrated, but those that are featured are refreshingly beautiful. New windows intermingle with older ones, making this section delightful to look at and occasionally engaging to read.

In sum, it can only be said that this publication is a mixed success. Its overshadowing sectarianism hampers its objectivity as art history. A sense of editorially-imposed limits on length haunts the chapters. Nonetheless, Farnsworth's research is worthwhile. Her biographical dictionary is an essential resource, and makes the book a valuable addition to the literature, as do the illustrations.

Julie L. Sloan

Jones, Robert O., D. *Maitland Armstrong: American Stained Glass Master.*

Tallahassee, Florida: Sentry Press, 1999; underwritten by the Stained Glass School of the Stained Glass Association in America. Hardcover, 325 pp., 43 col. plates & 89 b/w ills. ISBN 1 889574 16 3, $48.00 (US, available from the SGAA, 10009 East 62nd Street, Raytown, MO 64133, tel. 800-888-7422, see www.stainedglass.org for mailing costs).

David Maitland Armstrong (1836-1918) had become a successful New York lawyer and diplomat when, in the 1870s, he began to paint professionally. He shared a studio with sculptor Augustus Saint-Gaudens, became friends with many leading artists (such as John La Farge), exhibited widely, was a founding trustee of the Metropolitan Museum of Art, and organised the USA art exhibition at the Paris Universal Exposition of 1878.

Circa 1880, Armstrong joined the firm of another friend, Louis C. Tiffany, and participated in the development of opalescent or 'American Glass', according to Robert O. Jones, 'the first uniquely major American art form' (p. xix). In 1887, Armstrong established his own firm, Maitland Armstrong and Company (becoming also in 1888 the representative for Clayton & Bell in the USA). In 1890, he was joined by his daughter, Helen (1869-1948), who collaborated with her father until his death in 1918. She kept the firm going until 1930, working thereafter as a freelance artist.

Jones's book is based upon extensive archival material (held by members of the Armstrong family) and published sources. He identifies and discusses glass in over thirty sites in eleven states. About half the sites are in New York State and many of these are in New York City, although windows commissioned by George Vanderbilt for All Souls' Church in Ashville, North Carolina (1898-1911) will be familiar to some travellers.

With the aid of diagrams and period photographs, Jones documents how Armstrong created what Jones terms 'opalescent stained glass windows', convincingly challenging Virginia Raguin's statement that 'Maitland Armstrong... never actually touched the window' (*Reflections on Glass*, 2002, p. 42). His discussion of an 'allied arts' collaboration of architects and artists is suggestive, and his depiction of the artistic relationship of Maitland and Helen – she was the glass painter, responsible for flesh as well as figure design – is absorbing. The final chapter of the book is devoted to her work, which moved away from Renaissance iconography toward what Jones calls 'a more European, Gothic Styled design', realised in windows that combined opalescent and antique glass. Readers also meet Helen's older sister, Margaret (1867-1944), a gifted book designer, illustrator, biographer, and novelist.

Some textual and visual weaknesses compromise Jones's study. The book's organisation is awkward and repetitive, and readers endure pages of genealogical excavation only to encounter an Armstrong who is inhumanly perfect. Jones states that Armstrong's windows are artistically significant because they 'represent realistic subjects and... create ornament complimentary of the architectural setting' (p. 256), but he doesn't define his terminology or provide evidence to support his assertions. Important distinctions are ignored: quoting Louis Sullivan's *Autobiography* so as to suggest that Sullivan approved of the neo-classical architecture of the Chicago World's Fair of 1893 is either irresponsible or naïve. Aligning the Armstrongs with the Arts and Crafts movement is unwarranted.

Equally problematical is the inferior quality of many of the colour plates, which is compounded by incomplete captions and awkward placement in relation to the text. The site list (pp. xv-xvii) incorrectly identifies Columbia University's St Paul's Chapel as Faith Chapel. The reference to plate C-36 is missing from the text (p. 212).

There is a potentially wonderful book buried within this one. It needs a skilled editor, graphic designer, and photographer, and a more rigorous exploration of the art and architecture of the American Renaissance (James L. Sturm made a promising, well-illustrated start in 'Opalescent Glass and the Architecture of the "American Renaissance"', *Stained Glass From Medieval Times to the Present: Treasures to Be Seen in New York,* 1982). Despite its flaws, this book by Robert Jones contains much useful information about an important family of American glass artists.

Albert M. Tannler

Walker, Gay, *Bonawit, Stained Glass & Yale: G. Owen Bonawit's Work at Yale University & Elsewhere.*

Wilsonville, Oregon: Wildwood Press, 2000. Softcover, 42 pp., 44 col. and 4 b/w ills. [No ISBN], price $20 (US) plus $4.50 P&P to UK/Europe, (special discount to readers of this Journal, available from The Wildwood Press, 26761 SW 45th Drive, Wilsonville, Oregon 97070, USA).

Although the subject of this book, G. Owen Bonawit (1891-1971), was not quite in the forefront of the dramatic resurgence of traditional styles and techniques which transformed American stained glass in the 1900-1930 period, the contribution he made was both distinctive and interesting and it is here ably championed by Gay Walker. Bonawit is best known for his very extensive glazing schemes carried out in the 1930s for a number of Yale University's most prestigious buildings, among them the Harkness Memorial Tower and the Sterling Memorial Library. Designed or supervised by the architect James Gamble Rogers, they are among the finest examples of the 'Collegiate Gothic' style. This had evolved in the USA as a modern adaptation of the typical Oxford or Cambridge college, whose architectural features would impart to American academic institutions an instant patina of historical associations and venerable character. The addition of leaded lights and stained glass added to the convincing semblance of 'virtual' antiquity.

Bonawit, whom Rogers chose to make most of the leaded glass for his buildings, was ideally equipped for the task. His early training was in the New York workshop run by his uncle, Owen Bowen, in partnership with Otto Heinigke, followed by a short-lived but formative period of collaboration with the Scots-born Henry Wynd Young. The latter was of critical importance in the transmission of contemporary British stained glass trends to the USA in the 1900s.

Bonawit's Yale windows form part of an integrated decorative programme, orchestrated by James Gamble Rogers, which included sculpture in stone and wood, modelled plasterwork and decorative painting. Although Gay Walker does not use the term 'Arts & Crafts' in her account, this is probably how most British readers would characterise the idiom in which Bonawit worked – and which undoubtedly derives in part from his work with Heinigke & Bowen and Henry Wynd Young. It is a sort of expressionistic reinvention of the late medieval tradition of almost monochrome roundels or small panels set into expanses of leaded glass. The effect, however, diverges markedly from the delicate transparencies of Netherlandish glazing, for textured glasses are often used, the leading is chunkier and deliberately irregular, and the painting is more bold and graphic, with a decidedly modern linear quality.

Some of the illustrations show an innovative type of glazing developed in the 1920s and 30s and popular in the USA but rarely seen in the UK: this incorporates silhouettes of figures, animals or other motifs cut out of sheet lead or brass and inset into leaded glass. A selection of details showing glazing in the various Yale buildings, especially the Sterling Library, is very well illustrated in colour, revealing not only the skills of Bonawit's glass painters and glaziers but also the wide range of iconographic sources (from Persian miniatures to Arthur Rackham's illustrations) mustered for the hundreds of individual panels. Whilst some of the research was compiled by Yale librarians, Bonawit and his studio staff were also actively engaged in seeking out appropriate literary, allegorical or purely decorative imagery. One wonders if copyright was an issue when, at least in some cases, the more modern sources were transcribed with scarcely an alteration into vitreous form.

Apart from his many Yale commissions, Bonawit's studio produced windows and panels, as documented by Ms Walker, for a number of other non-ecclesiastical settings (notably the former Cunard Building in New York) as well as for several churches. His last commission, the five tower windows of New York's Church of the Ascension (1940-41), comprises 123 Biblical scenes and shows his mastery of the early-Gothic manner of Chartres, which became so favoured by American churches and their architects. Thereafter, Bonawit abandoned stained glass altogether to resume an early interest in photography, which he made his career for the next twenty years until his retirement.

In rescuing G. Owen Bonawit from relative obscurity, Gay Walker (who is not only the author but also the designer of this attractive publication) has revealed another facet of the extraordinary richness of America's stained glass history. But her book is not simply of art historical interest. The renewed enthusiasm for the skills and artistic potentialities of glass painting makes this book well worth acquiring for the excellence of its illustrations alone. For present-day designers and makers, it should also clearly demonstrate the creative possibilities of the historical tradition of decorative glazing, so delightfully explored by Bonawit and his co-workers.

Peter Cormack

Sloan, Julie L., *Light Screens, The Leaded Glass of Frank Lloyd Wright*. Exhibition catalogue, with introduction by David G. De Long.

New York: Rizzoli International Publications, 2001. Hardcover, 160 pp., 120 col. and 50 b/w ills. ISBN 0847823059, $39.95 (U.S.), plus $11.10 delivery to UK by economy (surface) letter post (4-6 weeks).

Sloan, Julie L., *Light Screens, The Complete Leaded-Glass Windows of Frank Lloyd Wright.*

New York: Rizzoli International Publications, 2001. Large format, slip-cased hardcover, 400 pp., 247 col. and 204 b/w ills., indexed. ISBN 0847823067, $175 (US), plus $29 delivery to UK as above (both titles may be ordered by credit card or cheque in US dollars from Art in Architecture Press, 54 Cherry St., North Adams, MA 01247, USA.; see www.aiap.com or email sales@aiap.com).

Frank Lloyd Wright (1867-1959) was a major and prolific American architect in the first half of the twentieth century. He designed many hundreds of buildings, primarily in the United States, and his stature and influence there can hardly be overestimated. During the first half of his career, from 1886-1923, Wright designed decorative glass schemes for nearly all of the apertures in well over half of his buildings.

These two rich books represent twenty years of research by an esteemed art historian and conservation consultant, Julie L. Sloan. There is already an extensive literature surrounding Wright's work and life and he himself wrote a great deal. However, as is so often the case, apart from studies of the glass in two or three particular buildings, little attention had been given to the large body of Wright's designs for decorative glass. Sloan set out to remedy this omission. She has done extensive new research to make a comprehensive study which undertakes to identify and record, as completely as possible to date, all of Wright's work in decorative glass, charting and analysing the development of his design schemes for glass.

Ever aware that the glass was always designed and intended as an architectural component rather than as freestanding works of art, Sloan discusses the glass in the context of Wright's architectural practice, emphasising the relationships between the panels and building designs. The result is truly a contribution to scholarship, bringing together thoughtful analysis with many examples not before published, offering an unprecedented coupling of images of the windows with images of their designs on paper.

The books were published to coincide with a major exhibition curated by Sloan, the first to survey Wright's designs for leaded glass windows for his buildings from 1885-1923. The exhibition has toured seven venues in the United States from 2001 to 2003. The smaller of the two volumes is published as a catalogue to this exhibition, but do not be put off by that description. It is very much a *catalogue raisonée*, of great interest on its own and, while lacking an index, is exceptionally good value for its substantial text and wealth of illustrations. Both books are extremely handsome, beautifully printed on good paper and seemingly well bound. My copies look pristine after a thorough reading.

Most of us will have some familiarity with windows by Frank Lloyd Wright and will correctly think in terms of rectilinear, geometric designs utilising large areas of clear glasses. Mostly, however, we will have seen published images of individual panels and will not necessarily have realised how many would have been incorporated in a single room of a single building, nor the overall patterning effect which this repetition would create. Sloan amply redresses this lack in our understanding.

Wright was passionate about the superiority of casement framing to sash window arrangements and frequently designed long rows of adjacent casements to form strips of openings which were essential to the overall design of the buildings and to his aim of 'bringing the outside in' without sacrificing the privacy of the life inside the buildings. Chapter 8 of *The Complete Leaded-Glass Windows* is particularly interesting as Sloan develops a structuralist approach to understanding the geometric language of Wright's windows, much in keeping with his own oft-quoted dictum of organic ornament: 'Part is to part as part is to whole.' The windows played a role in articulating the buildings; for a major period he used many horizontal strips of windows which were given dynamic tension and visual force by being filled with predominances of verticals in their design.

Wright was also very careful to provide textural elements to his exteriors and to this end chose particular glasses whose reflective qualities both maintained privacy and subtly articulated the exterior surface view. He especially favoured the surface variations offered by polished plate glass which was newly available at this period in North America at reasonably affordable prices. With a different tint and surface quality from the float glasses which have now largely supplanted it, its contemporary non-availability there is a major deterrent to the conservation of Wright's windows. Wright also valued the exterior qualities of various iridescent and opalescent glasses which he used in small pieces as accents, quite differently of course from their use for non-painted pictorial effects such as those favoured by Tiffany and La Farge.

The titles refer to 'the leaded glass' of Frank Lloyd Wright although many will recognise that most of the windows use zinc rather than lead calmes; these were often brass plated as well. Sloan is informative both on the range of terminology used for the various forms of decorative glazing in the United States during this period and on the techniques involved in glazing with zinc. She is clear about her broader use of the term 'leaded glass' and in every possible instance annotates illustrations with information about the materials used.

Sloan indicates that Wright favoured zinc because the calmes could be very thin, and that he believed that they were stronger than lead, assuring a client that they 'require no reinforcing bars and will last a life time or two'. Sloan acknowledges that he was wrong about this and that '...many of Wright's zinc-calmed [sic] windows are now bowing and sagging just like their leaded counterparts.' She footnotes that this is because 'zinc and brass calmes do not withstand weathering well and over the course of a century, they corrode and weaken.' She does not, however, mention that their very rigidity may make them less suitable carriers for glass than the more flexible lead nor does she make any comment upon the large number of cracks in the glass in Wright's windows today which might, at least in part, be explained thereby.

Overall within Sloan's text there is a hesitance to challenge, much less criticise, Wright's decisions. This is in large part admirable in a work with a scholarly aim; she sets out to survey and provide us with hitherto unstudied primary material, not to criticise it. Nonetheless, this may need to be considered within the context of North American discourse where Wright is seen as God, as Sloan reminded me in conversation. This can be somewhat disappointing and/or constraining when it comes to considering influences upon Wright's creative development. There is very little here about others designing at the same time elsewhere. Wright did not visit Europe until 1910 and surprise is expressed and explanations usually sought for any similarity between his and European work prior to this date – despite the availability of published images in the contemporaneous architectural press. Sloan does mention that it is now clear that Wright knew of the work of the Delaunays, Kandinsky, Kupka and the Vienna Secession 'despite his denial of familiarity with any European artwork.'

Nonetheless Wright was very much of his time as well as formative of it. In *Art Deco 1910-1939* Christopher Frayling speaks of 'the absorption of Modernism – in the form of basic geometric shapes, speed lines and assorted flat pattern – into the vocabulary of the decorative arts.' He is not speaking of Wright here but the description fits, my point being that Wright's work was concomitant with a much wider arena of development in the 'decorative idiom for modern life' (Frayling again) than is generally acknowledged in Sloan's text.

Finally Sloan tells us flatly that 'Wright's specific reasons for discontinuing the use of leaded glass in his buildings in the 1920s remain unknown.' The last chapter in each book is virtually identical and makes the point that Wright did continue to show an interest in and make innovations with fenestration design. Speculation and lament may have no place in scholarship, but the fact that Wright has not left his own statement on this does not make it any less of an important question. Also, a fact to regret in my view. The cold faces of unarticulated glazing in many of the later buildings, e.g. the Johnson Wax Building (1936), the House for Theodore Baird (1940), or the Clinic for Dr Kenneth Mayers (1956), to name a few (selected from a limited collection in a book of photographs of FLW exteriors) is reason to rue that this creative and energetic architect stopped designing leaded glass for his buildings when he did. Sloan's achievement is a handsome celebration of Wright's achievement so perhaps it is a tribute to both that reading these volumes leaves me wishing he had continued to design glass.

Adelle Corrin

Raguin, Virginia, with Pongracz, Patricia, *Reflections on Glass. 20th Century Stained Glass in American Art and Architecture.*

New York: American Bible Society, 2002. Softcover, 175 pp., 112 col. ills. ISBN 158516715 0, price $35 (US, available from: The Gallery at the American Bible Society, 1865 Broadway at 61st Street, New York, NY 10023, USA, or visit www.americanbible.org).

Reflections on Glass is the book accompanying an exhibition of the same title organised in 2002 at the Gallery of the American Bible Society in New York, previously the venue (in 1998) for the exhibition *Glory in Glass* which was also principally curated by Virginia Raguin. The earlier exhibition and book (the latter reviewed in Vol. XXIV of this *Journal*) provided a general survey of stained glass issues in the USA, whilst this volume offers a more focussed perspective.

The book has seven chapters, all but one contributed by Virginia Raguin. The fifth and seventh are useful more especially for their illustrations of American stained glass produced since the 1950s, including panels and windows by Ed Carpenter, Albinas Elskus, Ellen Mandelbaum, Ellen Miret, Sylvia Nicolas, Robert Pinart and Robert Sowers. The level of skill is generally at least as high as it would be in British equivalents, but one senses – particularly in the more recent commissions – a similar flailing in the post-war craft's stylistic vacuum, leading on occasions to some rather desperate commentary. One contemporary panel, for example, painted in a kitsch photo-realist technique, is likened to work by 'fifteenth-century Lowlands [*sic*] artists such as Jan van Eyck'. Nonetheless, there are some thoughtful passages about the problem of present-day stained glass aesthetics: Raguin, citing Robert Sowers, rightly emphasises the futility of Modernism's claims to a 'universality' comparable to the spiritual values and experience of medieval workers in the crafts.

The sixth chapter, written by Patricia Pongracz, is a straightforward account of 'Stained Glass Window Fabrication'. Here, one significant omission is any mention of 'slab' glass, the material which is so characteristic of the best American windows of the period, such as those by Charles Connick and J. Gordon Guthrie. Initially imported in considerable quantity from England, it was later manufactured in the USA, mainly by the Blenko firm of West Virginia (whose English-born founder had, before emigrating, been involved in the pioneering development of this type of glass in London in the 1880s). Raguin's text echoes the same *lacuna*. It does allude to Christopher Whall's use of slab glass and his influence on American designer-craftsmen, but fails to make clear the vital sequential links between this distinctively Arts & Crafts material and the style of craftsmanship it engendered, and the recognition by Connick and others that these furnished one of the key resources in their regeneration of the traditional craft.

Anyone who has read a little about American stained glass of the 1900s will know that it was the focus of much vigorous and highly-polarised debate, with many talented and eloquent advocates on either side. The central controversy was about the merits of America's home-grown invention, opalescent glass, as opposed to the traditional styles and materials of the European tradition. Crucially, the polemic centred on the *architectural* compatibility of glass by Tiffany, La Farge and their many followers and imitators. As America underwent a Second Gothic Revival in the early twentieth century – its first (in the Victorian period) had a much more limited impact than in Britain – the pictorialism of the opalescent school was deemed quite unsuitable for buildings which ever more ambitiously strove to evoke the spirit of medieval work. Raguin gives us little flavour of this ardent polemic in her account of the 1900-1910 period, nor (despite the claims of the book's title) does architecture feature at all significantly. In fact, although – bizarrely – Luis Domènech i Montaner's splendid Hospital de Pau in Barcelona is illustrated, there is not a single picture of a building by Ralph Adams Cram, Bertram Grosvenor Goodhue, Frank Lloyd Wright or any other major twentieth-century American architect.

Raguin does, however, make some good points about the way in which American glaziers, cut off from any regular and direct contact with large-scale medieval stained glass, managed to absorb the craft's ancient traditions through publications such as Viollet-le-Duc's *Vitrail* and Westlake's *History of Design in Painted Glass*. The extent to which a modern American 'glass man' could confidently identify with his medieval forebears is, as Raguin notes, shown best of all by Connick's 1937 book *Adventures in Light and Color*, in which his own work is 'indivisible from the historic windows he so admired'.

This is a much better-looking book than its 1998 predecessor, with a more expansive layout. The colour illustrations, most showing glass featured in the exhibition, are generally good, with those of recent work forming a useful survey of what was perceived to be noteworthy at a particular point in time. Unfortunately the historical chapters are marred by errors and inconsistencies: Harry Clarke, for example, was never a member of Dublin's Tower of Glass co-operative; and when the members of the Reynolds, Francis, Rohnstock partnership are listed, why only give the initials of two of them and not of W. M. Francis? It is a pity, too, that the bibliography is so sparse, seeming to ignore some recent pertinent literature, especially on the Opalescent *versus* Antique controversy and the link between Arts & Crafts and Second Gothic Revival glass.

Perhaps it is in the nature of exhibition-related books to end up as unsatisfactory hybrids, somewhere between a catalogue and a monograph. For readers new to the topic, this book can usefully be augmented by two earlier publications, James L. Sturm's *Stained Glass from Medieval Times to the Present: Treasures to be seen in New York* (1982) and Linda Papanicolaou's 'Colored Light' essay in *The Ideal Home 1900-1920: The History of Twentieth-Century American Craft* (1993).

Peter Cormack

Jones, Robert O., with the SGAA Stained Glass School, *Biographical Index of Historic American Stained Glass Makers.*

Raytown, MO: Stained Glass Association of America, 2002. Softcover, 142 pgs. No ISBN, $19.95 (US, $17.95 for SGAA members, available from the SGAA, 10009 East 62nd Street, Raytown, MO 64133, tel. 800-888-7422, see www.stainedglass.org for mailing costs).

This index is just that: an alphabetical listing of stained glass designers, craftspeople, and studios active in America from the Colonial period until fifty years ago. The aim of the publication, which claims to be 'the first of its kind', is to 'broadly define the history of stained glass in the United States in terms of the people and studios that practised the trade'. To be included, one had to be active in the US or Canada at least fifty years ago. The author, who is chair of the SGAA Historical Committee, does not make it clear why 1952 was selected as the cut-off date, nor why Canada is included in this definition.

Most of the contents were taken from back issues of *Stained Glass*, the organ of the Stained Glass Association of America, which has been published since 1906 (originally under the name of *The Monthly Visitor* and then the *Ornamental Glass Bulletin*). According to the introduction, *lacunae* in the magazine have been supplemented by research in other sources, both published and unpublished, which are listed in a short, peculiarly selective bibliography. Published works cited include such well-known resources as Sharon Darling's *Chicago Ceramics and Glass* (1979), the Metropolitan Museum of Art's *In Pursuit of Beauty* (1987), James Sturm's *Stained Glass From Medieval Times to the Present: Treasures to be Seen in New York* (1980), and the lamentably inaccurate *Stained Glass in America* by John Gilbert Lloyd (1963). Monographs on Frank Lloyd Wright, William Jay Bolton, and Henry Keck are supplemented by gazetteers from Rhode Island, Detroit, San Francisco, and Cleveland. Unpublished sources include the Rakow Library at the Corning Museum of Glass and the Winterthur Museum Library, the private papers of the author and several other individuals, and directories of such obscure locales as Jacksonville, Tallahassee, Pasco County, and Orlando, Florida (no other municipal archives are represented). Notably absent from this bibliography are works on Tiffany, La Farge, and the late nineteenth and early twentieth centuries, in spite of the undeniable fact that this was the height of the craft in the United States.

Following the introduction is a very short (one page) informational chapter on 'Researching Your Windows'. This provides common-sense advice aimed at building owners, suggesting a search through building records, local library and historical society records, and oral histories of donors' descendants. The elementary nature of this advice clearly indicates the intended audience for this volume: not art historians, architectural historians, or stained glass people in general, but a neophyte public.

Coverage is very uneven. Only a studio's address and years of activity are available for about half of the listings. The greatest amount of data is provided for those mid-twentieth century studios who were also heavily involved with the publication of *Stained Glass*, like Connick, Burnham, and Willet, which is to be expected, given the principal source of the book. For these, selected lists of commissions follow basic background information. Details on those working before the advent of the magazine are sparsest. The longest listing for any one firm may be for J. & R. Lamb, one of the country's oldest studios and deserving of such treatment; this attention is merited primarily because so many family members worked in the trade – the entry is actually made up of eight separate listings. This points up another problem – the absence of any cross-referencing or index. Fortunately for Lamb, the principals all had the family name, but if one wanted to know who worked at the Willet Studio, for example, it would be necessary to search every page.

Some important American glass designers are given short shrift. Louis Sullivan, whose Auditorium, Chicago Stock Exchange, and magnificent banks all included huge expanses of stained glass, is described only as having 'designed stained glass to complement his building projects', and none of these is named. The entry for Frank Lloyd Wright, designer of over 4500 windows in 185 buildings, mentions only one of his houses, and that one not particularly famous for its windows.

Most inexcusable is the entry for Louis Comfort Tiffany, for whom no list of commissions is given. Nor is his company given separate listings under each of its names (four in total) as is done for many other firms, like Connick, Willet, and

Lamb. Although he is acknowledged as the 'best known American stained glass Designer and Studio Owner', whose 'studio is the most written about' in 'books available from public libraries', the author provides none of these titles, either in the listing or the bibliography. The paltry five-line entry for Tiffany relegates him to the same obscurity as, say, the unknown Rembrandt Theodore Steele, whose entry, also five lines long, at least includes a commission. As a result, Mary Elizabeth Tillinghast, whose entry follows Tiffany's, looks like the more successful artist. Admittedly, the Stained Glass Association of America damned Tiffany with faint praise in their 1933 obituary, clearly reflecting the assertive opinions of Ralph Adams Cram, father of the Neo-Gothic in the United States (which then dominated the art), who vilified opalescent stained glass as 'bad, thoroughly and hopelessly bad' see *Church Building* (1924), p. 140. But surely the SGAA and the author himself cannot still be bound by such a dated opinion.

Poor proofreading may end up being the biggest impediment to the book's usefulness. A random sampling turns up such errors as two different spellings (and therefore listings) for artist Rowan LeCompte, which curiously do not contain quite the same information; since LeCompte is still living and it would have been easy to correct this, the error is particularly egregious. For Gray and Son, active 1916, 1918, Falls Creek, no state is provided – and because this studio is especially obscure, finding that state will be practically impossible. Under the Gorham Studio, Edward Peck Sperry is given as head of the stained glass studio, but under the listing for Sperry, the studio is named as Gordon. This tends to call into question the accuracy of all entries.

The author acknowledges that this method of researching – i.e., not using primary sources – is subject to the accuracy of its source material, for which he cannot verify. He excuses any errors with the assertion that primary source research was 'not feasible' for 'an index of this scope'. This is a debatable claim: a more inclusive effort, drawing on the knowledge of a number of independent scholars around the country who specialise in stained glass research, would probably yield better results than limiting the research to *Stained Glass*, which has never represented more than a small fraction of practitioners. But if the pages of that magazine provide the parameters of the project, what remains less reasonable, then, is the scope: since *Stained Glass* was published only from 1907 until the apparently arbitrary cut-off date of 1952 (and is actually still published today, making this terminus date that much more questionable), why did the author elect to go back to Colonial days? But since he did choose to go back that far, how does he justify the scatter-shot approach to his research in published sources, omitting some of the best known and relying on others of questionable value? Whether or not one likes the stranglehold Tiffany has on the public perception of American stained glass, how can he be virtually left out of a resource of the subject, on the apparent assumption that everyone reading this book will already know all about him, even though the intended audience is not really expected to know anything about stained glass?

In sum, while the goal of the book is admirable, the result is sadly lacking in accuracy, usefulness, and objectivity. It appears to have been rushed to press (an impression supported by two subsequent issues of *Stained Glass* – the first states that the editor, who did the design, editing, and layout, is going to start working on the book; the next, published three months later, says the book is published), and it suffers from this haste. Given the limitations of the source material, a more accurate title would have been 'Biographical Index of Stained Glass Artists from *Stained Glass Magazine*'.

Julie L. Sloan

Taylor, Richard, *How to Read a Church: A Guide to Images, Symbols and Meanings in Churches and Cathedrals.*

London: Rider Random House, 2003. Hardcover, 246 pp., 15 b/w images. ISBN 1 8441 3053 3, £10.

A more accurate title for this dry little work might be 'Catholic Images, Symbols and Meanings in English and Continental Churches and in Christian Art and Scripture: A Miscellany'. The emphasis on strictly liturgical images and the like, yet silence on secular, social or indeed the soldierly oddities characteristic of Anglican Churches indicates the author has chiefly considered a Catholic-minded audience, moreover one not particularly interested in artistic matters.

After short chapters of introduction and on God, Jesus and the Virgin Mary, Taylor describes the Four Evangelists (whose respective emblems are well illustrated by the pew end carvings at St John, Hampstead), and the Twelve Apostles. He then offers a somewhat idiosyncratic choice of 'later saints' who, it must be said, rarely feature in English parish churches. There can be few, if any, dedicated to St Anthony of Padua, St Theresa of Lisieux and St Veronica. Britain's own rich selection of familiar or obscure saints is overlooked: Alban, Edmund, Ethelburga, Etheldreda, Guthlac, Hugh of Lincoln, Margaret of Scotland, Pega, Remigius. Taylor describes the fourteen Stations of the Cross and the Papal Cross but says nothing of St George's Cross as the flag of England, nor is St Patrick, the Patron Saint of Ireland, even mentioned, let alone his red saltire cross!

One looks, too, in vain for misericordia, label stops, the barbarous detail of Norman archways and tympana, or the angelic adornments of hammerbeam roofs. The author may well have been to Rome: but has he ever been to Boston Stump, to Ely, to March; or further afield, to R. A. Cram's splendidly neo-Gothic St Thomas's Fifth Avenue, New York or K. F. Schinkel's Werderischer Kirche or has he seen the saints and screens in Bamberg, Havelberg, or Naumburg? I fancy not. Instead the sole memorable reference to Germany is: 'The swastika appears fairly frequently on Old Christian monuments in Rome, but the appalling associations of the last century mean that it is now little seen elsewhere.'

Taylor seems to be making a point by describing the excruciating details of the Crucifixion, yet selects as illustration not a limewood carving of unparalleled excellence by Tilman Riemenschneider but the mawkish and sanitised rood at St Dominic's, Gospel Oak. He then ignores rood screen dado decoration such as the saints depicted at Barton Turf and Ranworth. Hence his choices appear oblivious to quality in art.

Of stained glass there are but four images of poor Victorian work – the saints are identified; but neither artists nor manufacturers. Why not illustrate Chartres, Fairford, or York? Curiously, Taylor neglects much description of glass: in describing wheatsheaves, he sticks to symbolic meanings but neglects to mention this is the mark used by C. E. Kempe to sign his windows. The book is of limited help to students of stained glass.

The position of a church in reflecting local or national history escapes the author, who in particular ignores the secular significance since the Reformation and the Restoration of 1660 of Anglican parish churches and cathedrals. If one is presenting a book on images and symbols in such buildings, it really is negligence not to say something about British and Continental civic, ecclesiastical, family and military heraldry, hatchments, and royal arms. A whole rich dimension is therefore missing. What of, for example, the many American churches with Civil War and later memorials, or those in Northern (Protestant) Germany with their commemorations of the fallen of the Franco-Prussian and World Wars?

Notwithstanding omissions and a potentially misleading title, Taylor's book at a tenner makes a stocking filler or useful confirmation present with a difference – but it certainly does not supplant Jenkins, Pevsner or Clifton Taylor, and seems mainly directed towards committed Christians of Catholic leaning or Britons touring Catholic regions. To those new to the study of churches; or indeed those who tend to forgetfulness, this book is a useful aide-mémoire to complement (but not substitute) for the authors above. It is not for the car 'glove box' or pocket – though is pocketbook in size – but for the bedside or bookshelf at home.

H. S. Blagg

Stanton Harris, Martyn, *Practising Stained Glass Safely.*

Sheffield: The Society of Glass Technology, 2000. Softcover, A5, 48 pp., 19 col. and b/w ills. ISBN 0 900682 264, £5.50 (incl. P&P, available from the Society of Glass Technology, Don Valley House, Savile Street East, Sheffield S4 7UQ or see www.sgt.org).

If you are a practising glass artist or worker with a tendency towards hypochondria, you should read this book whilst in bed.

As a student, Martyn Stanton Harris became aware that health and safety practices in stained glass were lax. Subsequent visits to studios proved there was a general ignorance, lack of interest and a likely financial disincentive for establishing a healthy working environment. By bringing together information from many agencies, he tries to make people aware of the hazards of everyday working practices.

Every aspect of the craft comes under scrutiny. Each part has its cumulative dangers. An overview of materials leaves one feeling quite smug as there are no surprises here. However, this quickly evaporates when reading about the hazards of lead, work regulations, codes of practice, EU directives, commissions and blood-lead levels. There are myriad ways of inhaling, ingesting and transporting lead home to share with your family: a special bonus for children as they absorb it faster. Adverse effects on fertility are also explored. Symptoms are: anaemia, tiredness, headaches, constipation, difficulty sleeping, memory loss, irritability, diarrhoea, colic, and low blood pressure. Lead poisoning is a major hazard to an unborn child.

Glass paints and stains, etc. have a cocktail of glass powder, selenium, lead, cadmium, antimony and silver chloride. Glass cutting and sandblasting can cause silicosis, which is irreversible. Even firing glass has its problems with fibrefrax particles and heavy metal fumes. Some of our favourite authors come under fire in the section on hydrofluoric acid. Stanton Harris speculates here about Harry Clarke, whose intricate work with flashed glass may have been the cause of his death by tuberculosis at the early age of forty-one.

Illness can occur through large exposure to hazards over a short time or small exposure over a long time. Symptoms often appear like those of other illnesses and can be difficult to pin down. There are recommendations for ventilation and extraction systems, but I would have felt happier with more details about costs and availability. Common sense is promoted as the first line of defence.

If you work on your own, you should be aware of the danger you may be placing yourself in. If you have any employees, you are responsible for their health. If you are an employee, you should take the incentive to raise awareness of everyday hazards and avoid them. Buy this book and scare yourself properly.

Ginger Ferrell

Swash, Caroline, *14 Stained Glass Walks in London.*

Malvern: Malvern Arts Press Ltd., 2002. Decorative card covers with ring binding, 278 pp. [unpaginated], numerous maps and b/w text illustrations. ISBN 0 954 1055 0 8, £10.95 (available from publisher, email: malvernarts@btinternet.com).

This is an attractive and original book, designed for the pocket. The subject has been curiously neglected. There are plenty of books on London's architecture, but, with the possible exception of F. S. Eden's little paperback of 1939 (and that covered 'old' glass only), nothing has ever appeared devoted specifically to London's stained glass. Caroline Swash's spiritual forebear was however surely that lover of London churches T. Francis Bumpus, whose numerous writings published between 1883 and 1913 are full of observations on windows both old and new – often alas now destroyed. For the student of stained glass London presents a problem. Patronage and artistic excellence have always been concentrated here, but fanaticism, natural disasters, war, demolitions and, not least, changes in fashion, have all meant that the survival rate for stained glass has been exceptionally poor. Much beautiful and interesting glass has disappeared without trace, hardly anything, for example, surviving of the scores of windows installed in the capital in that romantic and formative period between about 1800 and 1840. Nevertheless, as the author makes clear in her brief introduction, the development of the art can still (just) be illustrated within central London, helped a little by museum holdings. Her fourteen walks lie mainly within the cities of London and Westminster, with forays west to Kensington and north to Highgate and Hampstead. A route map is supplied for each walk, together with information on opening times, or sometimes a contact number. Anyone who has tried to penetrate into some of the more unwelcoming London churches will appreciate the difficulties the author will have had in constructing these itineraries, and it is understandable that one or two of the suggested routes may appear a little convoluted.

Windows of all dates are described, from the thirteenth century onwards. The choice of examples is personal, but selected so as to illustrate fairly the various periods and styles and to engage the attention of those having only a rudimentary knowledge of the subject. The portraits of artists are an attractive feature. The text is concise and to the point, informative but never so wordy as to detract from the essential business of *looking* at the glass itself (but should a note not somewhere be added recommending binoculars as a valuable aid?). Many of the acknowledged nineteenth and twentieth century masterpieces are here, like Clayton & Bell's early windows in St Michael Cornhill (1858–9), the Brunel memorial window in Westminster Abbey designed by Henry Holiday and Richard Norman Shaw and made by Heaton, Butler & Bayne (1868), Christopher Whall's work in Holy Trinity, Sloane Street (1900–23), or J. Edward Nuttgens's East window in St

Etheldreda's, Ely Place (1953). There is one case only where I think a truly important window should have been included on an itinerary. This is at the Temple Church, where the southwestern window of the Round with its five medallions showing the early life of Christ was designed by Charles Winston and painted by Henry Hughes in 1852 to illustrate Winston's theory of the classical origins of Gothic art. It attracted a good deal of attention ('An indescribable something between Flaxman and Fuseli' said the *Ecclesiologist*). It was also the very first complete window painted on Winston's new glass, manufactured for him by James Powell & Sons, a stone's throw away at their Whitefriars factory.

Twentieth-century windows – say from the period of the Arts and Crafts onwards – are nearly all assigned to named artists, but earlier windows, even where singled out as being of special interest, are sometimes left anonymous. Information is of course less easy to come by, and problems of attribution remain, but it is perhaps worth noting for a future edition that the surviving border work of 1849–50 in St Mary-at-Hill (most of the glass here was regrettably purged by Seely & Paget in 1967) is in fact by Thomas Willement; that the 'Flower Sermon' window at St Katharine Cree is by William Morris Pepper & Co (1880); and that the author of the dramatic '*Judging of the Twelve Tribes*' window in St Edmund the King, Lombard Street, was Charles Hardgrave, who exhibited the design at the Royal Academy in 1886. It might also be mentioned that the Harvard memorial window of 1905 in Southwark Cathedral, the work of John La Farge, was made to a design by the American Beaux-Arts architect Charles F. McKim. There are occasional mis-attributions: the East window of St James's, Clerkenwell, is by Alexander Gibbs (not Heaton, Butler & Bayne). Dates are rather sparse and sometimes incorrect. Thomas Grylls (1845–1913) did not join the firm of Clayton & Bell 'during the 1850s' and he lived in Burgh House, Hampstead, from 1884 (not 'during the 1870s'). Henry Holiday's splendid West window in Southwark Cathedral is of 1893–4 (not 1910). And surely it is misleading to speak of the National Gallery as being 'newly founded' in the 1890s?

Windows have quite often been altered, for a variety of reasons. The author rightly deplores the substitution of plain glass for decorative borders and backgrounds in windows at St Mary Abbots (Kensington) and elsewhere – a destructive fashion prevalent forty or fifty years ago. Sometimes changes have been less obvious and can present pitfalls for the unwary. Much of what the visitor now sees in Lincoln's Inn chapel, for example, is not of the seventeenth century but of 1921 – a careful renewal by Kempe & Co following a zeppelin raid in 1915. The Brunel memorial window at Westminster was reduced in size when moved in 1952, and parts discarded, spoiling its original design. A worrying case is the East window of St Botolph, Bishopsgate, designed by F. W. Moody and made by Powell's in 1869 to replace a window of 1844 by Thomas Wilmshurst. As the author points out, it is a work of some significance in the history of Victorian taste: a rejection of medievalism in favour of the style of the High Renaissance. Aesthetically it is most successful. Yet we know that it was substantially altered by Osmond Bentley in 1912 to remove what he considered its Victorian crudity and bring it into harmony with his father's redecoration of the chancel. How would it have appeared to us originally?

A valuable feature of the book is the extensive and knowledgeable coverage of work executed since 1945, allowing us to view the art of stained glass as a continuum extending to the present day. Much is in secular buildings rather than in churches and will be unknown to most Londoners, or even to those of us with a particular interest in the subject. The author gives proper attention to that somewhat unfashionable period of the immediate post-war years when so much stained glass was installed in bomb-damaged churches. She praises for example the series of windows by Christopher Webb in St Lawrence Jewry, the striking glass by Carl Edwards in the Temple Church, and the moving and individual art of Brian Thomas in St Paul's Cathedral, St Vedast's and elsewhere, so sympathetic to the architecture of Wren. In lesser hands stained glass at this time could be tired and conventional. It did however possess the merit of succeeding better in historic contexts than some of the more exciting work that came after. The growth of interest in the stained glass panel as an 'art object' and the ease with which new, unprecedented styles could be debased or misapplied also brought dangers. It is a problem that is today as acute as ever and London can show some dismal failures, as well as the occasional triumph. Those armed with Caroline Swash's stimulating book will be able to form their own opinions on this and much else.

Mis-spellings are rather frequent, for example 'Bucknell' for Bucknall, 'Albert Gerente' for Alfred Gérente, 'Bain' (Bayne), and a good many more. 'William Farrer' should be Frederick William Farrar, once well known as the author of the schoolboy story *Eric, or Little by Little*, and who, incidentally, was Dean of Canterbury, and not of St Margaret's, Westminster. These are minor blemishes, easily put right in a reprint, which I am sure will be called for.

Michael Kerney

Little, Joyce (comp.), Goedicke, Angela and Washbourn, Margaret (eds.), *Stained Glass Marks & Monograms*.

London: NADFAS Church Recorders, 2002. Softcover, 145 pp., illustrated with many b/w line drawings. [No ISBN], £12.50 (including P&P, available from NADFAS Church Recorders, NADFAS House, 8 Guilford Street, London WC1N 1DA).

As someone whose admiration for the NADFAS Church Recorders is without reservation, I am perhaps not best qualified to review this publication. However, I suspect that many others will share my enthusiasm for the invaluable work of research and recording carried out (and described by Anne Haward in the last issue of this *Journal*) by these specialised volunteers, whose regional groups are all affiliated to the National Association of Decorative and Fine Art Societies. This latest edition of their *Marks & Monograms* book indicates unequivocally the organisation's real commitment to practical scholarship in the study of stained glass, especially in the bewilderingly vast fields of the Victorian and early twentieth-century craft.

As is evident from its spiral binding and no-nonsense format, the book is clearly designed to be used for 'field-work' and not simply to sit on the shelf gathering dust in company with more lavishly illustrated volumes. All but a few of its pages are devoted to an alphabetical list of individual designers/makers and firms with, where possible, an illustration of their particular mark or monogram as used in specific windows which have been recorded by Church Recorders or others. The geographic range covered is impressive, including almost all parts of the UK, so that many small-scale local studios are listed, among them such obscure firms as Done & Davies of Shrewsbury or W. Fourness of Leeds. Imported glass by foreign makers is also included, so one can track down work by C. Champigneulle (of Barle-Duc, Normandy) as far afield as Standish, Lancashire, and Wethersfield, Essex, or by U. de Matteis (of Florence) at Lastingham, Yorkshire, and Credenhill, Herefordshire. Details of studio addresses and, where possible, a brief history of the individual or firm are also given. In a number of cases, the data given here constitute the only published source of information.

Of course there are also the relatively well-known artists and firms, such as James Powell & Sons (Whitefriars) Ltd, whose white friar emblem is illustrated in three versions, or William Morris & Co. (Westminster) Ltd, whose rather undistinguished windows are all too often mistaken by the novice for the work of *the* Morris & Company, founded by the great Victorian artist-craftsman, poet and socialist. Although the latter firm never signed its windows and is therefore not listed, it might have been worth inserting some parenthetic mention simply to clarify the potential confusion.

Anyone interested in nineteenth- and twentieth-century stained glass should obtain a copy of this splendid directory. Once you look up a single name, you will – I guarantee – soon find yourself reading the entries for many others and, in the process, learning a great deal about the craft's fascinating and much-interconnected history over the last two hundred years.

Peter Cormack

Brown, Sarah and Strobl, Sebastian, *A Fragile Inheritance: The Care of Stained Glass and Historic Glazing: A Handbook for Custodians.*

London: Church House Publishing, 2002. Softcover, 68 pp., 31 col. ills. ISBN 0 7151 7600 5, £9.95 (available from Church House, Great Smith Street, London SW1P 3NZ, tel. 0207-898-1451, fax 0207-898-1449 or see www.chpublishing.co.uk).

This booklet is aimed principally at churchwardens, PCCs and those directly connected with the maintenance of stained glass in our churches: but everyone concerned with its upkeep or conservation will welcome such clear guidance on the routine problems that threaten the survival of stained glass (which, the authors wisely emphasise, extend beyond the condition of lead and glass to include failing ferramenta and wire guards).

In encountering the results of poor 'housekeeping' at the level of a Diocesan Advisory Committee one becomes aware that in the dissemination of this kind of information a gap remains between theory and practice. No doubt most members have observed disturbing examples of sloppy or heavy-handed work by under-qualified local glaziers, and wonder how they managed to slip through the conservation safeguards. It is imperative, therefore, that the church authorities redouble their efforts to ensure that this concise and informative booklet reaches those responsible 'on the ground'.

Colour photographs amplify the cogent descriptions of current 'best practice', and help to demonstrate the conservator's role. The text ends on a slightly more contentious note, however, in describing isothermal glazing, a process that the authors explain is 'largely reversible in the event of a less interventionist solution being found in the future'. While the isothermal system helps to create a secure atmospheric environment for stained glass, until it has been refined to diminish its impact on the visibility of the glass and the integrity of the masonry it should, in my opinion, be regarded as a last resort rather than the new orthodoxy. There are certainly conflicting views as to its merits, and its increasing application warrants an open and informed discussion before opinions become too entrenched.

Helpful appendixes show how to frame conservation reports, and the authors list further contact details and relevant websites; there is also brief but admirably clear technical advice on photographing stained glass – advice which should be more widely heeded.

Martin Harrison

Obituaries and appreciations

Professor Roy Newton OBE FRIBA FSA HON MA

Researcher whose fearless courting of controversy helped to rescue medieval stained glass

By detailed study of deteriorating medieval stained glass, which led him to controversial conclusions as to how the decay might be remedied, Roy Newton stirred up debate after debate in the 1970s. As he never shrank from stating his views with great forthrightness in a positive flurry of published papers, he provoked those who disagreed with him (of whom, at different times, there were many) to put their case equally forcefully. The disputes this engendered fostered a climate of debate that was salutary for stained-glass conservation in Britain, a field that had not previously been conspicuous for the pooling of ideas.

One major controversy sparked by Newton in the 1970s raged for a time over whether externally or internally ventilated glazing systems were better for countering condensation on medieval stained glass. Newton, who himself advised conservationists to opt for external ventilation, fuelled discussion by publishing papers and articles on the subject in Britain and overseas. Although it is now established that internal ventilation generally has the better record, Newton's surviving externally ventilated systems at Canterbury Cathedral, one of the establishments that followed his advice in the 1970s, work only marginally less well than the cathedral's more recent internally ventilated versions.

Equipped with a doctorate in plant physiology from Imperial College, London, Ronald Gordon Newton (always known as Roy) made his early career in the rubber industry. He was employed by the British Rubber Manufacturers Research Association, and when war broke out in 1939 he was called upon to advise the Ministry of Supply on the use of rubber in radar camouflage for submarines and in inflatable wave reducers for D-Day's Mulberry harbours.

His real fascination was with research, however, and by the mid-1950s he had left the rubber industry for an area new to him, glass technology, as director of the British Glass Industry Research Association in Sheffield. Here he collected and analysed data from the industry not only in Britain but also internationally. To him, this was an early example of the importance of pooling knowledge in an industry where secretiveness had become something of an affliction. An indefatigable collector and analyst of statistics, Newton instituted a number of highly detailed research projects in his 19 years with the association.

His Ballidon experiment – started in 1970 and, astonishingly, scheduled to continue until the year 2482 – was one that turned out to have wider implications than he imagined. His main purpose in burying different types of glass in a limestone quarry at Ballidon in the Peak District was to improve archaeological dating methods by observing the long-term and short-term incidence of corrosion and leaching.

It became clear, however, that the project was also relevant to the latest research on the disposal of radioactive waste by setting it in glass, encapsulating the glass in steel and burying it in deep repositories, where it is hoped that it will remain inert for thousands of years. As recently as last year, Newton himself, although well into his retirement, attended one of the regular unearthings from the Ballidon site when the items recovered for analysis included two types of glass, buried in 1986, that were designed for (although not actually containing) radioactive waste.

A developing interest in medieval stained glass led to Newton's editing, from 1972 to 1978, of the newsletter of the Corpus Vitrearum Medii Aevi (the international art-historical project which researches, records and publishes details of surviving medieval window glass). In 27 issues of that newsletter, and in an even greater number of individually published papers, he launched a wide-ranging and long-lasting debate on stained-glass conservation. His publications not only promulgated his own studies and ideas, but crucially, through a number of critical bibliographies, drew attention to the researches of others around the world.

Taking early retirement from the research association in 1974, Newton was well placed, on becoming honorary visiting professor in the physics department of the University of York, to study the causes of glass deterioration at York Minster; but he widened his brief to cover the glass at Canterbury Cathedral, too, and later continued his work in the department of ceramics, glasses and polymers at Sheffield University.

In 1989 he published some of his results in *The Conservation of Glass*, which he wrote with the glass restorer Sandra Davison. He was president of the Society of Glass Technology, 1973-75, and in 1983 was awarded one of the society's rare honorary fellowships.

His meticulous collecting and analysing of data extended in his spare time to ornithology, archaeology and genealogy – all of which he pursued avidly, without realising that others might not be as interested as he. With his first wife he had worked on the rook survey of the British Isles, and ever afterwards visitors to his home, whether ornithologically inclined or not, ran the risk of being expected to pore with every appearance of interest over maps of rook migration. In his last years, he conducted a statistical survey of the origin and distribution of the Bagshaws, the family of his third wife, Joy, but still found time to correspond with his glass-conservation colleagues and published his final professional paper at the age of 79.

He was appointed OBE in 1969. Twice widowed, Newton is survived by Joy, whom he married in 1971, and by the two sons of his second marriage. A promoter of research to the last, he donated his body to medical science.

Roy Newton, OBE, glass technologist, was born on November 19, 1912. He died on May 9, 2003, aged 90.

This obituary appeared in The Times on Tuesday, 3 June 2003 and is reprinted with permission.

Canon Maurice Ridgway FSA
(19 January 1918 – 20 December 2002)

Maurice Hill Ridgway was born in Stockport, the son of a vicar. Between 1941 and 1983 he served as curate and then vicar of four Cheshire parishes in succession. A traditional Anglican cleric, he combined care for his flock with an interest both active and scholarly in the preservation of church buildings and artefacts, serving for many years on the Chester and later the St Asaph Diocesan Advisory Committees. In 1966 he became an honorary Canon of Chester Cathedral.

He is best known for his publications on silver and church plate (the silver gallery at the Grosvenor Museum in Chester is named after him) and for his work on Welsh rood lofts and screens, undertaken with the late Fred Crossley. However, his achievements in other fields, too numerous to summarise here, should not be allowed to obscure his contribution to the study of ancient glass.

In 1941 he became curate of St Wilfrid's, Grappenhall, which possesses the finest fourteenth-century stained glass in Cheshire. This aroused his interest in the subject. During the latter years of the Second World War he managed to combine his clerical duties (which at one time included the position of chaplain to several hundred Wrens, a job his fellow curates must have envied) with a thorough survey of the surviving and lost glass of Cheshire and North Wales. He compiled an extensive collection of material, comprising personal observations and descriptions sometimes augmented by drawings or photographs, references from books and manuscripts, letters, articles and newspaper cuttings. This provides a detailed picture of the state of Cheshire's ancient glass half a century ago, against which subsequent losses can be measured. Few other counties have such a useful yardstick. In 1988 he deposited his collection on permanent loan to the British Society of Master Glass Painters' archive, an act typical of his desire to help other researchers. These included the late Mostyn Lewis, who drew heavily on his fieldwork and expertise in his own *Stained Glass in North Wales up to 1850* (1970). In later years, Canon Ridgway welcomed enquirers into his home, showing patience, good humour and impressive powers of recollection when cross-examined. He would reply conscientiously to written enquiries in a slightly shaky hand, his letters displaying courtesy, dry humour and attention to detail.

Between 1947 and 1962 he published a number of articles which provide an excellent survey of Cheshire's indigenous pre-Victorian stained glass. Had the CVMA project been established in Britain at an earlier date, he would undoubtedly have authored the volumes covering Cheshire and probably North Wales too. After 1962 he withdrew from the field to concentrate on other antiquarian interests. He felt that he had by then covered the subject of Cheshire's ancient glass, and given that he had recorded virtually all the modest volume of indigenous material remaining, the opinion is justified. Even so, letters from his friend Claude Blair reveal that in the early 1970s he was still engaged in identifying the sources of the seventeenth-century window at Farndon (SEE ARTICLE, p. 75). His continued interest in the subject was evidenced by his deep disappointment on learning of the losses of Cheshire glass which occurred during the last half-century.

He had a good eye for inscriptions and was a careful copyist, a particularly valuable skill in the days when the quality of photographs was below today's standard. His notes contain many watercolours based upon his drawings and tracings of medieval glass which show its appearance better than a black and white photograph could have done. In a letter acknowledging receipt of Canon Ridgway's drawing of a fifteenth-century figure of St Olaf originally from Chester Cathedral, J. A. Knowles commented that although 'it is a very difficult thing to express any opinion from a drawing only, in this case the drawing is so spirited that it is possible to offer one or two remarks'. His watercolour of this panel is even more valuable now that the glass itself has been lost.

He was not infallible, notably in his article on Grappenhall which appeared in the 1950-51 edition of the *JBSMGP*. This dated the medieval glazing, which is typical of the period 1330-40, to the late fourteenth century on the basis of a crude seventeenth-century sketch of the lost donors' attire. However, such an error was easier to make at a time before the many coloured images of early fourteenth-century English glass which are now familiar to scholars were generally available. It is also disappointing that his notes barely mention the large quantity of non-indigenous ancient glass to be found in Cheshire, which fell outside his self-imposed remit, although he pursued with commendable diligence glass of Cheshire origin which had left the county.

Canon Ridgway, photograph copyright Chester City Council, reproduced courtesy of Simon Warburton, Grosvenor Museum, Chester.

Canon Ridgway's interest in stained glass was practical as well as academic. In 1947 he excavated the site of a glass house at Kingswood in Delamere Forest and in 1952-53 the sanctuary of Bunbury church, of which he was then vicar, uncovering fragments from the lost fourteenth-century East window. His restoration of the bomb-damaged Bunbury church included both the commissioning of new windows from Christopher Webb and the purchase and installation in the vestry windows of ancient glass formerly in Marple Hall, which would otherwise have perished when the hall was demolished.

Fittingly for a glass historian, his wife Audrey was a member of the Newton family whose shield still remains in a north window of Wilmslow church which they glazed in 1523. Audrey and their five children survive him.

Writing to a new correspondent, the Canon good-humouredly acknowledged his own mortality, remarking '...being now over eighty, you catch me before I pop off!'. Like everyone else who benefited from his expertise and generosity, I am very glad to have caught him before he popped off. Future students of Cheshire and Welsh stained glass will not be so lucky, but he has left a rich legacy in the form of his articles, which are valuable, and his collections, which are invaluable.

Penny Hebgin-Barnes

THE OPEN CHURCHES TRUST

All Hallows, Allerton Road, Liverpool

Nearly ten years ago Lord Lloyd-Webber created and funded The Open Churches Trust at a time when three out of five parish churches were kept locked between Evensong on a Sunday and flower ladies and cleaners opened up on a Saturday.

The locked church syndrome was doing great harm to the perception of local communities of why these churches were there. Locked churches gave a message that they existed only for Sunday worshippers.

Today, this situation is transformed. Tens of thousands of people every day pop into churches for peace, quiet, reflection and prayer. Several million people each year visit places of worship, because tourism is suddenly recognising the assets of these thousands of wonderful listed buildings. No day passes without more doors opening.

The comments of first-time visitors to a church are invariably about the wonderful stained glass windows. This is a remarkable first impression.

The Trust has proved to be a catalyst which has persuaded many PCCs and their equivalents that an open place of worship rapidly becomes a community asset and so a community responsibility. Once the community is involved, congregations swell.

Any open church can become a member of the Trust and benefit from its help and advice in making your place of worship user- and visitor-friendly.

For more information, please contact:
The Open Churches Trust, 22 Tower Street, London WC2H 9TW
(Website: www.openchurchestrust.org.uk)
E-mail: oct@reallyuseful.co.uk

Sam Fogg

works of art, sculpture, manuscripts

We are always looking to
acquire stained glass of the
middle-ages or Renaissance
whether windows or small
fragments.

15D Clifford St, London W1S 4JZ
t: 020 7534 21 00
f: 020 7534 21 22
e: info@samfogg.com
www.samfogg.com

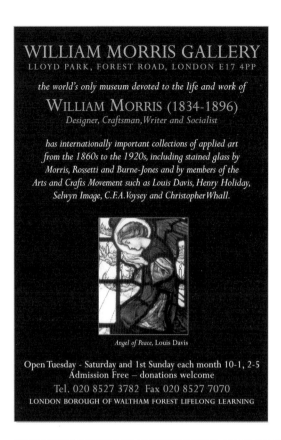

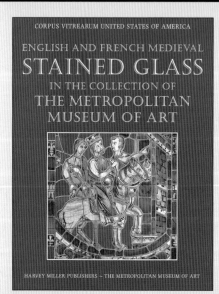

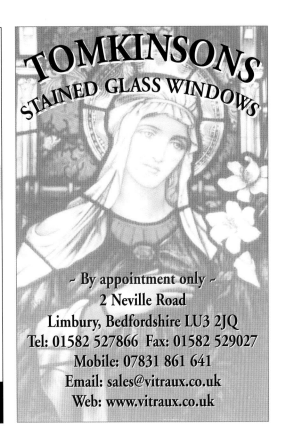

Hetley
Stained Glass Suppliers

AVAILABLE AT GLASSHOUSE FIELDS, LONDON

are the largest stocks of Mouthblown 'antique' glass in the UK.

We hold over 300 colours in the **Lamberts** range and an excellent selection of **St Just** flashed and restoration glasses. Our **Desag** 'Antique Cathedral' is excellent for restoration purposes, and we also hold an extensive range of **Spectrum, Wissmach** and **Kokomo** glasses.

We now have a comprehensive range of FUSING glasses and materials available from stock.

We can also supply all your **tool** and **accessory** requirements and offer a good selection of **books.**

We are stockists for Stillemans Lead.

We offer a nationwide delivery service, mail order service and overseas shipping.

OPENING TIMES:
Monday - Friday: 8.30am-4.30pm Saturday: 9.00am-2.00pm Closed Bank Holiday weekends

James Hetley & Co. Ltd.,
Glasshouse Fields, London E1W 3JA

Tel: 020 7780 2343 Fax: 020 7790 2682
e-mail: sales@hetleys.co.uk   www.hetleys.co.uk

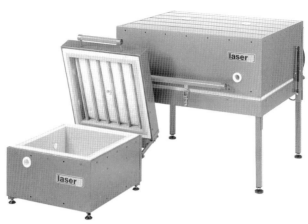

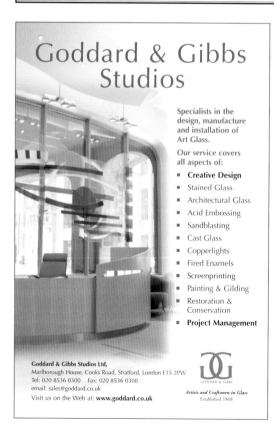

Notes on Contributors

DR TIM AYERS is Secretary and project manager of the Corpus Vitrearum Medii Aevi in Great Britain. A book on the medieval stained glass of Wells Cathedral will be published in the CVMA series in spring 2004 and he is working on the glass at Merton College, Oxford.

TONY BENYON is a glass painter.

H. S. BLAGG is patron of the livings of two South Nottinghamshire parishes in the Vale of Belvoir and sits on the Southwell Diocesan Glebe Committee. Widely travelled, he has a particular interest in early 20th-century stained glass.

CHRIS BROOKS (1949-2002) was Professor of Victorian Culture at the University of Exeter. His many publications include *The Great East Window of Exeter Cathedral* (with David Evans) and *The Gothic Revival*. A full obituary appeared in the last issue of this Journal.

JAMES BUGSLAG received his doctorate from the University of East Anglia in 1992. He teaches in the School of Art at the University of Manitoba, in Winnipeg, and is a member of the Canadian Committee of the CVMA and the Managing Editor of *RACAR (Revue d'art canadien/Canadian Art Review)*. His current research is mainly divided between the stained glass of Chartres Cathedral and a collection of late medieval German panel paintings in the Winnipeg Art Gallery.

MARY CALLÉ has been an active guide in Winchester Cathedral since 1976, specialising since 1994 in the study of its medieval glass. A former trustee of the Friends of Winchester Cathedral, she founded the Outreach group (now the Cathedral Roadshow), which takes knowledge of the Cathedral into the diocese and beyond.

DR MARTIN CHERRY is Chief Buildings Historian at English Heritage. He has published in the fields of late-medieval history, medieval secular architecture and Victorian church architecture.

PETER CORMACK FSA, HON FMGP is a museum curator and historian of 19th- and 20th-century stained glass. He is an honorary director on the board of the Charles J. Connick Stained Glass Foundation.

ADELLE CORRIN AMGP is a contemporary stained glass artist and tutor. She is also the Glass Information Officer for the Worshipful Company of Glaziers and Painters of Glass.

HELEN DUNSTAN MA is part of a specialist dealership in nineteenth-century British design.

ANNA EAVIS is the Head of NMR Services at the National Monuments Record in Swindon. She is also working on a catalogue of the medieval glazing of New College, Oxford for the CVMA.

GINGER FERRELL AMGP is a contemporary stained glass artist practising in Deptford, London.

ADAM GOODYEAR trained at Swansea College of Art and established his own studio in 1984. He has designed and built windows for churches in Yorkshire, Westmorland and Scotland.

J. W. F. (BILL) HARRIMAN BSc., MAE is a firearms and weapons historian. A member of the Academy of Experts, he practises as a forensic firearms examiner and lectures on firearms law to legal professionals and the police. He is also the Director of Firearms of the British Association for Shooting and Conservation based near Chester. He is one of the panel of experts for the BBC TV programme 'Antiques Roadshow' and writes the weekly 'Gunroom' column for *Shooting Times* and *Country Magazine*.

MARTIN HARRISON HON FMGP is a freelance author, curator, designer and art historian. He is the author of *Victorian Stained Glass* (1980, revised edition forthcoming) as well as many books on photography, and is a Trustee of the Stained Glass Museum, Ely. He is currently writing a book about Francis Bacon.

DR PENNY HEBGIN-BARNES is a member of the CVMA Great Britain Committee and author of their summary catalogue volume *The Medieval Stained Glass of the County of Lincolnshire* (1996). She has written numerous articles and advises the Pevsner revisers on the medieval glass in the county of Lancashire.

PETER HOWELL taught Classics for thirty-five years in the University of London. He is a former Chairman of the Victorian Society.

MICHAEL KERNEY is a retired academic: a geologist and zoologist, and co-author of a standard work on European land snails that has appeared in several languages. A life-long interest in architecture has in recent years focussed on that of the Gothic Revival, and on the stained glass it produced.

RUTH KERSLEY GREISMAN BA FINE ART, PGCE, AMGP studied sculpture at Newcastle-upon-Tyne University and taught art in schools. A short course run by Paul San Casciani led her to study stained glass at Central Saint Martins. She works as a glass artist, teaches art part-time in an autistic unit and creates windows with children in schools.

NEIL MOAT works for English Heritage, and writes and lectures as an amateur art historian, with a specialist interest in stained glass and church architecture of the 19th and 20th centuries. He is a member of the Diocesan Advisory Committees for the Care of Churches, for the (Anglican) Dioceses of Newcastle, and of Durham.

JOSEPH MCBRINN is a PhD candidate at the National College of Art and Design in Dublin and is currently the recipient of an Irish Research Council of Humanities and Social Sciences scholarship. He is interested in the history of Irish and British stained glass 1890-1940 and its relationship with mural painting.

DAVID O'CONNOR is a lecturer in the School of Art History and Archaeology, University of Manchester, where he teaches MA options on Stained Glass of York Minster and Victorian Glass. He works on stained glass in York for the Corpus Vitrearum, and is Chairman of the Council for the Care of Churches Stained Glass Committee.

DR MICHAEL PEOVER became interested in stained glass as a physicist, responsible for national standards of light and colour. His particular interest is 18th-century collectors and the continental glass they imported at that time. He is currently researching the glass at Sir John Soane's Museum.

PAUL SHARPLING is a retired language teacher and translator, who developed his interest in stained glass as an undergraduate at Cambridge and later as a postgraduate at Oxford. The author of *Stained Glass in Rutland Churches*, he has conducted extensive research into the stained glass of the Diocese of Peterborough, and is currently engaged in a similar project in the Diocese of Leicester. He has translated numerous articles on stained glass from a wide range of European languages.

JULIE L. SLOAN is a stained glass consultant in North Adams, Massachusetts. She has a Master of Science degree in historic preservation from Columbia University and is the author of *Conservation of Stained Glass in America* and numerous articles. She is also adjunct professor of historic preservation at Columbia, where she has taught stained glass restoration since 1985. She recently curated an exhibition and wrote two major books on the leaded glass of Frank Lloyd Wright, and is currently working on John La Farge and American stained glass history. She regularly consults on the restoration of stained glass windows throughout the USA, including H. H. Richardson's Trinity Church in Boston.

LEONIE SELIGER MA is Senior Conservator at the Cathedral Studios, Canterbury Cathedral. During her eleven years at the Cathedral, she has been involved in many important projects such as the conservation of the Cathedral's North Oculus Window and the cleaning of the Great East Window at Gloucester Cathedral.

DR SEBASTIAN STROBL ACR is Head of Stained Glass Conservation at the Cathedral Studios, Canterbury Cathedral and Secretary of the International Technical Committee of the CVMA. He is a Fellow of the Society and served on the Council for 10 years until 2002.

CAROLINE SWASH FMGP is a London-based painter, writer and stained glass artist. She is currently running the glass course at Central Saint Martins College of Art and Design.

ALBERT M. TANNLER is Historical Collections Director at the Pittsburgh History & Landmarks Foundation. He writes about 19th- and 20th-century architecture and design and has co-edited a book about American Renaissance architect Henry Hornbostel.

ALAN YOUNGER FMGP is a Vice-President of the Society, a Trustee of the Stained Glass Museum, Ely, a Brother of the Art Workers Guild and a part-time senior lecturer at the American International University in London. He has designed and made stained glass for numerous churches and cathedrals, including Durham, Chester, St Albans, Southwark, Gloucester and Westminster Abbey.

The British Society of Master Glass Painters 2002

The Society was inaugurated by Charter in 1921. Both as the professional body for practitioners of stained glass in Britain and as the focus for the study of stained glass history and conservation, it seeks to promote interest in all aspects of the craft and to act as an information exchange. The Society's *Journal* has been published since 1924.

President
His Grace the Duke of Grafton KG, DL, Hon FRIBA, FSA

Vice-Presidents
The Master of the Worshipful Company of Glaziers *ex officio*
Dr Michael Archer OBE, MA, FSA
Alfred Fisher FMGP
Lawrence Lee FMGP
Dr Hilary G. Wayment OBE, LittD, FSA
Alan Younger FMGP

Chairman of the Council
Caroline Benyon FMGP, ACR

Council
Susan Ashworth AMGP
Rodney Bender FMGP
Philip Broome AMGP
Harry Cardross AMGP
Thomas Carlile CBE, BSc, FCGI, FEng, FIMechE
Stephen Clare
Adelle Corrin AMGP
Robert Glaze
Douglas Hogg FMGP
Mel Howse AMGP
Derek Hunt AMGP
Peter London MBE, CStJ, MBBS, FRCS, MFOM, FACEM (Hon)
Kathy Shaw AMGP
Dr Sebastian Strobl FMGP, ACR
Andrew Taylor AMGP

Hon Treasurer
David Kuenssberg FCA

Hon Solicitor
Graham Field BA

Hon Secretary
Ruth Cooke BA (Econ.)

Hon Librarian
Dr Michael Peover

Hon Editor of Journal
Sandra Coley MA

Hon Editor of Newsletter
Chris Wyard MA

Registered in England and Wales 173764
Registered Office of the Society 6 Queen Square, London WC1N 3AR

Please visit the Society's Web Site at **www.bsmgp.org.uk**

The British Society of Master Glass Painters

The Society is intended for all those with an interest in stained glass. Benefits of the annual subscription include the Society's publications (*The Journal of Stained Glass*, published towards the end of the calendar year of membership, and the quarterly *Newsletter*), the Society's Library, and invitations to all the Society's events including lectures and the annual conference.

MEMBERSHIP APPLICATION 2004

New members join as ORDINARY members. Article 6 of the BSMGP Constitution states '**Ordinary Membership is not a professional qualification and does not entitle its holders to quote membership'.** (NB Designers/craft members can apply for other levels of membership after joining. Please contact the Secretary for details.) Subscription rates are as follows:

Please tick

ORDINARY member	£30.00 (£35.00 overseas*)	[ ]
ORDINARY member *(aged over 70 years)*	£18.00 (£22.00 overseas*)	[ ]
ORDINARY student member	£15.00 (£20.00 overseas*)	[ ]
(min. 10 hours per week in college.	....	
Please state institution, course title,	....	
duration and tutor)	....	[ ]
INSTITUTIONAL subscriber	£20.00 (£24.00 overseas*)	
(Journal entitlement only)		

*Please add £5 equivalent to this amount if paying in currency other than Sterling.

Name: ....

Address: ....

....

Telephone: .... Fax:.............................. E-mail: ....

Signature: .... Date: ....

My main interest in stained glass is as MAKER/DESIGNER/CONSERVATOR/AMATEUR CRAFTSMAN/HISTORIAN (please state special interest)/TUTOR (please state locality or institution)/ OTHER (please state):

....

Please return this completed form with a cheque made payable to BSMGP and an A4 s.a.e. to the Secretary: *Chris Wyard, P.O. Box 15, Minehead, Somerset* TA24 8ZX, TEL. 01643 862807
Email: secretary@bsmgp.org.uk

The British Society of Master Glass Painters

MEMBERSHIP APPLICATION